POLITICAL CAMPAIGN COMMUNICATION:

A Bibliography and Guide to the Literature

by

Lynda Lee Kaid

Keith R. Sanders

Robert O. Hirsch

The Scarecrow Press, Inc.

Metuchen, N.J.   1974

Library of Congress Cataloging in Publication Data

Kaid, Lynda Lee.
   Political campaign communication.

   1. Electioneering—United States—Bibliography.
2. Communication—Social aspects—United States—
Bibliography. 3. United States—Politics and
government—1945-   —Bibliography. I. Sanders,
Keith R., joint author. II. Hirsch, Robert O.,
joint author. III. Title.
Z7165.U5K34   016.329'01'0973   73-22492
ISBN 0-8108-0704-1

PREFACE

This bibliography and guide to the literature on political campaign communication has been prepared with the needs of two groups in mind. We hope that our professional and scholarly colleagues in the field will find the introduction valuable because it sets, in some detail, the parameters of the bibliography and may save some of them the necessity of retracing our steps. Likewise, we hope that the bibliography in Section Two will contain at least a few references new to even the best informed specialist and that the French and German Supplement will arouse the curiosity of many who have heretofore confined their reading to the English language literature.

The annotations in Section Four and the Guide to the Literature were prepared for quite a different audience. Undergraduate and graduate students, novice candidates or anyone else with a newly acquired interest in campaigning will, we hope, find these two sections helpful in gaining some initial perspective on the field. We are quite well aware that our professional and scholarly colleagues will probably not find in them much that is new.

A great many people aided in the data gathering and writing stages of this project. We owe particular thanks to our friend, Alan Cohn, Director of the Humanities Library at Southern Illinois University, for his invaluable aid at every stage in the compilation and preparation of this volume.

To Professors Erwin Atwood, John Jackson, and William Smith, who read and commented on parts of the manuscript, we express our appreciation. For his contribution to our interest in the subject and to an earlier version of this work, we owe many thanks to our colleague, Professor Thomas Pace.

iii

Larry and Sheila Kokkeler spent many hours checking the accuracy of the citations in the bibliography; The Office of Research and Projects, Southern Illinois University, provided financial support; Kay Parrish did her usual able job of typing the final manuscript; Cliff Jones and Bob Cureton helped proofread and provided moral support; and Carol Sanders' patience, quiet encouragement, and editing skills helped make the most tedious aspects of the task seem easier and more worthwhile.

In fact, so impressed are we with the quality of the help we received, from the above mentioned persons and from many others, that we have decided to forgo the usual disclaimer and to assert confidently that in the unlikely event that some user finds an error in this volume it cannot be attributed to the compilers.

TABLE OF CONTENTS

1. INTRODUCTION

During the past two decades there has been increasing interdisciplinary interest in political campaign communication. This dramatic upsurge in scholarly interest in American political campaigns has been prompted in part by some major controversies such as the influence of the "image-makers" and the "mediated campaign." Speech-communication scholars, political scientists, sociologists, psychologists, and mass media scholars have all found the study of political campaigns of interest; and with the advent of television-oriented campaigning, the role of communication in political campaigns has received special attention.

In spite of this increase in scholarly activity, no comprehensive bibliography presently exists in this area. On the one hand, some highly specialized bibliographies exist on such topics as political socialization; and, on the other, some general bibliographies exist on such broad topics as mass communication. However, no attempt has been made to collect under a single, consistently applied definition the literature from the many disciplines related to political campaign communication.

Two recent bibliographies in related areas have been compiled by Robert Agranoff, Political Campaigns: A Bibliography and Elections and Electoral Behavior: A Bibliography. [1] These bibliographies are broad in scope but do not approach a comprehensive listing of available materials. Neither contains more than about 200 entries. Their value is further limited by the fact that the entries were not gathered under a clear, systematically-applied definition.

A more comprehensive bibliography, Political Communication: A Bibliography, was compiled by Keith R. Sanders, Robert O. Hirsch, and Thomas Pace. [2] This bibliography was derived over the course of several years by professors and research assistants at the Center for Communications Research, Southern Illinois University. This

collection consists of over 1000 entries. The material contained in it covers a broad area of political communication
but is not limited to the communications process in American political campaigns and was not compiled in accordance
with a clear, systematically applied definition of the area.
Although this bibliography is a significant contribution because
of its breadth and because it includes many relatively ob-
scure but important items, it has a major weakness. As
its compilers indicate, it does not provide the scholar with
a listing of the sources which have and have not been consulted in the compilation.

Building on the work of Sanders, Hirsch and Pace,
Kaid[3] compiled a bibliography of over 700 entries on political campaign communication. Although this bibliography
was more carefully defined and provided the user with an
index, it is not widely available and does not cover popular
literature or materials published outside the United States.

The lack of a comprehensive, widely-available, well-
defined bibliography on a subject of such increasing, contemporary importance is a serious handicap to researchers
in the area. Presently, each researcher in each field must
begin anew the search for relevant citations. This is an
unnecessary task which consumes time better spent on other
matters and sometimes results in a less than comprehensive
review and investigation of the relevant literature. Thus,
the bibliography presented here was compiled in response
to a rather comprehensive definition of the subject matter,
contains annotations of 50 books published between 1950 and
1972, provides a brief German and French supplement, and
offers suggestions for those who wish to stay abreast of
the field in a concluding "Guide to the Literature" section.

Definition

The first important step in compiling a bibliography
is to define carefully the entries to be included. In the case
of political campaign communication, the task is a difficult
one because the process of political campaigning and the
operation of communication variables in that process are
complex and varied. A great deal of thought was given to
this problem, with special attention to the manner in which
political campaign communication has been operationally defined and used in major works in the field. The final decision on works to be included in this bibliography was based

on the following broad criterion:

> This bibliography consists of entries relevant to the communications process as it operates in a political campaign or similar context in the United States from 1950 through 1972. [4]

The entries include books, articles in periodicals and journals, pamphlets, public documents (primarily hearings and reports of the U.S. Congress and specific federal agencies), and unpublished materials (primarily dissertations, theses, and papers presented at meetings and conventions). No attempt was made to cover the indexes of newspapers, although relevant material in major newspapers such as the New York Times and the Wall Street Journal was included when cited in other indexes or bibliographies. The texts of actual political campaign speeches or broadcasts were also omitted.

The "communication process" is meant to encompass the communication variables of source, channel, message, and receiver as well as their interrelationships. Although the emphasis is placed on source and channel variables, the bibliography also includes material which evaluates, analyzes and describes the message and its role in the political campaign and material which is concerned with analyzing and explaining the effects of channel, source, and message variables on the receiver, or voter.

Communication variables can function in ways very similar to their operation in an actual political campaign without actually being in a political campaign. For this reason, citations related to political communication in a context similar to that of a political campaign were included. For instance, a study which indicates that television is the most credible source of public affairs information would provide important information, even though the study may not have been done in an actual political campaign.

Finally, the bibliography is generally limited to material on political campaign communication in the United States from 1950 through 1972. [5] The time-span of 1950 through the present was chosen primarily because the early 1950's mark the beginning of the television era in political campaigning. The impact of television on the information exposure and processing habits of Americans has been such that most empirically oriented researchers will find items

concerning periods prior to 1950 to be of only incidental
value. Material which was published after 1950 but which
obviously dealt with political campaigning before that date
was usually excluded.

The general definition provided useful guidelines for
gathering material; but in practice, more specific criteria
regarding what should and should not be included were
necessary. As a result, the following specific guidelines
for inclusion were formulated in advance, based in part on
prior familiarity with the subject matter and the interdisciplinary nature of the literature in the field:

1. Descriptive, analytical, and evaluative works on
actual political campaigns, including primary and general
election campaigns at local, state, and national levels.

2. Works on the role and effects of the communications media in political campaigns and on the relative use
and credibility of the mass media as information sources in
political campaigns and in other relevant contexts.

3. Works on the flow of information in political contexts, particularly items on the multi-step flow of communication and on interpersonal communication.

4. Works on public opinion polling and computers
when related to political campaigns.

5. Works on public opinion and the political attitudes of communications receivers, including works on psychological factors related to receiver perceptions of communications.

6. Works related to the role and effects of public
speaking and debating in political campaigns.

7. Works related to the general messages and content of political communication, especially in the context of
"issues" versus "image" of political candidates and parties.

8. Works on "practical politics" when related to the
role of communication.

9. Works on the financing and high cost of political
campaigning, including works discussing government regulation of campaign expenditures, media expenditures, and

media use in political campaigns (equal time).

Consistent with the above stated guidelines, the following were excluded:

1.   Works on political parties and on demographic characteristics of the electorate except when they are related to a communication variable (such as "media use patterns of Spanish-Americans").

2.   Works on methodologies used in research in political campaign communication unless the material itself provides information on the operation of a communication variable in a political campaign context.

Procedure for Collecting Citations

Because of the interdisciplinary nature of the subject matter of this bibliography, a wide variety of indexes and other sources had to be consulted in order to cover the subject matter comprehensively:

1.   The collection process began with the general bibliographies on political communication compiled by Sanders, Hirsch and Pace and by Kaid.   From these bibliographies, entries considered relevant to the definition and guidelines outlined above were included in this bibliography.

2.   The search for new entries to the bibliography entailed the use of many indexes.   For each index utilized it was necessary to arrive at a list of headings to be consulted consistently throughout the various volumes of the index.   An examination of a few recent volumes provided initial guidelines, but it was often necessary to drop or add headings as one went along due to changes in terminology over time.   The following is a list of all indexes and sources consulted[6] as well as the major headings used:

Social Science and Humanities Index--until April, 1965, The International Index of Periodicals, 1950-March, 1973 (under political campaign; political candidate; political; mass media; voting; electioneering; elections; television; newspapers; journalism and politics; radio and politics; communication; presidential campaign; and presidential candidates).

Library of Congress Catalogue--Books, Subject Index, 1960-71 (under political party; political psychology; politics, practical; campaigns; television in politics; public relations in politics; radio in politics; and advertising campaigns).

Public Affairs Information Service Index, 1950-April 21, 1973 (under campaigns; elections; local elections; candidates; communication; mass media; newspapers, periodicals; radio; television; political; presidential candidates; presidential campaigns; and voting).

Psychological Abstracts, 1950-January, 1973 (under communications; mass communications; opinion; political behavior; politics; voting; television; radio; and information).

Dissertation Abstracts, 1950-December, 1972 (under journalism; psychology; mass communication; social psychology; speech; sociology; and political science).

Journalism Abstracts, 1963-71 (under all categories).

Bibliographic Index, 1951-August, 1972 (under communication; journalism; political parties; political science; television; elections; and voting).

Sociological Abstracts, 1953-October, 1972 (under campaign; candidate; television; news; voting; radio; political; and politics; mass media).

Table of Contents and Index of the Quarterly Journal of Speech, Speech Monographs, Speech Teacher, Southern Speech Journal, Western Speech, Central States Speech Journal, Today's Speech, through 1969 (issue by issue, rather than with the index).

Monthly Catalogue of Government Documents, 1950-January, 1973 (under political campaigns; campaign finance; campaign regulation; and political broadcasting).

Journalism Quarterly, "Articles on Mass Communication in U.S. and Foreign Journals: A Selected Annotated Bibliography," (quarterly bibliography, title varies), 1950-Fall, 1972.

Index to Legal Periodicals, 1950-January, 1973 (under politics; television; radio; and elections).

The Readers' Guide to Periodical Literature, 1950-March 10, 1973 (under advertising, political; campaign; candidates, political; elections; communication; mass media; newspapers and politics; political advertising; political attitudes; political campaigns; political forecasts; political parties; political psychology; politics; politicians; radio broadcasting, political uses; television in politics; and voting).

The Vertical File Index, 1950-March, 1973 (under elections; communication; mass media; newspapers, political campaigns; political conventions; political candidates; political parties; radio; television; voting; politics; presidential campaigns; presidential candidates; United States--politics and government).

Education Index, 1950-April, 1973 (under advertising; campaign; candidate; communication; elections; political attitudes; political conventions; political parties; political psychology; politics; public speaking; radio; television; voting; and presidential campaigns).

Canadian Periodicals Index, 1950-1972 (under communication; political campaigning; elections; mass media; television; United States--politics and government; presidential campaign; presidential candidates; and newspapers in/and politics).

British Humanities Index, 1962-July/September, 1972 --Subject Guide to Periodicals, 1950-1961 (under communication(s); elections; political; politics; television and politics; United States--politics and government; and mass media).

Speech Abstracts, Vol. I-III, 1970-1972.

British Books in Print, 1972 (under campaigns; elections; electoral; communication; mass media; mass communication; party; politics; political; television; radio; and newspapers).

ABC POL SCI, 1970-May, 1973.

3. In addition to the indexes consulted, a number of other sources were used in compiling the final bibliography. Of major use were extensive bibliographies compiled in related areas and programs from recent conventions.

4. The last procedure followed in the collection process was to select some recent, seemingly comprehensive
books and articles and check the footnotes and bibliographies
against the entries provided by the indexes.   This was
originally intended to increase the number of entries in the
final bibliography and to uncover any citations which might
have been missed by the indexing processes of the various
indexes consulted.   However, this procedure was of limited
value except as a verification measure.   Very few new
entries were gained through this procedure.

In the collection procedure, every attempt was made
to collect only those entries which were within the parameters of the original definitions and guidelines.   Often, this
decision had to be made solely in terms of the title of the
work since it was impossible to check the specific content
of every item.   In many cases, however, familiarity with
the work or the presence of an abstract or summary in the
index made possible a more informed decision.

5.   Finally, the accuracy of the citations (author,
title, date of publication, etc.) was checked against the
original work when the original was available.   When the
original was not available, most citations were checked
against at least one other reference to the work.

The final bibliography contains over 1500 entries.
These are arranged in alphabetical order by author and
numbered in order to simplify the indexing process.

Method of Indexing Citations

Several possible methods of organizing the bibliography were considered.   One common method for such tasks
has been a "key word" indexing system whereby the bibliography would be indexed according to selected words in
the title.   Unfortunately, despite its simplicity, such a
system may not truly reflect the content of individual works.
For instance, the article by Edward Barrett entitled "The
Force, the Faults, the Future" would be categorized under
force, faults, and future in a key word index although the
actual content of the article concerns the Kennedy-Nixon
debates in 1960.   Consequently, an indexing system was
chosen for this bibliography which reflects the apparent content of the work as well as its title.

The system used here is not intended to be a comprehensive indexing of every reasonable interpretation of the contents of every work in the bibliography.   It is intended as an organized guide to the main contents of the items included.

The index contains headings which are as specific as the compilers' knowledge and information about the entries permit.   In the absence of other information, an entry was indexed according to key words in the title. Works relating to more than one concept were listed under related concepts.

Again, as in the case of the decision to include or not include an entry in the bibliography, the decision of where and how to index an entry was sometimes based only on the title of the work.   However, the accuracy and the completeness of the indexing process were aided considerably by the fact that whenever possible brief notes were taken during the collection process on each entry card regarding the specific content and relevance of the material contained in the item.   This information, along with the general familiarity of the compilers with the subject matter, was quite valuable in the indexing process.

Finally, we caution the user of this bibliography that, although it provides a good general guide to the literature on the subject, it is not exhaustive.   A highly specialized research topic such as the role of interpersonal communication in political campaigns would require a more detailed search of the general literature on interpersonal communication than is contained in this bibliography.

It is also limited by our heavy dependence on prepared indexes for gathering citations.   Some items are missed by these indexes, and some appear under seemingly inappropriate categories.

Notes

1.   Both 1972 bibliographies are available in monograph form from the Center for Governmental Studies, Northern Illinois University, DeKalb, Illinois.

2.   (Carbondale, Illinois: College of Communications and Fine Arts, Southern Illinois University, 1972).

3.   Lynda Lee Kaid, "A Selected, Indexed Bibliography on
      Political Campaign Communication" (unpublished M. S.
      Thesis, Department of Speech, Southern Illinois Uni-
      versity, 1972).

4.   These definitions and guidelines as well as 700 of the
      entries in this bibliography were taken from the bib-
      liography by Kaid, cited earlier.

5.   All indexes were not available through 1972; and those
      that were available did not always include all ma-
      terials published through that date.   Consequently,
      an effort was made to include the most recent issues
      of all indexes.

6.   Indexes consulted in compiling the German and French
      supplement are listed in that section.

2. BIBLIOGRAPHY

001 Abcarian, Gilbert and Soule, John W. Social Psychology and Political Behavior. New York: Merrill, 1971.

002 Abels, Jules. The Degeneration of Our Presidential Election. New York: The Macmillan Co., 1968.

003 Abelson, Robert P. "Computers, Polls, and Public Opinion--Some Puzzles and Paradoxes," Transaction, 5 (Sept., 1968), pp. 20-27.

004 _____. "The Goldwater Machine and Beyond." Paper presented at the American Political Science Association Convention, Chicago, September, 1971.

005 _____, and Berstein, Alex. "A Computer Simulation Model of Community Referendum Controversies," Public Opinion Quarterly, 27 (1963), pp. 93-122.

006 Abney, F. Glenn. "The Cost of Democracy in Mississippi," Public Administration Survey, 20 (Sept., 1972), pp. 1-6.

007 Abrams, M. "Opinion Polls and Party Propaganda," Public Opinion Quarterly, 28 (1964), pp. 13-19.

008 Abramson, M. "Want to be Elected?" National Civic Review, 50 (Dec. 1961), pp. 595-600.

009 Academy of Television Arts and Sciences. "TV and Politics: A Forum." New York: Academy of Television Arts and Sciences, 1960.

010 Ace, Goodman. "The Grand Old Players," Saturday Review, 49 (August 20, 1966), p. 8.

11

011   Ackerman, Donald H., Jr.   "The Write-in Vote for
      Dwight Eisenhower in the Spring, 1952, Minnesota
      Primary: Minnesota Politics on the Grass-root
      Level." Unpublished Ph.D. dissertation, Syracuse
      U., 1954.

012   Adamany, David W.   "The Media in Campaigning," The
      League of Women Voters of the United States Quart-
      erly, 47 (Autumn, 1972), pp. 46-47.

013   _____. "Money in American Politics: The Costs of
      Campaigning; What's the Problem?" Washington,
      Conn.: Center for Information on America, Oct.,
      1971.

014   Adler, Kenneth P.   "Mass Media Responsibility to
      Political Elites," Journal of Communication, 8
      (Summer, 1958), pp. 51-55.

015   Adler, Renata.   "Who's Here? What Time Is It?"
      New Yorker, 48 (Sept. 16, 1972), pp. 114-18+.

016   "Admen Join the Race; Contenders for Presidential
      Nomination Enlist Madison Avenue Teams," Busi-
      ness Week, July 6, 1968, p. 21.

017   "Ads Play Top Role in Election Drama," Printers' Ink,
      281 (Nov. 2, 1962), pp. 13-15.

018   "Advancing the Art," Newsweek, 79 (Jan. 31, 1972),
      p. 15.

019   "Advantage to the Incumbent," Time, 100 (July 10,
      1972), pp. 17-18.

020   Agranoff, Robert.   Elections and Electoral Behavior:
      A Bibliography. DeKalb, Ill.: Center for Govern-
      mental Studies, Northern Illinois University, 1972.

021   _____. "The Minnesota Democratic-Farmer-Labor-
      Party Organization: A Study of the 'Character' of
      a Programmatic Party." Unpublished Ph.D. disser-
      tation, University of Pittsburgh, 1967.

022   _____, ed.   The New Style in Election Campaigns.
      Boston: The Holbrook Press, 1972.

023 _____ . Political Campaigns: A Bibliography.
De Kalb, Ill.: Center for Governmental Studies,
Northern Illinois University, 1972.

024 Albig, William. Modern Public Opinion. New York:
McGraw-Hill Publishers, 1956.

025 Albjerg, Victor. "Truman and Eisenhower: Their Ad-
ministrations and Campaigns," Current History, 47
(Oct., 1964), pp. 221-28.

026 Alexander, Herbert E. "Communication and Politics:
The Media and the Message," Law and Contemporary
Problems, 34 (1969), pp. 255-77.

027 _____ . Financing the 1960 Election. Princeton,
N.J.: Citizen's Research Foundation, 1962.

028 _____ . Financing the 1964 Election. Princeton,
N.J.: Citizen's Research Foundation, 1966.

029 _____ . Financing the 1968 Election. Boston: Heath
Publishing Co., 1971.

030 _____ . "The Folklore of Buying Elections: Just How
Important Are Corporations, Unions, and the Rich to
Political Campaigns?" Business and Society Review,
Summer, 1972, pp. 48-53.

031 _____ . "Money, Politics and Public Reporting."
Princeton, N.J.: Citizen's Research Foundation,
Feb., 1960.

032 _____ . "Political Broadcasting in 1968," Television
Quarterly, 9 (Spring, 1970), pp. 41-50.

033 _____ . "Political Broadcasting: What's Its Impact
on Elections?" Washington, Conn.: Center for Information on America, 1964.

034 _____ ; Bullitt, Stimson; and Goldin, Hyman H. "The
High Cost of TV Campaigns," Television Quarterly,
5 (1966), pp. 47-65.

035 _____ , and Denny, Laura L. "Regulation of Political
Finance." Institute of Governmental Studies, U. of
California at Berkeley, 1966.

036   _____, and Meyers, Harold B. "The Switch in Cam-
           paign Giving, " Fortune, 72 (Nov., 1965), pp. 170-
           72+.

037 Allard, Erik, and Rokkan, Stein (eds.). Mass Politics;
     Studies in Political Sociology. New York: Free
     Press, 1970.

038 Allen, A. J. "Voting Recollections and Intentions in
     Reading: An Opinion Poll Experiment, " Parliamen-
     tary Affairs, 20 (1967), pp. 170-77.

039 Allen, George E. Presidents Who Have Known Me.
     New York: Simon and Schuster, 1970, pp. 260-70.

040   _____. "Shake Well before Voting, " New York
           Times Magazine, Nov. 5, 1950, p. 20+.

041 Allen, Thomas H. "Mass Media Use Patterns in a
     Negro Ghetto, " Journalism Quarterly, 45 (1968), pp.
     525-31.

042 Alley, Anne G. "A Demographic Study of the 1967
     Gubernatorial Campaign Speaking of Louie Broady
     Nunn." Unpublished Ph.D. dissertation, Southern
     Illinois U., 1969.

043 "Alliteration Is Reputation; Empress Specialty Co., New
     York, " New Yorker, 28 (April 19, 1952), pp. 23-24.

044 Alper, S. William, and Leidy, Thomas R. "The Im-
     pact of Information Transmission through Television, "
     Public Opinion Quarterly, 33 (1969-70), pp. 556-62.

045 American Institute for Political Communication. The
     Credibility Problem. Washington, D.C.: American
     Institute for Political Communication, 1972.

046   _____. Media and Non-Media Effects on the Forma-
           tion of Public Opinion. Washington, D.C.: Ameri-
           can Institute for Political Communication, 1969.

047   _____. The New Methodology: A Study of Political
           Strategy and Tactics. Washington, D.C.: American
           Institute for Political Communication, 1967.

048   . The 1968 Campaign: Anatomy of a Crucial
          Election. Washington, D.C.: American Institute for
          Political Communication, 1970.

049 American Newspaper Publishers Association. "Less
          Bias in Newspapers than in Readers," News Re-
          search Bulletin, Jan. 20, 1972, pp. 5-8.

050 Anderson, James A. "An Analysis of the Methodologies
          Used in Media Credibility Studies or: 'The medium
          they believe depends on the question you ask.' "
          Paper presented at the International Communication
          Association Convention, Phoenix, Arizona, April 22-
          24, 1971.

051 Anderson, Lynn R., and Bass, Alan R. "Some Ef-
          fects of Victory or Defeat upon Perception of Po-
          litical Candidates," Journal of Social Psychology,
          73 (1967), pp. 227-40.

052 Anderson, Patrick. "Issue vs. Image," New Republic,
          158 (April 27, 1968), pp. 32-35.

053 Anderson, Robert O. "The Characterization Model for
          Rhetorical Criticism of Political Image Campaigns,"
          Western Speech, 37 (1973), pp. 75-86.

054   . "A Rhetoric of Political Image Communica-
          tion." Unpublished Ph.D. dissertation, U. of Mis-
          souri-Columbia, 1971.

055 Anderson, Ronald Eugene. "Group Homogeneity and
          Stimulus Evaluation in Political Campaigns." Un-
          published Ph.D. dissertation, Stanford U., 1970.

056 Anderson, Totton J. (ed.). "The 1960 Elections in the
          West," Western Political Quarterly, 14 (1961), pp.
          287-385.

057   , and Lee, E. C. "The 1964 Election in Cali-
          fornia," Western Political Quarterly, 18 (1965), pp.
          451-74.

058 Anderson, Walt. Campaigns: Cases in Political Con-
          flict. Pacific Palisades, California: Goodyear Pub-
          lishing Co., Inc., 1970.

059   Andrews, William G.   "American Voting Participation,"
      Western Political Quarterly, 19, no. 4 (1966), pp.
      639-52.

060   Angel, Duane D.   "The Campaign Speaking of George
      Romney: 1962 and 1964." Unpublished Ph.D. dis-
      sertation, Purdue U., 1965.

061   Apple, R. W.   "The Funding of a President," New
      Statesman, 82 (Dec. 3, 1971), pp. 770, 772.

062   Archibald, Samuel J. (ed.).   The Pollution of Politics.
      Washington, D.C.: Public Affairs Press, 1971.

063   "The Architect of a Triumph on Television," Broad-
      casting, 59 (Nov. 14, 1960), pp. 32+.

064   "Are Political Conventions a TV Flop?" United States
      News and World Report, 4 (Sept. 7, 1956), p. 35.

065   "Are Political Spots on Television Unfair?" United
      States News and World Report, 57 (Sept. 28, 1964),
      p. 10.

066   Arrendell, Charles.   "Predicting the Completeness of
      Newspaper Election Coverage," Journalism Quarterly,
      49 (1972), pp. 290-95.

067   Arrendell, Odes C.   "Coverage of the 1968 Democratic
      and Republican Presidential Campaign by Texas Daily
      Newspapers: An Evaluation Related to Social Re-
      sponse Theory." Unpublished Ph.D. dissertation,
      U. of Texas at Austin, 1969.

068   Atkin, Charles K. "The Effect of Imbalanced Political
      Campaign Coverage on Voter Exposure Patterns."
      Paper presented at the Association for Education in
      Journalism Convention, Washington, D.C., August,
      1970.

069   _____ .   "How Imbalanced Campaign Coverage Af-
      fects Audience Exposure Patterns," Journalism
      Quarterly, 48 (1971), pp. 235-44.

070   _____ .   "The Impact of Political Poll Reports on
      Candidate and Issue Preference," Journalism
      Quarterly, 46 (1969), pp. 515-21.

071 _____. "Interpersonal Communication as a Deter-
        minant of Mass Media Exposure Patterns." Paper
        presented at the International Communication Associ-
        ation Convention, Phoenix, Arizona, April 22-24,
        1971.

072 _____. "Some Effects of Public Opinion Polls on
        Voter Images and Intentions." Paper presented at
        the Association for Education in Journalism Con-
        vention, Lawrence, Kansas, August, 1968.

073 _____; Crouch, Wayne W.; and Troldahl, Verling C.
        "The Role of the Campus Newspaper in the New
        Youth Vote." Paper presented at the International
        Communication Association Convention, Montreal,
        April 25-29, 1973.

074 _____, et al. "Electronic Politics and the Voter:
        Conventional Wisdom and Empirical Evidence."
        Paper presented at the International Communication
        Association Convention, Phoenix, Arizona, 1971.

075 _____, et al. "Patterns of Voter Reception and Re-
        sponse to Televised Political Advertising in Two
        Gubernatorial Campaigns." Paper presented at the
        Association for Education in Journalism Convention,
        Carbondale, Ill., August, 1972.

076 Atwood, L. Erwin, and Sanders, Keith R. "Mass Com-
        munication and Ticket-Splitting in the 1972 General
        Election." Paper presented at the International
        Communication Association Convention, Montreal,
        April 25-29, 1973.

077 The Australian Royal Commission on Television. "Con-
        trol of Political Broadcasting in English-Speaking
        Countries," Journal of Broadcasting, 2 (1958), pp.
        123-36.

078 Aycock, A. "Campaigning with Catchwords," New York
        Times Magazine, Nov. 29, 1959, p. 62+.

079 "Bad Samples and Political Polls," Science News, 94
        (August 24, 1968), p. 179.

080   Bagdikian, Ben H. "Election Coverage '72: The Fruits
      of Agnewism," Columbia Journalism Review, 11
      (Jan./Feb., 1973), p. 9+.

081   Bagdikian, H. "TV, the President's Medium," Columbia
      Journalism Review, 1 (1962), pp. 34-38.

082   Baird, A. Craig. "Political Speaking in 1952: A Sym-
      posium," Quarterly Journal of Speech, 38 (1952),
      pp. 265-99.

083   Baker, Michael J. "Constitutional Remedy for the High
      Cost of Broadcast and Newspaper Advertising in
      Political Campaigns," California Law Review, 60
      (1972), pp. 1371-1415.

084   Baker, Russell. Our Next President: The Incredible
      Story of What Happened in the 1968 Elections. New
      York: Atheneum Publishers, 1968.

085   Balmer, Donald. "Financing State Senate Campaigns:
      Multnomah County, Oregon, 1964." Princeton,
      N.J.: Citizen's Research Foundation, 1966.

086   Banks, Jimmy. Money, Marbles and Chalk: The
      Wondrous World of Texas Politics. Austin, Texas:
      Texas Publishing Company, 1971.

087   Bantz, Charles. "The Rhetorical Vision of the ABC
      Evening News: June 12 to July 10, 1972," Mo-
      ments in Contemporary Rhetoric and Communication
      (Temple U.), 2 (Fall, 1972), pp. 34-37.

088   Barber, Stephen. "The Cost of Running for President,"
      Daily Telegraph, Nov. 30, 1971, p. 9.

089   Barclay, Martha Thomson. "Distaff Campaigning in the
      1964 and 1968 Presidential Elections," Central
      States Speech Journal, 21 (1970), pp. 117-22.

090   Barnes, P. "Candidates on Television," New Republic,
      157 (July 22, 1967), pp. 7-8.

091   Barr, Carolyn E. "Newspaper vs. Television Coverage
      of the California Gubernatorial Race in the Bay
      Area." Unpublished M.J. thesis, U. of California
      at Berkeley, 1967.

092   Barrett, Edward W.   "The Force, the Faults, the Fu-
      ture," Television, Jan., 1961, pp. 58-60.

093   Barrow, Lionel.   "Factors Related to Attention to the
      First Kennedy-Nixon Debate," Journal of Broad-
      casting, 5 (1961), pp. 229-38.

094   Barrow, Roscoe L.   "Regulation of Campaign Funding
      and Spending for Federal Office," Journal of Law
      Reform, 5 (Winter, 1972), pp. 159-92.

095   Bart, Peter.   "The Adman in Politics," Saturday Re-
      view, April 11, 1964, p. 81.

096   Barthelmes, Wes.   "No News is Bad News," Common-
      weal, 97 (Oct. 20, 1972), pp. 54-56.

097   Basset, Edward P.   "Political News, Newspapers, and
      Politicians: The Roles Newspapers Played in Iowa's
      1964 First District Congressional Campaign." Un-
      published Ph.D. dissertation, U. of Iowa, 1967.

098   Batlin, Robert.   "San Francisco Newspapers' Campaign
      Coverage: 1896, 1952," Journalism Quarterly, 31
      (1954), pp. 297-303.

099   "The Battle of the Ads: Humphrey Looks a Loser,"
      Sunday London Times, Oct. 20, 1968, p. 10.

100   "Battle Page," Time, 64 (Oct. 18, 1954), p. 48.

101   Bauer, Otto Frank.   "A Study of the Political Debate
      Between Dwight D. Eisenhower and Adlai E. Steven-
      son in the Presidential Campaign of 1956." Unpub-
      lished Ph.D. dissertation, Northwestern U., 1959.

102   Bauer, Raymond, and Bauer, Alice.   "America, Mass
      Society, and the Mass Media," Journal of Social Is-
      sues, 16 (1960), pp. 3-66.

103   Baur, E. J.   "Opinion Change in a Public Contro-
      versy," Public Opinion Quarterly, 26 (1962), pp.
      212-26.

104   Baus, Herbert M., and Ross, William B.   Politics
      Battle Plan.   New York: Macmillan, 1968.

105   Baxter, Dick H.   "Interpersonal Contact and Exposure
       to the Mass Media during a Presidential Campaign."
       Unpublished Ph.D. dissertation, Columbia U., 1951.

106   Bay, Ch.   "Politics and Pseudopolitics: A Critical
       Evaluation of Some Behavioral Literature," Ameri-
       can Political Science Review, 59 (1965), pp. 39-51.

107   Beal, George M.; Hartman, John J.; and Lagomarcino,
       Virgil.   "An Analysis of Factors Associated with
       School Bond Elections," Rural Sociology, 33 (Sept.,
       1968), pp. 313-27.

108   Beall, C. P.   "The 1962 Election in Wyoming," Western
       Political Quarterly, 16 (1963), pp. 477-82.

109   Beam, George D.   Usual Politics.   New York: Holt,
       Rinehart and Winston, 1970.

110   "Beating the Celebrity Takes Time (on TV)," Broad-
       casting, 78 (May 11, 1970), p. 51.

111   Beaton, Leonard.   "Good Television, Bad Politics,"
       Listener, 84 (August 27, 1970), pp. 261-63.

112   Beattie, William R.   "A Readability-Listenability
       Analysis of Selected Campaign Speeches of Adlai
       E. Stevenson in the 1952 and 1956 Presidential
       Campaigns," Central States Speech Journal, 10
       (Spring, 1959), pp. 16-18.

113   Beck, D.   "Polarization of Political Attitudes in the
       1968 Presidential Campaign."   Paper presented at
       the Speech Association of America Convention,
       New York City, Dec., 1969.

114   Becker, Jerome D., and Preston, Ivan L.   "Media
       Usage and Political Activity," Journalism Quarterly,
       46 (1969), pp. 129-34.

115   Becker, John F., and Heaton, Eugene E., Jr.   "The
       Election of Senator Edward W. Brooke," Public
       Opinion Quarterly, 31 (1967), pp. 346-58.

116   Becker, Jules, and Fuchs, Douglas A.   "How Two Ma-
       jor California Dailies Covered Reagan vs. Brown,"
       Journalism Quarterly, 44 (1967), pp. 645-53.

117   Becker, S. L.   "Politics and Broadcasting, " National
      Association of Secondary School Principals Bulletin,
      50 (Oct., 1966), pp. 48-53.

118   Becker, Samuel L.   "Presidential Power: The Influ-
      ence of Broadcasting, " Quarterly Journal of Speech,
      47 (1961), pp. 10-18.

119   _____, and Lower, Elmer W.   "Broadcasting in
      Presidential Campaigns, " The Great Debates, ed.
      Sidney Kraus. Bloomington, Ind.: Indiana Uni-
      versity Press, 1962.

120   Bedggood, David R.   "The Measurement of Political At-
      titudes and the Concept of Ideology: USA and NZ, "
      Political Science, 24 (April, 1972), pp. 15-23.

121   Behn, Dick (ed.).   "Politics '72: A Survey of the 1972
      Elections, from Presidential to State-Legislative
      Races...," Ripon Forum, 8 (July, 1972), pp. 13-36.

122   Behrens, John C.   "Freelance Job Idea: Political
      Ghostwriting, " Writers' Digest, 49 (Nov., 1969), pp.
      48-53.

123   Belson, William A.   "Selective Perception in Viewing a
      TV Broadcast, " Audio-Visual Communication Review,
      6 (Winter, 1958), pp. 23-43.

124   Benavides, Rosalinda.   "Texas Daily Press Coverage of
      the 1968 Gubernatorial Campaign." Unpublished M.A.
      thesis, U. of Texas at Austin, 1969.

125   Bendiner, Robert.   "Quickie 'Results' Could Sway the
      Election, " Life, 57 (Sept. 18, 1964), pp. 125-33.

126   Benham, T. W.   "Polling for a Presidential Candidate:
      Some Observations on the 1964 Campaign, " Public
      Opinion Quarterly, 29 (1965), pp. 185-99.

127   Bennett, Ralph K.   "Television and the Candidates, "
      The National Observer, May 20, 1968, p. 1+.

128   Bennett, T.   "Government Publicity and Democratic
      Press Theory." Unpublished Ph.D. dissertation,
      U. of Illinois, 1962.

129   Berelson, Bernard, and Janowitz, Morris (eds.). A
      Reader in Public Opinion and Communication. Glen-
      coe, Ill.: Free Press, 1953.

130   _____; Lazarsfeld, Paul; and McPhee, William.
      Voting: A Study of Opinion Formation in a Presi-
      dential Campaign. Chicago: University of Chicago
      Press, 1954.

131   Berger, A. "Politics of Entertainment," Nation, 205
      (Oct. 30, 1967), pp. 422-24.

132   Berger, John. "The Political Uses of Photo-Montage,"
      New Society, 14 (Oct. 23, 1969), pp. 652-53.

133   Berlak, H. "The Construct Validity of a Content Analy-
      sis System for the Evaluation of Critical Thinking in
      Political Controversy." Unpublished Ph.D. disserta-
      tion, Harvard U., 1964.

134   Bernd, Joseph L. "A Study of Primary Elections in
      Georgia." Unpublished Ph.D. dissertation, Duke U.,
      1957.

135   "Beware the Witching Hours." Washington, D.C.:
      Fair Campaign Practices Committee, 1968, 11 pp.

136   "Big Money, Talent and Effort Devoted to Politicking
      on Television," National Journal, 2 (Oct. 3, 1970),
      pp. 2135-44.

137   Bilik, Eugene Wyckoff. "The Image Candidate: An
      Appraisal of Political Broadcast Regulation Based
      on TV Coverage of the 1961 Mayoral Campaigns in
      New York City." Unpublished Ph.D. dissertation,
      New York U., 1966.

138   Bird, J. "Trudeau, Kennedy: Campaign Twins," Fi-
      nancial Post, 62 (April 6, 1968), p. 7.

139   Bishop, George F.; Barclay, Andrew M.; and Rokeach,
      Milton. "Presidential Preferences and Freedom-
      Equality Value Patterns in the 1968 American Cam-
      paign," Journal of Social Psychology, 88 (Dec.,
      1972), pp. 207-12.

140 Bishop, Robert L.; Boersma, Mary; and Williams, John. "Teenagers and News Media: Credibility Canyon," Journalism Quarterly, 46 (1969), pp. 597-99.

141 _____, and Brown, Robert L. "Michigan Newspaper Bias in the 1966 Campaign," Journalism Quarterly, 45 (1968), pp. 337-38.

142 Black, Edwin. "Electing Time," Quarterly Journal of Speech, 59 (1973), pp. 125-29.

143 _____. "Trends in Political Persuasion in the United States." Paper Presented at the Central States Speech Association Convention, Minneapolis, April, 1973.

144 Blackman, Edwin T. "Patterns of Information-seeking in Presidential Campaigns." Unpublished Master's thesis, U. of North Carolina, 1968.

145 Blaustein, A. I., and Sussman, P. Y. "McGovern: The Man, the Press, the Machine, the Odds," Nation, 215 (Oct. 16, 1972), pp. 328-35.

146 Bliven, Bruce. "Politics and TV," Harper's Magazine, 205 (Nov., 1952), pp. 27-33.

147 Blum, Eleanor. Reference Books in the Mass Media: An Annotated, Selected Booklist Covering Book Publishing, Broadcasting, Films, Newspapers, Magazines, and Advertising. Urbana, Ill.: University of Illinois Press, 1962.

148 Blumberg, N. B. "Newspaper Bias in the 1952 Presidential Campaign," Nieman Reports, 8 (July, 1954), pp. 14-16.

149 Blumberg, Nathan B. One Party Press? Coverage of the 1952 Presidential Campaign in Thirty-Five Daily Newspapers. Lincoln, Neb.: The University of Nebraska Press, 1954.

150 Blume, Norman. "Group Cohesion in Political Campaigning; A Case Study," Social Science, 37 (October, 1962), pp. 221-30.

151 _____, and Lyons, Schley. "The Monopoly News-
      paper in a Local Election, The Toledo Blade,"
      Journalism Quarterly, 45 (1968), pp. 286-92.

152 Blumler, Jay G., and McQuail, Denis. "Television and
      Politics," New Society, 12 (Dec. 5, 1968), pp. 834-
      35.

153 _____, and McQuail, Denis. Television in Politics:
      Its Uses and Influence. London: Faber and Faber,
      Ltd., 1969.

154 Blydenburgh, John C. "A Controlled Experiment to
      Measure the Effects of Personal Contact Campaign-
      ing," Midwest Journal of Political Science, 15 (1971),
      pp. 365+.

155 _____. "Two Attempts to Measure the Effects of
      Precinct-level Campaigning Activities." Unpublished
      Ph.D. dissertation, U. of Rochester, 1969.

156 Bode, Kenneth A. "The South Dakota Poll: A Critical
      Analysis," Public Affairs (South Dakota), Feb. 15,
      1970.

157 Bogardus, E. "Sociology of Presidential TV Press
      Conference," Sociology and Social Research, 46
      (1962), pp. 181-85.

158 Bogardus, Emory S. "Television and the Political
      Convention," Sociology and Social Research, 37
      (1953), pp. 115-21.

159 Bogart, Leo L. "American Television: A Brief Survey
      of Research Findings," Journal of Social Issues, 18
      no. 2 (1962), pp. 36-42.

160 _____. Silent Politics: Polls and the Awareness of
      Public Opinion. New York: Wiley-Interscience,
      John Wiley and Sons, Inc., 1972.

161 Bolen, John H. "Daily Newspaper Coverage of the 1970
      Texas Gubernatorial Campaign." Unpublished M.A.
      thesis, U. of Texas at Austin, 1970.

162 Bonafede, Dom. "Nixon Models Campaign Organization
      after His Successful Version of 1968," National Jour-
      nal, 3 (Sept. 11, 1971), pp. 1876-84.

163 Bone, H. A. "Campaign Methods Today," Annals of
     the American Academy, 283 (Sept., 1952), pp. 127-
     40.

164 Bone, Hugh A., and Ranney, Austin. Politics and
     Voters. New York: McGraw-Hill Book Co., 1967.

165 Bonnati, Robert (ed.). Winning Elections with the New
     Politics. New York: Popular Library, 1971.

166 Boodish, H. M. "Electing the Next President of the United
     States," Social Studies, 55 (Oct., 1964), pp. 190-92.

167 Boorstin, Daniel J. The Image. New York: Atheneum,
     1962.

168 _____. "Selling the President to the People: The
     Direct Democracy of Public Relations," Commen-
     tary, 20 (1955), pp. 421-27.

169 Booth, P. "The New Politics Goes Local," Nation,
     204 (May 29, 1967), pp. 682-85.

170 "Boredom and TV Politicking," Nation, 187 (Nov. 8,
     1958), p. 330.

171 Borgestad, James T. "The Opinions of Media Con-
     sumers during the 1972 Presidential Campaign,"
     Moments in Contemporary Rhetoric and Communica-
     tion (Temple U.), 2 (Fall, 1972), pp. 45-52.

172 Bormann, Ernest G. "The Eagleton Affair: A Fantasy
     Theme Analysis," Quarterly Journal of Speech, 59
     (1973), pp. 143-59.

173 _____. "A Rhetorical Analysis of the 1972 Political
     Campaign as a Communication System," Moments in
     Contemporary Rhetoric and Communication (Temple
     U.), 2 (Fall, 1972), pp. 10-12.

174 Bouchard, Thomas J., and Stuster, Jack. "The Lost-
     Letter Technique: Predicting Elections," Psycho-
     logical Reports, 25 (1969), pp. 230-34.

175 Boulding, Kenneth E. The Image. Ann Arbor, Michi-
     gan: University of Michigan Press, 1956.

176   Bowen, Lawrence, et al. "How Voters React to Elec-
      tronic Political Advertising: An Investigation of the
      1970 Election Campaigns in Wisconsin and Colorado."
      Paper presented at the Annual Conference of the
      American Association for Public Opinion Research,
      Pasadena, Calif., May 19-22, 1971.

177   Bowers, Thomas A. "An Analysis of Information Con-
      tent in Newspaper Political Advertising in Selected
      Senatorial, Gubernatorial and Congressional Cam-
      paigns of 1970." Unpublished Ph.D. dissertation,
      Indiana U., 1971.

178   _____. "Issue and Personality Information in News-
      paper Political Advertising," Journalism Quarterly,
      49 (1972), pp. 446-52.

179   Bowman, Georgia B. "A Study of the Reporting by 27
      Metropolitan Newspapers of Selected Speeches of
      Adlai Stevenson and Dwight Eisenhower in the 1952
      Presidential Campaign." Unpublished Ph.D. disser-
      tation, U. of Iowa, 1957.

180   Bowman, Lewis, and Boynton, G. R. "Recruitment
      Patterns Among Local Party Officials: A Model and
      Some Preliminary Findings in Selected Locales,"
      The American Political Science Review, 60 (1966),
      pp. 667-76.

181   Boyarsky, Bill. The Rise of Ronald Reagan. New
      York: Random House, 1968.

182   Boyd, R. W. "Presidential Elections: An Explanation
      of Voting Defection," American Political Science Re-
      view, 63 (1969), pp. 498-514.

183   Brademas, J. "Candidate's Compleat Guide to Political
      Evasion," Grade Teacher, 86 (Oct., 1968), pp. 30+.

184   Bradford, R., and Elliott, W. "Politics and Television:
      A Fable," Television's Impact on American Culture,
      ed. William Y. Elliott. East Lansing, Mich.:
      Michigan State University Press, 1956, pp. 183-94.

185   Bradley, Rulon L. "The Use of the Mass Media in the
      1960 Election." Unpublished Ph.D. dissertation, U.
      of Utah, 1962.

186 Brandes, Paul D. "The Attitude of College Audiences to Speakers of Political Extremes," Southern Speech Journal, 32 (1967), pp. 282-88.

187 "Britain: Television: Politics on the Box," Economist, 230, n. 6542 (Jan. 11, 1969), p. 46.

188 Brock, Bernard L. "1968 Democratic Campaign: A Political Upheaval," Quarterly Journal of Speech, 55 (1969), pp. 26-35.

189 _____. "Unifying Issues and Image in Political Argument." Paper presented at the Central States Speech Association Convention, Chicago, April, 1972.

190 Broder, Davis S. "Great Speeches Aren't Necessarily Good Politics," New York Times Magazine, March 29, 1964, p. 7+.

191 _____. The Party's Over: The Failure of Politics in America. New York: Harper and Row, 1972.

192 _____. "Political Reporters in Presidential Politics," Washington Monthly, 1 (Feb., 1969), pp. 20-33.

193 Brooks, William D. "A Field Study of the Johnson and Goldwater Campaign Speeches in Pittsburgh," Southern Speech Journal, 32 (1967), pp. 273-81.

194 _____. "A Study of Images of Congressman Robert Ellsworth and Senator James Pearson in Five Selected Cities in Kansas." Research Report, The Communication Research Center, University of Kansas, 1966, 5 pp.

195 _____. "A Study of the Relationships of Selected Factors to Changes in Voting Attitudes of Audiences Listening to Political Speeches of President Johnson and Senator Goldwater." Unpublished Ph.D. dissertation, Ohio U., 1964.

196 Broughton, Ida A. M. "A Content Analysis of Daily and Weekly Newspaper Coverage of the 1968 Louisiana Sixth Congressional District Democratic Primary Campaign." Unpublished M.A. thesis, Louisiana State University, 1969.

197   Brown, Dennis E.   "The San Francisco Press in Two
      Presidential Campaigns: A Study of the Effects of
      Newspaper Concentration on Diversity in Editorial
      Page Comment." Unpublished Ph.D. dissertation,
      U. of Missouri, 1971.

198   Brown, J. G.   "Presidential Campaign Items, 1789-
      1956," Hobbies, 65 (August, 1960), pp. 28-29.

199   Brown, Robert L.   "Goldwater's Agency," Sales Man-
      agement, 93 (Sept. 18, 1964), pp. 36-38+.

200   Brown, Robert U.   "Ike Press Support 67%; Stevenson
      Backed by 14%," Editor and Publisher, 85 (Nov. 1,
      1952), p. 9.

201   Brown, William B.   The People's Choice: The Presi-
      dential Image in the Campaign Biography.   Baton
      Rouge: Louisiana State University Press, 1960.

202   Brown, William R.   "Television and the Democratic
      National Convention in 1968," Quarterly Journal of
      Speech, 55 (1969), pp. 237-46.

203   Browning, R. P., and Jacob, Herbert.   "Power Motiva-
      tion and the Political Personality," Public Opinion
      Quarterly, 28 (1964), pp. 75-90.

204   Brundage, Gloria Swegman.   "Rationale for the Applica-
      tion of the Fairness Doctrine in Broadcast News,"
      Journalism Quarterly, 49 (1972), pp. 531-37.

205   Bruno, Jerry, and Greenfield, Jeff.   Advance Man: An
      Offbeat Look at What Really Happens in Political
      Campaigns.   New York: William Morrow and Co.,
      1971.

206   Bryant, Barbara E.   "Message Manipulation Effects on
      Attitude Change and Comprehension in Communication
      of a Complex Political Issue." Paper presented at
      the International Communication Association Conven-
      tion, Phoenix, April, 1971.

207   _____ .   "Message Manipulations in Communication
      of a Complex Political Issue." Unpublished Ph.D.
      dissertation, Michigan State University, 1970.

208   Bryant, Donald C. (ed.). "Rhetoric and the Campaign
       of 1956," Quarterly Journal of Speech, 43 (1957),
       pp. 29-54.

209   Bryson, L. "Signs and Symbols in the Presidential
       Campaign," Commonweal, 64 (April 6, 1956), pp.
       14-16.

210   Buckley, Tom. "The Three Men Behind Rockefeller,"
       New York Times Magazine, October 30, 1966, pp.
       34-35+.

211   Burch, D. "Speaking Out: Presidential Campaigns Are
       a Sham," Saturday Evening Post, 238 (March 27,
       1965), p. 12+.

212   Burdick, Eugene, and Broadbeck, A. J. "Social De-
       terminism and Electoral Decision: The Case of
       Indiana," American Voting Behavior, eds. Eugene
       Burdick and A. J. Brodbeck. Glencoe, Ill.: Free
       Press, 1959, pp. 281-99.

213   _____, et al. The Eighth Art: Twenty-Three Views
       of Television Today. New York: Holt, Rinehart and
       Winston, 1962.

214   Burkhart, James A., and Kendrick, Frank J. The New
       Politics: Mood or Movement? Englewood Cliffs,
       N.J.: Prentice-Hall, 1971.

215   _____, et al. Strategies of Participation. Cam-
       bridge, Mass.: Winthrop Publishers, 1972.

216   Burnham, W. D. "American Voting Behavior in the
       1964 Election," Midwest Journal of Political Science,
       12 (1968), pp. 1-40.

217   Burnham, Walter Dean. Critical Elections and the Main-
       springs of American Politics. New York: Norton,
       1970.

218   Bush, C. "The Analysis of Political Campaign News,"
       Journalism Quarterly, 28 (1951), pp. 250-52.

219   Butcher, H. K. "How to Be a Politician," National
       Municipal Review, 47 (May, 1958), pp. 216-19.

220   Butler, David. "Polls and Elections," Spectator, no.
        7072 (1964), pp. 36-37.

221   "Buttons Pick the Victor," Business Week, July 25,
        1964, p. 34.

222   Byrne, Donn; Bond, Michael H.; and Diamond, Michael
        J.   "Response to Political Candidates as a Function
        of Attitude Similarity-Dissimilarity," Human Rela-
        tions, 22 (June, 1969), pp. 251-62.

223   "Cable TV Enters Presidential Race," United States
        News and World Report, 72 (March 13, 1972), p. 66.

224   Caldwell, Donald W. "An Analysis of Selected News-
        paper Coverage of the 1968 National Democratic Con-
        vention." Unpublished M.S.J. thesis, West Virginia
        University, 1969.

225   Califano, Joseph, Jr. "The Political Airwaves: The
        Conspiracy of TV Advertising and Politics in Re-
        making Images Is Disturbing," New Democrat, 3
        (March, 1972), pp. 16-17.

226   "The Campaign: A Matter of Inches?" Time, 72 (Nov.
        3, 1958), pp. 15-16.

227   "Campaign Buttons and Bows: A Sign Picture Article,"
        Sign, 32 (Nov., 1952), pp. 15-17.

228   "Campaign Buttons Write our Political History," Col-
        liers, 138 (Oct. 26, 1956), pp. 42-43.

229   "Campaign by Talkathon," Newsweek, 40 (August 25,
        1952), p. 76.

230   "Campaign Costs: More Specialization, More Dollars,"
        Congressional Quarterly Weekly Report, 29 (Sept.
        11, 1971), pp. 1912-16.

231   "Campaign Coverage: An Appraisal of 1960--and Im-
        plications for 1964: How Fair Were Newspapers in
        the 1960 Campaign?" Columbia Journalism Review,
        1 (1961), pp. 6-19.

232 "Campaign Coverage '64," Quill, 52 (August, 1964),
     pp. 12-18.

233 "Campaign Guide to Publicity." Washington, D.C.:
     Democratic National Committee, 1954, 96 pp.

234 "Campaign Issue; Biased Reporting?" United States
     News and World Report, 57 (August 3, 1964), p. 40.

235 "Campaign Mud," Reporter, 35 (Nov. 17, 1966), p.
     20+.

236 "Campaign '72: Newspaper Endorsements: Nixon, 753;
     McGovern, 56," Congressional Quarterly Weekly Re-
     port, 30 (Nov. 4, 1972), pp. 2898-99.

237 "Campaign '72: Political Advertising: Making It Look
     Like News," Congressional Quarterly Weekly Report,
     30 (Nov. 4, 1972), pp. 2900-04.

238 "Campaign '72: The Media Woods," Nation, 214 (June
     19, 1972), pp. 771-73.

239 "Campaign Spending Controls under the Federal Election
     Campaign Act of 1971," Columbia Journal of Law
     and Social Problems, 8 (Spring, 1972), pp. 285-320.

240 "Campaign Spending Regulation: Failure of the First
     Step," Harvard Journal of Legislation, 8 (May, 1971),
     pp. 640-74.

241 "Campaign Traditions Up-To-Date," Economist, 164
     (July 5, 1952), pp. 22-24.

242 "Campaigning on TV," Washington, D.C.: National
     Association of Radio and Television Broadcasters,
     1952, 18 pp.

243 "Campaigns in the West," Economist, 173 (Oct. 23,
     1954), pp. 302-03.

244 Campbell, Angus. "Has Television Reshaped Politics?"
     Columbia Journalism Review, Fall, 1962, pp. 10-13.

245 _____; Gurin, Gerald; and Miller, Warren E. "Po-
     litical Issues and the Vote: November, 1952,"
     American Political Science Review, 47 (1953), pp.
     359-85.

246 _____; _____; and _____. "Television and the
        Election," Scientific American, 188 (May, 1953), pp.
        46-48.

247 _____; _____; and _____. The Voter Decides.
        Evanston, Ill.: Row, Peterson Co., 1954.

248 _____, and Miller, W. E. "The Motivational
        Basis of Straight and Split Ticket Voting," Ameri-
        can Political Science Review, 51 (1957), pp. 293-
        312.

249 _____, et al. The American Voter. New York:
        John Wiley and Sons, 1960.

250 _____, et al. Elections and the Political Order.
        New York: John Wiley and Sons, 1966.

251 Canby, William C., Jr. "The First Amendment Right
        to Persuade: Access to Radio and Television,"
        U.C.L.A. Law Review, 19 (1972), p. 723+.

252 "A Candidate Is Not A Product," Fair Comment (Quar-
        terly of the Fair Campaign Practices Committee),
        1965.

253 "Candidates Debate--Now," The New York Times, July
        14, 1968, Section 5E, p. 10.

254 "Candidates vs. Newsmen," Time, 60 (Sept. 22, 1952),
        p. 98+.

255 Canham, E. D. "The American Press and the 1952
        Presidential Campaign," Confluence, 2 (March, 1953),
        pp. 108-16.

256 Canon, Dwayne Tipton. "The 1970 Nonpartisan Primary
        Race for State Superintendent of Public Instruction in
        California: An Analytic Case Study of the Canon Cam-
        paign." Unpublished Ph.D. dissertation, Claremont
        Graduate School, 1972.

257 Carey, Kevin W. "Tom Swift and his Electric Elec-
        torate: Legislation to Restrict Election Coverage,"
        Notre Dame Lawyer, 40 (1965), pp. 191-202.

258 Carlson, Earl, and Habel, Daniel A. "The Perception of Policy Positions of Presidential Candidates," Journal of Social Psychology, 79 (1969), pp. 69-77.

259 Carlsson, Gosta. "Time and Continuity in Mass Attitude Change: The Case of Voting," Public Opinion Quarterly, 29 (1965), pp. 1-15.

260 Carney, Francis M., and Way, H. Frank, Jr. (eds.). Politics 1972. Belmont, Calif.: Wadsworth Publishing Co., 1971.

261 Carson, S. "'Ike' and 'Mike'--TV and the Election," Nation, 175 (Nov. 15, 1952), pp. 448-49.

262 Carter, H. "Hushpuppies, Stew and Oratory," New York Times Magazine, June 18, 1950, pp. 12-13+.

263 Carter, P. "Local Scene: Where the Pork Barrel Still Rules, 1968 Senate and House Races," Newsweek, 70 (July 10, 1967), p. 39.

264 Carter, R. E., Jr., and Clark, P. "Public Affairs Opinion Leadership Among Educational Television Viewers," American Sociological Review, 27 (1962), pp. 792-99.

265 Carter, Richard F. "Bandwagon and Sandbagging Effects: Some Measures of Dissonance Reductions," Public Opinion Quarterly, 23 (1959), pp. 279-87.

266 _____, and Greenberg, Bradley S. "Newspapers or Television: Which Do You Believe?" Journalism Quarterly, 42 (1965), pp. 29-34.

267 "A Case for Bookburning," Christian Century, 81 (Nov. 11, 1964), p. 1415.

268 "The Case for Political Debates on TV?" New York Times Magazine, Jan. 19, 1964.

269 Cass, Don Pirie. How to Win Votes and Influence Elections. Chicago: Public Administration Service, 1962.

270 "Cast of Thousands," Newsweek, 71 (April 8, 1968), pp. 43-44.

271   Cater, Douglass. "Notes from Backstage," Reporter,
       23 (Nov. 10, 1960), pp. 19-20.

272   "CATV Has Good Political Season," Variety, Nov. 13,
       1968, p. 121.

273   Chaffee, Steven H.; Ward, Scott L.; and Tipton,
       Leonard. "Mass Communication and Political
       Socialization," Journalism Quarterly, 47 (1970),
       pp. 647-59.

274   Chang, Lawrence K., and Lemert, James B. "The In-
       visible Newsman and Other Factors in Media Com-
       petition," Journalism Quarterly, 45 (1968), pp. 436-
       44.

275   "Charge-a-Vote," Newsweek, 71 (April 29, 1968), p. 76.

276   "Charisma, Calluses and Cash," Time, 88 (Oct. 14,
       1966), pp. 37-38.

277   Chartrand, Robert L. Computers and Political Cam-
       paigning. New York: Spartan Books, 1972.

278   _____. "The Use of Automatic Data Processing in
       Politics," Congressional Record, 113 (July 27, 1967),
       pp. A3829-A3834.

279   Chase, Edward T. "Politics and Technology," Yale
       Review, 52 (March, 1963), pp. 321-39.

280   Chase, H., and Lerman, A. (eds.). Kennedy and the
       Press. New York: Crowell, 1965.

281   Cherney, Sheldon. "An Analysis of the Use of Humor
       in Presidential Campaign Speeches, 1940-1952." Un-
       published Ph.D. dissertation, University of Southern
       California, 1956.

282   Chesebro, James W. "Toward a Generic Conception of
       Presidential Campaigns," Moments in Contemporary
       Rhetoric and Communication (Temple U.), 2 (Fall,
       1972), pp. 4-5.

283   Chester, Edward W. Radio, Television and American
       Politics. New York: Sheed and Ward, 1969.

284 _____. "The Radio and Television Styles of Ameri-
    can Presidents." Paper presented at the Speech As-
    sociation of America Convention, New York City,
    Dec. 27-30, 1969.

285 Chester, Lewis; Hodgson, Godfrey; and Page, Bruce.
    An American Melodrama: The Presidential Cam-
    paign of 1968. New York: Viking Press, 1969.

286 "Choosing Sides," Newsweek, 70 (Nov. 20, 1967), p. 94.

287 Christenson, Reo M., and McWilliams, Robert O.
    Voice of the People: Readings in Public Opinion and
    Propaganda. New York: McGraw-Hill, 1967.

288 Christoph, James B. "The Press and Politics in
    Britain and America," Political Quarterly, 34 (April-
    June, 1963), pp. 137-50.

289 Churgin, Jonah R. "Anatomy of a Presidential Primary:
    An Analysis of New Hampshire's Impact on American
    Politics." Unpublished Ph.D. dissertation, Brown
    University, 1970.

290 Clark, Carroll Hamilton. "Some Aspects of Voting Be-
    havior in Flint, Michigan--A City with Nonpartisan
    Municipal Elections." Unpublished Ph.D. disserta-
    tion, University of Michigan, 1952.

291 Clark, Wesley C. "The Impact of Masscommunications
    (sic) in America," Annals of the American Academy
    of Political and Social Science, 378 (1968), pp. 68-
    74.

292 Clarke, George T., and Ewald, Bill. "Media, Money
    and Markets," Challenge, 8 (July, 1960), pp. 29-37.

293 Clarke, Peter, and Ruggels, Lee. "Preferences Among
    News Media for Coverage of Public Affairs," Jour-
    nalism Quarterly, 47 (1970), pp. 464-71.

294 Clausen, A. R. "Political Predictions and Projections:
    How Are They Conducted? Do They Influence the
    Outcome of Elections?" Washington, Conn.: Center
    for Information on America, 1966, 14 pp.

295 Cleary, James W., and Haberman, Frederick W. (eds.).
     Rhetoric and Public Address: A Bibliography, 1947-
     1961. Madison and Milwaukee: University of Wis-
     consin Press, 1964.

296 Cleary, R. "Elections and Image Building," Today's
     Education, 60 (Dec., 1971), pp. 30-32+.

297 Clem, Alan L. "Analysis of the 1958 Congressional
     Campaign in the Third District of Nebraska." Un-
     published Ph.D. dissertation, American University,
     1960.

298 Clevenger, Theodore, Jr. "Communication and the
     Survival of Democracy," Address, Dec. 30, 1972,
     Vital Speeches, 39 (Feb. 1, 1973), pp. 239-42.

299 _____, and Knepprath, Eugene. "A Quantitative
     Analysis of Logical and Emotional Content in Se-
     lected Campaign Addresses of Eisenhower and Steven-
     son," Western Speech, 30 (1966), pp. 144-50.

300 Clotfelter, James. "Communication Theory in the
     Study of Politics," Studies in Journalism and Com-
     munication, 7 (1968).

301 Clyde, Robert W.; Hemmerle, William J.; and Ban-
     croft, T. A. "An Application of 'Post Stratifica-
     tion' Technique in Local TV Election Predictions,"
     Public Opinion Quarterly, 27 (1963), pp. 467-72.

302 Coffin, T. "Sales Techniques Give Politics New
     Twist," Nation's Business, 44 (April, 1956), pp.
     86-89.

303 Coleman, James, and Waldorf, Frank. "A Study of
     Voting Systems with Computer Techniques." Balti-
     more: Johns Hopkins University, 1966.

304 _____, et al. "Computers and Election Analysis:
     The New York Times Project," Public Opinion Quar-
     terly, 28 (1964), pp. 418-46.

305 Colldeweih, Jack Howard. "The Effects of Mass Media
     Consumption on Accuracy of Beliefs about the Candi-
     dates in a Local Congressional Election." Unpub-
     lished Ph.D. dissertation, U. of Illinois, 1968.

306 "Combining all Channels to Reach a Mass Public; J. W. Kluge's Metromedia," Business Week, Sept. 18, 1965, pp. 80-82+.

307 Commager, Henry Steele. "Is It the Man or Is It the Issue?" New York Times Magazine, Oct. 12, 1952, p. 13+.

308 _____. "Washington Would Have Lost a TV Debate," New York Times Magazine, Oct. 30, 1960, pp. 13, 79-80.

309 The Committee for Economic Development. "Financing a Better Election System." New York: The Committee for Economic Development, 1968.

310 Compton, D. "Super-Veep," Atlantic, 219 (April, 1967), p. 118+.

311 "Computerized Army: Nixon's Campaign Organization," Time, 92 (Oct. 25, 1968), p. 26.

312 "Computers Try the Campaign Trail," Business Week, Jan. 20, 1968, p. 84+.

313 Congressional Quarterly Weekly Report. "Campaign Management Grows into National Industry," Congressional Quarterly Weekly Report, 26 (April 5, 1968), pp. 706-14+.

314 _____. "Political Pollsters Head for Record Activity in 1968," Congressional Quarterly Weekly Report, 26 (May 3, 1968), pp. 992-1000.

315 Connelly, F. Marlin. "Some Questions Concerning Lyndon Johnson's Rhetoric in the 1964 Presidential Campaign," Southern Speech Journal, 37 (1971), pp. 11-20.

316 "Conventions: Change on Tap?" Broadcasting, 51 (August 27, 1956), p. 28.

317 Converse, Philip E. "Information Flow and the Stability of Partisan Attitudes," Public Opinion Quarterly, 26 (1962), pp. 578-99.

318 Conway, M. M. "Voter Information Sources in a Non-
     Partisan Local Election," Western Political Quarter-
     ly, 21 (1968), pp. 69-77.

319 Cook, Samuel DuBois. "Political Movements and Or-
     ganizations," Journal of Politics, 26 (1964), pp. 130-
     53.

320 Cooke, Alistair. "Choosing a Leader--U.S. Style,"
     Listener, 70 (October 17, 1963), pp. 595+.

321 _____. "Cunning Campaign of Reagan," Guardian,
     June 7, 1966, p. 12.

322 _____. "Image-Makers Beware," National Review,
     22 (Oct. 20, 1970), pp. 1103-04.

323 _____. "Mr. Nixon's Invisible Campaign for Presi-
     dency," Guardian, Jan. 11, 1960, p. 7.

324 _____. "Oracles under a Cloud," Guardian, Nov.
     26, 1966, p. 9.

325 _____. "The Smear Campaign Gathers Force,"
     Guardian, Sept. 2, 1960, p. 9.

326 Cooper, Joseph B. "Perceptual Organization as a Func-
     tion of Politically Oriented Communication," Journal
     of Social Psychology, 41 (1955), pp. 319-24.

327 Coplin, William D. (ed.). Simulation in the Study of
     Politics. Chicago: Markham Publishing Co., 1968.

328 Cordier, Hubert V. "Campaigning with Television:
     The Speaking of Senator Paul H. Douglas in the
     1954 Campaign." Unpublished Ph.D. dissertation,
     U. of Illinois, 1955.

329 Cornwell, E. "The Johnson Press Relations Style,"
     Journalism Quarterly, 43 (1966), pp. 3-9.

330 _____. "Presidential News: The Expanding Public
     Image," Journalism Quarterly, 36 (1959), pp. 275-
     83.

331 "Corruption in the Campaign," New Republic, 167 (Oct.
     28, 1972), pp. 5-7.

332 "Cost of Campaigning, Rockefeller Style," United States
     News and World Report, 65 (July 29, 1968), p. 26.

333 Costigan, James. "Communication Theory in the Works
     of Marshall McLuhan." Unpublished Ph.D. disserta-
     tion, Southern Illinois University, 1969.

334 _____. "Media Exposure, Political Preference, and
     Candidate Image." Unpublished Paper, Speech Dept.,
     Southern Illinois University, 1969.

335 Cotler, Gordon. "That Plague of Spots from Madison
     Avenue," Reporter, 7 (Nov. 25, 1952), pp. 7-8.

336 Cotter, Neil (ed.). Practical Politics. Boston: Allyn
     and Bacon, 1968.

337 Cottin, Jonathon. "Advance Men Ensure Campaigners
     against Silent Mikes, Short Stories," National Jour-
     nal, 4 (June 3, 1972), pp. 924-30.

338 _____. "Political Spending Law Will Have Impact
     on Candidates, Business, Labor," National Journal,
     4 (1972), pp. 276-82.

339 "Covering the Candidate," Newsweek, 64 (July 20, 1964),
     pp. 71-72.

340 Cox, Kenneth Z. "Broadcasters as Revolutionaries,"
     Television Quarterly, 6 (1967), pp. 13-19.

341 Coyle, Edward. "Behind the Scenes in Political Ad-
     vertising--1962," Western Advertising, Sept., 1962,
     pp. 17-18+.

342 Craig, H. R. "A Rhetorical Criticism of the Principal
     Network Speeches on the Issues of Corruption and
     Subversion in the 1952 Presidential Campaign." Un-
     published Ph.D. dissertation, University of Iowa,
     1955.

343 Craig, Robert E. "Voting Behavior in a Presidential
     Primary: The New Hampshire Democratic Presiden-
     tial Primary of 1968." Unpublished Ph.D. disserta-
     tion, U. of North Carolina at Chapel Hill, 1971.

344   Cranford, R.   "The Nebraska Press Coverage of the
      1960 Presidential Campaign."   Unpublished Ph.D.
      dissertation, U. of Nebraska, 1964.

345   Cranson, Pat.   "Political Convention Broadcasts: Their
      History and Influence," Journalism Quarterly, 37
      (1960), pp. 186-94.

346   Crawford, K.   "New and Improved," Newsweek, 71
      (June 24, 1968), p. 38.

347   _____.   "Television Politics," Newsweek, 76 (July
      20, 1970), p. 24.

348   _____.   "They Vote Against," Newsweek, 69 (May 1,
      1967), p. 30.

349   Crick, B.   "The Science of Politics in the United
      States," Canadian Journal of Economics and Political
      Science, 20 (August, 1954), pp. 308-20.

350   Crosby, J.   "TV and the 1952 Election," American
      Magazine, 153 (April, 1952), p. 21+.

351   _____.   "TV's Future Effect on Politicians,"
      Reader's Digest, 58 (Jan., 1951), pp. 4-5.

352   Crossley, Archibald M., and Crossley, 'Helen M.
      "Polling in 1968," Public Opinion Quarterly, 33
      (1969), pp. 1-16.

353   Crossman, R. H. S.   "Political Cabaret," Guardian,
      May 10, 1963, p. 22.

354   Crotty, William J.   "Party Effort and Its Impact on
      the Vote," American Political Science Review, 65
      (1971), pp. 439-50.

355   _____   (ed.).   Public Opinion and Politics: A Reader.
      New York: Holt, Rinehart, and Winston, Inc., 1970.

356   Cummings, Milton C. (ed.).   The National Election of
      1964.   Washington, D.C.:   The Brookings Institution,
      1966.

357 Cunningham and Walsh. Television and the Political
    Candidate, A Report Prepared by the Research De-
    partment. New York: Cunningham and Walsh, Inc.,
    1959.

358 Cusack, M. "The Emergence of Political Editorializing
    in Broadcasting," Journal of Broadcasting, 8 (1963),
    pp. 53-62.

359 Cutright, Phillips. "Measuring the Impact of Local
    Party Activity on the General Election Vote," Public
    Opinion Quarterly, 27 (1963), pp. 372-86.

360 Dahl, Robert A. "Who Participates in Local Politics
    and Why?" Science, 134 (1961), pp. 1340-48.

361 Danbury, Thomas, and Berger, Charles. "The Diffu-
    sion of Political Information and Its Effect on Candi-
    date Preference." Paper presented at the Associa-
    tion for Education in Journalism Convention, Syra-
    cuse, New York, August, 1965.

362 Danforth, K. "Dodging the Dragon's Tail: The Advance
    Man's Work," Time, 92 (Oct. 25, 1968), p. 28+.

363 Danielson, Wayne, and Adams, John B. "Completeness
    of Press Coverage of the 1960 Campaign," Journalism
    Quarterly, 38 (1961), pp. 441-52.

364 _____, and Wilhoit, G. C., Jr. A Computerized
    Bibliography of Mass Communication Research, 1944-
    64. New York: Magazine Publisher's Association,
    Inc., 1967.

365 Danish, Roy. "The Shaping of the Television Medium."
    Speech before the Speech Association of America,
    New York City, Dec. 30, 1965.

366 Darby, John M., and Cooper, Joel. "The 'clean for
    Gene' Phenomenon: The Effect of Students' Ap-
    pearance on Political Campaigning," Journal of Ap-
    plied Social Psychology, 2 (1972), pp. 24-33.

367 Darcy, Robert. "Communications and Political Atti-
    tudes." Unpublished Ph.D. dissertation, University
    of Kentucky, 1971.

368 _____ . "Communications and Political Attitudes:
     An Experimental Investigation." Paper presented at
     the American Political Science Association Conven-
     tion, Washington, D.C., September, 1972.

369 David, P. T. "Presidential Election Campaigns: Could
     They Be Done Better?" Washington, Conn.: Center
     for Information on America, 1967, 4 pp.

370 Davies, J. C. "Charisma in the 1952 Campaign,"
     American Political Science Review, 48 (1954), pp.
     1083-1102.

371 Davis, James. "A Political Scientist Views the Cam-
     paign." Paper presented at the Central States
     Speech Association Convention, Minneapolis, April,
     1973.

372 Davis, James W., Jr. Presidential Primaries: Road
     to the White House. New York: Crowell, 1967.

373 Davis, N. G. "Freedom of the Press in Texas: A
     Comparative Study of State Legal Controls on Mass
     News Media." Unpublished Ph.D. dissertation, U.
     of Minnesota, 1954.

374 Dawson, P. A., and Zinser, J. E. "Broadcast Ex-
     penditures and Electoral Outcomes in the 1970 Con-
     gressional Elections," Public Opinion Quarterly, 35
     (1971), pp. 398-402.

375 Day, John F. "Do the Pollsters Control Your Vote?"
     New Leader, 43 (August 29, 1960), pp. 3-5.

376 Day-Lewis, Sean. "Politics and the Box," Daily Tele-
     graph, June 16, 1970, p. 11.

377 Dean, Richard Lawrence. "Aspects of Persuasive Ap-
     peal in Stevenson's Campaign Speeches," Speaker,
     37 (May, 1955), pp. 19-22.

378 "Debating the Great Debate: Symposium," Nation, 191
     (Nov. 5, 1960), pp. 342-47.

379 Deedy, J. "News and Views," Commonweal, 89 (Nov.
     22, 1968), p. 266.

380 Defleur, Melvin L. "Experimental Studies of Stimulus Response Relationships in Leaflet Communication." Unpublished Ph.D. dissertation, U. of Washington, 1954.

381 De Grazia, Alfred. "The Limits of External Leadership over a Minority Electorate," Public Opinion Quarterly, 20 (1956), pp. 113-28.

382 Delson, Jane. "Ethos or 'Image' in Contemporary Political Persuasion with Particular Reference to Lyndon B. Johnson, 1964." Unpublished Ph.D. dissertation, U. of California at Los Angeles, 1967.

383 Dematier, Royce D., et al. (eds.). The Rumble of California Politics, 1848-1970. New York: John Wiley and Sons, Inc., 1970.

384 Democratic National Committee. A Campaign Guide to Political Publicity: A Handbook for Candidates. Washington, D.C.: Democratic National Committee, 1955.

385 Department of Marketing, Miami University. "Influence of Television on the Election of 1952." Oxford, Ohio: Oxford Research Associates, 1954.

386 De Santis, Vincent P. "The Presidential Election of 1952," Review of Politics, 15 (April, 1953), pp. 131-50.

387 "Design in Politics: The Candidate Identity Program," Print, 22 (Sept./Oct., 1968), pp. 30-35.

388 De Toledano, Ralph, and Brennan, Phillip V., Jr. Claude Kirk--Man and Myth. New York: Pyramid Books, 1970.

389 Deutschmann, Paul. "Viewing, Conversation and Voting Intentions," The Great Debates, ed. Sidney Kraus. Bloomington, Indiana: Indiana U. Press, 1962, pp. 232-52.

390 Devlin, Lawrence Patrick. Contemporary Political Speaking. Belmont, Calif.: Wadsworth Publishing Co., Inc., 1971.

391   _____. "Hubert H. Humphrey: His Speaking Princi-
       ples and Practices in Campaign and General Audience
       Speaking to 1966." Unpublished Ph.D. dissertation,
       Wayne State U., 1968.

392   _____. "Professional Political Speechwriting and
       Rhetorical Criticism." Paper presented at the
       Speech-Communication Association Convention, Chica-
       go, Dec. 27-30, 1972.

393   DeVries, Walter, and Tarrance, V. Lance, Jr. The
       Ticket-Splitter: A New Force in American Politics.
       Grand Rapids, Mich: William B. Eerdmans Pub-
       lishing Co., 1972.

394   Dexter, L. A. "Candidates Must Make the Issues and
       Give Them Meaning," Public Opinion Quarterly, 19
       (1955-56), pp. 408-14.

395   _____. "The Use of Public Opinion Polls by Political
       Party Organizations," Public Opinion Quarterly, 18
       (1954), pp. 53-61.

396   Diamond, Edwin. "Chicago Press: Rebellion and Re-
       trenchment," Columbia Journalism Review, 7 (Fall,
       1968), pp. 10-17.

397   Diamond, S. "Language and Politics: An Afterword,"
       Political Science Quarterly, 84 (1969), pp. 380-85.

398   Dickens, Milton, and Williams, Frederick. "Mass
       Communication," Review of Educational Research,
       34 (April, 1964), pp. 211-21.

399   Dickerson, George. "Politics and the Sexual Image,"
       Mademoiselle, 63 (Oct., 1966), pp. 172-73+.

400   Dickinson, W. B., Jr. "Politicians and the Press,"
       Editorial Research Reports, Sept. 2, 1964, pp. 643-
       60.

401   "Dirty Politics: A Bumper Crop of Complaints in
       1972," Congressional Quarterly Weekly Report, 30
       (Nov. 18, 1972), pp. 3046-47.

402   "Dirty Politics and Backlash," Life, 61 (Oct. 7, 1966),
       p. 8.

403 Dishman, Robert B. "The Eisenhower Pre-Convention Campaign in New Hampshire, 1952," New England Quarterly, 26 (1953), pp. 3-26.

404 "Divided Opinion," Newsweek, 75 (Jan. 19, 1970), p. 59.

405 Dizney, H. F., and Roskens, R. W. "An Investigation of the 'Bandwagon Effect' in a College Straw Election," Journal of Educational Sociology, 36 (Nov., 1962), pp. 108-14.

406 "Do Agencies Belong in Politics: Consensus of 408 Advertising Executives," Printers' Ink, 270 (March 25, 1960), p. 51.

407 Doig, I. "Kefauver versus Crime: Television Boosts a Senator," Journalism Quarterly, 39 (1962), pp. 483-90.

408 Dominick, J. R. "Television and Political Socialization," Educational Broadcasting Review, 6 (1972), pp. 48-55.

409 Donohew, Lewis. "Decoder Behavior on Incongruent Political Material: A Pilot Study," Journal of Communication, 16 (1966), pp. 133-42.

410 _____, and Palmgreen, Phillip. "A Reappraisal of Dissonance and the Selective Exposure Hypothesis," Journalism Quarterly, 48 (1971), pp. 412-20.

411 Donovan, Robert J. "Television and the 1952 Campaign," Reporter, 6 (March 4, 1952), pp. 38-39.

412 Doob, Leonard, et al. "Opinion Polls, Computers, and the National Election." New Haven, Conn.: Yale U., Yale Reports, 1964.

413 Dordick, Herbert S., and Lyle, Jack. "Access by Local Political Candidates to Cable Television: A Report of an Experiment." Santa Monica, Calif.: The Rand Corp., Nov., 1971.

414 Dorr, C. E. "Presidential Campaign Insignia," Hobbies, 57 (July, 1952), pp. 18-21.

415 Dorris, Celia A. "A Rhetorical Analysis of the 1954
     Campaign Speaking of Richard L. Neuberger." Un-
     published Ph.D. dissertation, U. of Oregon, 1970.

416 Douglas, Jack. "The Verbal Image: Student Percep-
     tions of Political Figures," Speech Monographs, 39
     (1972), pp. 1-15.

417 Douglas, Paul H. "Is Campaign Oratory a Waste of
     Breath?" New York Times Magazine, Oct. 19,
     1958, pp. 26, 72-73.

418 Downs, Anthony. An Economic Theory of Democracy.
     New York: Harper, 1957.

419 Dreistadt, Roy. "How to Answer the 'ifs' of Election
     Results by a New Survey Approach," Psychology, 8
     (Aug., 1971), pp. 19-21.

420 Dreyer, Edward C. "Media Use and Electoral Choices:
     Some Political Consequences of Information Exposure,"
     Public Opinion Quarterly, 35 (1971-72), pp. 544-53.

421 _____. "Political Party Use of Radio and TV in the
     1960 Campaign," Journal of Broadcasting, 8 (1964),
     pp. 211-17.

422 _____. "A Study of the Patterns of Political Com-
     munication in the South." Unpublished Ph.D. dis-
     sertation, U. of North Carolina at Chapel Hill, 1968.

423 _____, and Rosenbaum, Walter A. (eds.). Political
     Opinion and Electoral Behavior: Essays and Studies.
     Belmont, Calif.: Wadsworth Publishing Co., 1970.

424 Driberg, Tom. "The First TV Election," New States-
     man, 61 (March 10, 1961), pp. 374-76.

425 Duffy, Ben. "Adventures in Politics," Media/Scope,
     April, 1961, pp. 51-56.

426 Dunn, Delmer D. Financing Presidential Campaigns.
     Washington, D.C.: Brookings Institution, 1972.

427 Dursin, Henry L. "Public Issues: Who Cares about What?
     How the Interests of Opinion Leaders Differ from Those
     of the General Public," Public Relations Journal, 23
     (1967), pp. 24-25.

428 Duscha, Julius. "How Do You Fight Shirley Temple?"
     Reporter, 37 (Nov. 2, 1967), pp. 21-23.

429 Dustin, David S. "Attitudes toward Political Candidates,"
     Psychological Reports, 16 (1965), p. 1212.

430 Dybvig, Homer Eugene. "An Analysis of Political
     Communication through Television Commercials Pro-
     duced by the Robert Goodman Agency, Inc." Un-
     published Ph.D. dissertation, Southern Illinois Uni-
     versity, 1970.

431 Easton, David. A Systems Analysis of Political Life.
     New York: Wiley and Sons, 1965.

432 Ecroyd, Donald H. "The Alabama Governor's Primary,
     1954: A Case Study," Southern Speech Journal, 24
     (1959), pp. 135-43.

433 Edelman, Murray. Politics as Symbolic Action: Mass
     Arousal and Quiescence. Chicago: Markham Pub-
     lishing, 1971.

434 _____. The Symbolic Uses of Politics. Urbana,
     Ill.: U. of Illinois Press, 1964.

435 Edsall, Thomas B. "Maryland: The Governor Raiseth,"
     Washington Monthly, 3 (Feb., 1972), pp. 25-28+.

436 Edwards, Lee. Reagan: A Political Biography. San
     Diego: Viewpoint Books, 1967.

437 Efron, Edith. "The Great Television Myth," TV Guide,
     May 6, 1967, pp. 8-13.

438 Eggers, Paul. "The Candidate's Point of View."
     Report presented at the Seminar in Political Cam-
     paign Communication, Southern Illinois University,
     Carbondale, Ill., July 26, 1969.

439 Einhorn, Hillel J.; Komorita, S. S.; and Rosen, Ben-
     son. "Multidimensional Models for the Evaluation
     of Political Candidates," Journal of Experimental
     Social Psychology, 8 (1972), pp. 58-73.

440   Eisenber, Ronald A. "Vehicles of Communication Em-
        ployed by Robert Taft, Jr., Candidate for Congress,
        1966 Congressional Elections." Unpublished master's
        thesis, Bowling Green State U., 1965.

441   Eisenberg, Ralph. "Gubernatorial Politics in Virginia:
        The Experience of 1965," University of Virginia
        News Letter, March, 1969.

442   Elam, Maxine S. "The Texas Press in a Guberna-
        torial Primary, 1968: A General Content Analysis."
        Unpublished M.A. thesis, U. of Texas at Austin,
        1969.

443   Eldersveld, Samuel J. "Experimental Propaganda
        Techniques and Voting Behavior," American Po-
        litical Science Review, 50 (1956), pp. 154-65.

444   _____, and Dodge, Richard W. "Personal Contact
        or Mail Propaganda?" Public Opinion and Propa-
        ganda, ed. Daniel Katz. New York: Dryden Press,
        1954.

445   "Election Year in the United States," Statist, 173 (1960),
        Supplement, pp. 31-35.

446   "Elections, Computers, and the First Amendment,"
        Columbia Journal of Law and Social Problems, 2
        (June, 1966), pp. 17-36.

447   "Elections Made Easy," Television Age, 9 (April 30,
        1962), p. 31+.

448   "Electronic Politics: The Image Game," Time, 96
        (Sept. 21, 1970), pp. 43-44+.

449   "Electronic Stumping," Time, 68 (Sept. 17, 1956), p. 56.

450   "Electronics Give Incumbents an Edge," Business Week,
        Sept. 15, 1962, pp. 31-32.

451   "Electrons for Nixon," Newsweek, 72 (Sept. 30, 1968),
        p. 28.

452   "Eleventh Hour Radio-TV Volleys Climax Turbulent Cam-
        paign," Broadcasting, 47 (Nov. 1, 1954), p. 27.

453   Elfin, Mel, and Zweig, Leonard.   "The Battle of Po-
        litical Symbols," Public Opinion Quarterly, 18 (1954),
        pp. 205-10.

454   Eli, Jack.   "A Study of Political Attitudes and Voting
        Behavior in the 1970 Tennessee Gubernatorial Elec-
        tion." Unpublished Ph.D. dissertation, Southern
        Illinois U., 1971.

455   Eller, J. N.   "New Emphasis on People in Politics,
        Return to the Grass Roots," America, 107 (Dec.
        15, 1962), p. 1238.

456   Ellinghen, Ronald C.   "Inter-Media Usage Patterns of
        Politically Conservative, Liberal, Neutral Persons."
        Unpublished M.A. thesis, U. of Georgia, 1970.

457   Elliott, Elbert E.   "The Rhetoric of Spiro T. Agnew:
        A Study of Political Controversy." Unpublished Ph.D.
        dissertation, Southern Illinois U., 1972.

458   Ellsworth, J. W.   "Rationality and Campaigning: A
        Content Analysis of the 1960 Presidential Campaign
        Debates," Western Political Quarterly, 18 (1965),
        pp. 794-802.

459   Emery, Edwin.   "Press Support for Johnson and Gold-
        water," Journalism Quarterly, 41 (1964), pp. 485-
        88.

460   Emmett, B. P.   "The Design of Investigations into the
        Effects of Radio and Television Programmes and
        Other Mass Communications," Journal of the Royal
        Statistical Society, 129 (1966), pp. 26-59.

461   "Endorsing of Candidates by Celebrities," New Yorker,
        44 (Aug. 10, 1968), p. 19.

462   Erikson, Robert S.   "The Advantage of Incumbency in
        Congressional Elections," Polity, 3 (1971), pp. 395+ .

463   _____, and Zavoina, William J.   "Issues and Voters
        in the 1970 Florida Election," Governmental Re-
        search Bulletin (Institute of Governmental Research,
        Florida State U.), 8 (Nov., 1971), pp. 1-4.

464   Erskine, Hazel. "The Polls: Opinion of the News
      Media," Public Opinion Quarterly, 34 (1970-71), pp.
      630-43.

465   Eulau, Heinz. The Behavioral Persuasion in Politics.
      New York: Random House, 1963.

466   _____, and Schneider, Peter. "Dimensions of Po-
      litical Involvement," Public Opinion Quarterly, 20
      (1956), pp. 128-42.

467   Ewald, B. "Television and Politics; Who Projects the
      Image of a Winner?" Newsweek, 56 (Sept. 5, 1960),
      pp. 18-21.

468   Eysenck, H. J. The Psychology of Politics. London:
      Routledge and Kegan Paul, Ltd., 1954.

469   Fagen, Richard R. Politics and Communication. Bos-
      ton: Little, Brown, and Co., 1966.

470   Fairlie, Henry. "Misreporting the Campaign," Specta-
      tor, Sept. 23, 1972, p. 465.

471   Farber, Maurice L. "Toward a Psychology of Political
      Behavior," Public Opinion Quarterly, 24 (1960), pp.
      458-64.

472   Farney, Dennis. "A Modern Machine: How Savvy Matt
      Reese, a Political Consultant, Gets Out Winning
      Vote," Wall Street Journal, March 23, 1972, p. 1.

473   Farnsworth, A. "Political Propaganda and Income Tax,"
      The Solicitor, 21 (Sept., 1954), pp. 213-15.

474   Fayard, Judy. "Would You Vote for this Man? Film-
      ing of the Candidate, with Report by J. Fayard and
      the Spencer-Roberts Firm," Life, 73 (July 28, 1972),
      pp. 45-48+.

475   "FCC Rules Create Problems for Performer-Campaign-
      ers," Congressional Quarterly Weekly Report, 28
      (Sept. 25, 1970), pp. 2336-38.

476   Federal Communication Commission. "Survey of Po-
         litical Broadcasting, Primary and General Election
         Campaigns of 1966." Washington, D.C.: Federal
         Communications Commission, June, 1967.

477   _____. "Survey of Political Broadcasting, Septem-
         ber 1-November 8, 1960." Washington, D.C.:
         Federal Communications Commission, April, 1961.

478   Felknor, Bruce. Dirty Politics. New York: Norton
         Publication, 1966.

479   Fenton, John H. "For Cleaner Elections," National
         Municipal Review, 47 (Sept., 1958), pp. 384-87.

480   Fenton, R. W. "Candidates, Campaign, and Ballot
         Box," Public Relations Journal, 22 (March, 1966),
         pp. 25-28.

481   Ferguson, Beverly. "The Rhetorical Visions of the
         1972 Campaign: An Analysis of Consumer Communi-
         cation," Moments in Contemporary Rhetoric and Com-
         munication (Temple U.), 2 (Fall, 1972), pp. 38-44.

482   Ferguson, LeRoy, and Smuckler, Ralph. Politics in
         the Press. East Lansing, Mich.: Michigan State
         U. Press, 1954.

483   Ferguson, Sherry Devereaux. "A Study of the Good
         Will Speaking of a U.S. Congressman," Southern
         Speech Journal, 38 (1973), pp. 235-43.

484   Fingerhut, Vic. "A Limit on Campaign Spending--Who
         Will Benefit?" Public Interest, 25 (Fall, 1971), pp.
         3-13.

485   Finkelstein, Sidney. Sense and Nonsense of McLuhan.
         New York: International Publishers, 1968.

486   Finney, Robert G. "Television News Messages and
         Their Perceived Effects in a Congressional Election
         Campaign." Unpublished Ph.D. dissertation, Ohio
         State U., 1971.

487   Fishbaugh, C. W. "Political Badges," Hobbies, 65
         (June, 1960), pp. 120-21.

488   Fishbein, Martin, and Coombs, Fred S.   "Modern At-
        titude Theory and the Explanation of Voting Choice."
        Paper presented at the American Political Science
        Association Convention, Chicago, Sept., 1971.

489   Fisher, H. N. D.   "How the 'I Dare You!' Candidate
        Won," Public Relations Journal, 25 (April, 1969),
        pp. 26-29.

490   Fisher, Walter R.   "Reaffirmation and Subversion of
        the American Dream," Quarterly Journal of Speech,
        59 (1973), pp. 160-67.

491   Flanigan, William H.   "Partisanship and Campaign
        Participation."   Unpublished Ph.D. dissertation,
        Yale U., 1966.

492   _____.   Political Behavior and the American Elec-
        torate.   Boston: Allyn and Bacon, 1972.

493   Fleitas, D. W.   "Bandwagon and Underdog Effects in
        Minimal-Information Elections," American Political
        Science Review, 65 (1971), pp. 434-8.

494   Fleming, T. J.   "Selling the Product Named Hubert
        Humphrey," New York Times Magazine, Oct. 13,
        1968, pp. 45-47+.

495   Flood, Lawrence G.   "Voting in Primary Elections:
        The Case of Hillsborough, North Carolina."   Un-
        published Ph.D. dissertation, U. of North Carolina
        at Chapel Hill, 1970.

496   Flournoy, H. L.   "1958 Knowland Campaign in Cali-
        fornia--Design for Defeat," (abstract), Western Po-
        litical Quarterly, 12 (1959), pp. 571-2.

497   Foote, Cone and Belding.   "The Public's Reaction to
        Political Advertising," A Report Prepared by the Re-
        search Department.   New York: Foote, Cone and
        Belding, Jan., 1971.

498   Frank, Stanley.   "Campaigns Can Change Elections,"
        Nation's Business, 40 (Sept., 1952), pp. 25-27,
        74-77.

499   Freadman, Paul. "Broadcasting and Politics," University of Western Australia Annual Law Review, 2 (1952), pp. 281-300.

500   Free, Lloyd A., and Cantril, Hadley. The Political Beliefs of Americans: A Study of Public Opinion. New Brunswick, N.J.: Rutgers U. Press, 1967.

501   Freedman, Jonathan L., and Sears, David O. "Selective Exposure," Advances in Experimental Social Psychology, Vol. 2, ed. Leonard Berkowitz. New York: Academic Press, 1965.

502   _____, and _____. "Voters' Preferences Among Types of Information" (abstract of paper presented at American Psychological Association Convention, Philadelphia, Aug. 29-Sept. 4, 1963), American Psychologist, 14 (1963), p. 375.

503   Freeley, Austin J. "Ethos, Eisenhower and the 1956 Campaign," Central States Speech Journal, 9 (Spring, 1958), pp. 24-26.

504   Frenkel-Brunswik, E. "Interaction of Psychological and Sociological Factors in Political Behavior," American Political Science Review, 46 (March, 1952), pp. 44-65.

505   Freshley, Dwight L. "Gubernatorial Ghost Writers," Southern Speech Journal, 31 (1965), pp. 95-105.

506   Friedenthal, Jack H., and Medalie, Richard J. "The Impact of Federal Regulation on Political Broadcasting: Section 315 of the Communication Act," Harvard Law Review, 72 (1959), pp. 445-93.

507   Friedrich, Carl J. "Political Pathology," Political Quarterly, 37 (1966), pp. 70-85.

508   Friel, Charlotte. "The Influence of Television in the Political Career of Richard M. Nixon, 1946-1962." Unpublished Ph.D. dissertation, New York U., 1968.

509   Friendly, Fred. "The Spirit of '76 and the Next President of the United States," Washington University Magazine, 43, no. 2 (Winter, 1973), pp. 35-37.

510 Fritchey, Clayton. "Toward TV Debates," New York Post, May 15, 1968, p. 55.

511 Froman, L. A. "A Realistic Approach to Campaign Strategies and Tactics," The Electoral Process, ed. M. Kent Jennings and L. Harmon Zeigler. Englewood Cliffs, N.J.: Prentice-Hall, 1966.

512 Froman, L. A., Jr., and Skipper, J. K., Jr. "Factors Related to Misperceiving Party Stands on Issues," Public Opinion Quarterly, 26 (1962), pp. 265-72.

513 Fuchs, Douglas A. "Does TV Election News Influence Voters?" Columbia Journalism Review, 4 (Fall, 1965), pp. 39-41.

514 _____ . "Election Day Newscasts and Their Effects on Western Voter Turnout," Journalism Quarterly, 42 (1965), pp. 22-28.

515 Fulford, R. "On Marshall McLuhan: What One Communications Expert Discerns--But Has Trouble Getting Across," McLean's Magazine, 77 (June 20, 1964), p. 53.

516 Fulford, Robert. "Television Notebook," Canadian Forum, 42 (March, 1963), pp. 275-77.

517 "Funding Campaigns," Economist, 239 (May 1, 1971), p. 53.

518 Gale, George. "The Abuse of Television," Spectator, May 2, 1970, p. 584.

519 Gallup, George. "Polls and the Political Process-- Past, Present and Future," Public Opinion Quarterly, 29 (1965-66), pp. 544-49.

520 Gannon, James P. "Is GOP Campaign Rhetoric Too Hot?" Wall Street Journal, 180 (Sept. 8, 1972), p. 8.

521 _____ . "Rerunning Nixon: A New Ad Agency Has One Client and One Aim: To Reelect President," Wall Street Journal, 179 (March 6, 1972), p. 1+.

522 _____. "Will '72 Sloganeers Produce a 'Tippecanoe and Agnew, Too'?" Wall Street Journal, 179 (Feb. 22, 1972), p. 1+.

523 Garceau, O. "Research in the Political Process," American Political Science Review, 45 (March, 1951), pp. 69-85.

524 Gardner, Allan D. "Political Ads: Do They Work?" Wall Street Journal, 179 (Feb. 1, 1972), p. 10.

525 Gardner, Gerald. Robert Kennedy in New York. New York: Random House, 1965.

526 Gartner, Michael. "Campaign Financing: A Dubious Law," Wall Street Journal, 179 (April 5, 1972), p. 16.

527 Gauer, H. How to Win in Politics. Chumleigh, England: Athena Publishing Co., n.d.

528 Geller, H. "Political Broadcasts--A Few Short Steps Forward," Catholic University Law Review, 20 (Spring, 1971), pp. 449-62.

529 Gelman, David, and Kempton, Beverly. "New Issues for the New Politics: An Interview with Richard N. Goodwin," Washington Monthly, 1 (Aug., 1969), pp. 18-29.

530 Gelman, Morris J. "TV and Politics: '62," Television Magazine, 19 (Oct., 1962), pp. 64-67+.

531 Gent, George. "Somehow It Works: On N.B.C., A Study of Campaigns, U.S. Style," The New York Times, May 11, 1968, p. 70.

532 George, Alexander L. "Comment on 'Opinions, Personality and Political Behavior,'" American Political Science Review, 52 (1958), pp. 18-26.

533 Gerbner, George. "Ideological Perspectives and Political Tendencies in News Reporting," Journalism Quarterly, 41 (1964), pp. 495-508.

534   Gieber, Walter. "California Campaign Reporting (1962 Contest between Nixon and Brown)," Columbia Journalism Review, 2 (Winter, 1963), pp. 17-19.

535   Gilkinson, H., et al. "Conditions Affecting the Communication of Controversial Statements in Connected Discourse: Forms of Presentation and the Political Frame of Reference of the Listener," Speech Monographs, 20 (1953), pp. 253-60.

536   Gillette, Glen. "Marketing a Political Candidate," Western Advertising, 83 (Aug., 1964), pp. 11-13+.

537   Gilman, Irving. "The Marketing of a Political Candidate," Printers' Ink, 289 (Oct. 16, 1964), p. 58.

538   Gilmour, Ian. "The Campaigners," Spectator, no. 6906 (Nov. 4, 1960), pp. 680-82.

539   Glaser, William A. "Television and Voting Turnout," Public Opinion Quarterly, 29 (1965), pp. 71-86.

540   Glass, Andrew J. "Candidates Use Opinion Polls to Plan Campaigns for 1972," National Journal, 3 (Aug. 14, 1971), pp. 170-74.

541   _____. "Effective Media Campaign Paved Way for McGovern Win in California," National Journal, 4 (June 10, 1972), pp. 966-74.

542   _____. "Low-cost TV and Radio Facilities Prove Popular in Election Year," National Journal, 2 (July 11, 1970), pp. 1482-87.

543   Goetcheus, V. M., and Mansfield, H. C. "Innovations and Trends in the Study of American Politics," Annals of the American Academy, 391 (Sept., 1970), pp. 177-87.

544   Goldberg, A. S. "Discerning a Causal Pattern Among Data on Voting Behavior," American Political Science Review, 60 (1966), pp. 913-22.

545   Goldberg, P. A., and Stark, M. J. "Johnson or Goldwater? Some Personality and Attitude Correlates of Political Choice," Psychological Reports, 17 (1965), pp. 627-31.

546 Goldberg, Toby. "A Selective Bibliography of the
       Writings of and about Marshall McLuhan," Journal
       of Broadcasting, 12 (1968), pp. 179-82.

547 Goldblatt, D. "The Mechanics of Politics," Con-
       temporary Review, 205, no. 1186 (1964), pp. 563-66.

548 Golden, L. L. "TV: New Hazard for Politicians,"
       Saturday Night, 67 (March 1, 1952), pp. 7, 17.

549 Goldman, Ralph. Contemporary Perspectives on Poli-
       tics. New York: Van Nostrand Reinhold Co., 1972.

550 Goldstein, W. "Network Television and Political Change:
       Two Issues in Democratic Theory," Western Political
       Quarterly, 20 (1967), pp. 875-87.

551 Gonchor, Ruch M. "William F. Buckley on the 1965
       New York City Mayorality Campaign Debate." Un-
       published master's thesis, Temple U., 1967.

552 "Good Old Dirty Tricks?" Time, 100 (Oct. 30, 1972),
       p. 12.

553 Goodman, I. Robert. "Getting Across with Advertising,"
       Ways to Win. Washington, D.C.: Republican Na-
       tional Committee, 1968.

554 Goodman, Walter. "Candidates and the Camera," New
       Republic, 132 (May 9, 1955), pp. 13-16.

555 "GOP Admen Have the Edge," Business Week, Aug. 5,
       1972, p. 20.

556 "GOP Backs a New Kind of Candidate; Younger, More
       Attractive, More Positive than the Old Guard,"
       Business Week, Oct. 8, 1966, pp. 45-47.

557 "GOP Ignored Ad Men and Lost," Printers' Ink, 273
       (Dec. 2, 1960), pp. 43-44.

558 "GOP 'Morals' Film Back in Can," Broadcasting, 68
       (Oct. 26, 1964), p. 58.

559 Gordon, L. V. "Image of Political Candidates: Values
       and Voter Preference," Journal of Applied Psycho-
       logy, 56 (1972), pp. 382-87.

560   Gore, W. J., and Peabody, R. L. "The Functions of
      the Political Campaign: A Case Study," Western Po-
      litical Quarterly, 11 (1958), pp. 55-70.

561   Gosnell, H. F. "Does Campaigning Make a Difference?"
      Public Opinion Quarterly, 14 (1950), pp. 413-18.

562   Gould, Jack. "Candidates on TV--The Ideal and Oth-
      ers," New York Times Magazine, Oct. 28, 1962,
      pp. 26-27+.

563   _____. "TV Techniques on the Political Stage,"
      New York Times Magazine, April 25, 1954, pp. 12-
      13, 42, 44.

564   _____. "The X of the Campaign--TV 'personality,'"
      New York Times Magazine, June 22, 1952, p. 14,
      40-41.

565   Gould, L. J., and Steele, E. W. (eds.). People,
      Power and Politics. New York: Random House,
      1961.

566   Graber, D. "Press as Opinion Resource During the
      1968 Presidential Campaign," Public Opinion Quar-
      terly, 35 (1971), pp. 168-82.

567   Graber, Doris S. "Personal Qualities in Presidential
      Images: The Contribution of the Press," Midwest
      Journal of Political Science, 16 (1972), pp. 46-76.

568   Graff, Henry F. "From Tippecanoe to Scranton, Too,"
      New York Times Magazine, July 5, 1964, pp. 11,
      16.

569   Graham, P. L. "High Cost of Politics," National
      Municipal Review, 44 (1955), pp. 346-51.

570   Grant, Don. "Dailey Says Ad Function in Nixon Cam-
      paign to 'Set Record Straight,'" Advertising Age,
      Feb. 7, 1972, p. 6+.

571   Green, Wayne E. "Time for Everyone: A TV Staff in
      Florida Struggles to Provide Candidates Air Space,"
      Wall Street Journal, 179 (March 10, 1972), p. 1+.

572 Greenberg, Bradley S. "Media Use and Believability:
Some Multiple Correlates," Journalism Quarterly,
43 (1966), pp. 665-70.

573 _____. "The Political Candidate Versus the Tele-
vision Performer." Paper presented to the Pacific
Chapter, American Association for Public Opinion
Research, Los Angeles, Jan., 1962.

574 _____. "Voting Intentions, Election Expectations
and Exposure to Campaign Information," Journal of
Communications, 15 (Sept., 1965), pp. 149-60.

575 Greenstein, Fred I. Personality and Politics. Chicago:
Markham Publishing Co., 1969.

576 Gregg, James E. "Newspaper Editorial Endorsements
and California Elections, 1948-62," Journalism
Quarterly, 42 (1965), pp. 532-38.

577 _____. "Newspaper Endorsements and Local Elections in California," California Government Series
No. 12, U. of California at Davis, May, 1966.

578 Grupp, Fred W., Jr. "Newscast Avoidance among Political Activists," Public Opinion Quarterly, 34
(1970), pp. 262-66.

579 _____. "Social Correlates of Political Activists:
The John Birch Society and the ADA." Unpublished
Ph.D. dissertation, U. of Pennsylvania, 1968.

580 Guback, Thomas H. "Political Broadcasting and Public
Policy," Journal of Broadcasting, 12 (1968), pp.
191-211.

581 Gunderson, Robert Gray. "Political Phrasemakers in
Perspective," Southern Speech Journal, 26 (1960),
pp. 22-26.

582 Guthrie, G.; Becker, S.; and Siegel, S. "Preferences
and Differences in Preference for Political Candidates," Journal of Social Psychology, 53 (1961), pp.
25-32.

583 "Gutter Politics and the First Amendment," Valparaiso
Law Review, 6 (Winter, 1972), p. 185.

584 Gwyn, R. "Admen and Scientists Run This Election,"
     Financial Post, 56 (April 28, 1962), pp. 25-26.

585 Haas, R. "Political Handshake: Non-Verbal Persuasion
     in Image Construction," Quarterly Journal of Speech,
     58 (1972), pp. 340-43.

586 Haberman, Frederick W. "The Election of 1952: A
     Symposium," Quarterly Journal of Speech, 38 (1952),
     pp. 397-414.

587 Hage, G. S. "Anti-Intellectualism in Newspaper Com-
     ment on the Elections of 1828 and 1952." Unpub-
     lished Ph.D. dissertation, U. of Minnesota, 1957.

588 Hahn, Dan. "The Effects of Television on Presidential
     Campaigns," Today's Speech, 18 (1970), pp. 4-17.

589 _____, and Gonchar, R. M. "Political Myth: The
     Image and the Issue," Today's Speech, 20 (Summer,
     1972), pp. 57-65.

590 Halberstam, David. The Unfinished Odyssey of Robert
     Kennedy. New York: Random House, Inc., 1969.

591 Hale, William H. "The Politicians Try Victory Through
     Air Power," Reporter, 15 (Sept. 6, 1956), pp. 16-
     20.

592 Haley, Evetts. A Texan Looks at Lyndon. Canyon,
     Texas: Palo Duro Press, 1964.

593 Hall, Gary Jon. "An Analysis of the Role and Function
     of Communication in the 1959 Prohibition Repeal
     Campaign in Oklahoma: Focal Point, Oklahoma
     County." Unpublished Ph.D. dissertation, Southern
     Illinois U., 1971.

594 Hall, Leonard W. "How Politics is Changing," Politics
     U.S.A.: A Practical Guide to the Winning of Public
     Office, ed. Andrew M. Scott and Earle A. Wallace.
     Garden City, N.Y.: Doubleday, 1969.

595 Halloran, James D. The Effects of Mass Communica-
     tion. Leicester, England: Leicester U. Press, TV
     Research Committee, 1964.

596   Hamill, Pete. "When the Client Is a Candidate," New
      York Times Magazine, Oct. 25, 1964, pp. 30-31+.

597   Hammerback, John C. "Barry Goldwater's Rhetoric of
      Rugged Individualism," Quarterly Journal of Speech,
      58 (1972), pp. 175-83.

598   "Hand-shaking Campaigns," Economist, 173 (Oct. 16,
      1954), pp. 215-16.

599   "Hard-to-Cover Campaign," Newsweek, 80 (Oct. 23,
      1972), pp. 118-19.

600   Harding, H. F. "John F. Kennedy: Campaigner,"
      Quarterly Journal of Speech, 46 (1960), pp. 362-64.

601   _____. "The Voter Decides," Quarterly Journal of
      Speech, 46 (1960), pp. 429-33.

602   _____, et al. "Rhetoric in the Campaign of 1956,"
      Quarterly Journal of Speech, 43 (1957), pp. 29-54.

603   Harlan, Douglas S. "Party and Campaign in a Con-
      gressional Election: A Case Study of Reciprocal
      Dependency." Unpublished Ph.D. dissertation, U.
      of Texas at Austin, 1968.

604   Harris, B. A. "A Rhetorician in the Tunney Cam-
      paign," Quarterly Journal of Speech, 58 (1972), pp.
      84-87.

605   Harris, Charles E., and Court, Leonard. "Free
      Speech Implications of Campaign Expenditure Ceil-
      ings," Harvard Civil Rights-Civil Liberties Law Re-
      view, 7 (1972), pp. 214-59.

606   Harris, Louis. "Election Polling and Research," Public
      Opinion Quarterly, 21 (1957), p. 108, 116.

607   _____. "Polls and Politics in the United States,"
      Public Opinion Quarterly, 28 (1963), p. 3.

608   _____. "Some Observations on Election Behavior
      Research," Public Opinion Quarterly, 20 (1957), pp.
      379-91.

609   Harris, T. George. Romney's Way: A Man and an Idea. Englewood Cliffs, N.J.: Prentice-Hall, 1967.

610   Hart, Jim A. "Election Campaign Coverage in English and U.S. Daily Newspapers," Journalism Quarterly, 42 (1965), pp. 213-18.

611   Hartnett, R. C. "Political Motives of Voters," America, 92 (Nov. 6, 1954), p. 144.

612   "Has a New Type of Political Campaign Arrived?" Christian Century, 67 (Nov. 22, 1950), p. 1381.

613   Hastings, Philip K. "The Independent Voter in 1952: A Study of Pittsfield, Massachusetts," American Political Science Review, 47 (1953), pp. 805-10.

614   _____. "The Non-Voter in 1952: A Study of Pittsfield, Massachusetts," Journal of Psychology, 38 (1954), pp. 301-12.

615   Haun, Martha J. W. "A Study in Demagoguery: A Critical Analysis of the Speaking of George Corley Wallace in the 1968 Presidential Campaign." Unpublished Ph.D. dissertation, U. of Illinois, 1971.

616   Hauth, Luster E. "George Wallace: Rhetoric of a Left-Winger." Paper presented at the Speech-Communication Association Convention, San Francisco, Dec. 27-30, 1971.

617   "Have Clout, Will Travel; The President's Campaign Manager," Newsweek, 80 (July 17, 1972), pp. 21-22.

618   Hayes, I. M. "Financing Presidential Campaigns." College Park, Md.: U. of Maryland Library, 1953, 12 pp.

619   Hazard, P. D. "Broadcasting and the Elections," Senior Scholastic, 73 (Oct. 10, 1958), p. 29T.

620   Hazlitt, H. "Labels versus Policies," Newsweek, 64 (Nov. 30, 1964), p. 85.

621   _____. "Words Against Words," Newsweek, 64 (August 3, 1964), p. 67.

622   Heard, Alexander.   The Costs of Democracy.   Chapel
      Hill, N.C.:   U. of North Carolina Press, 1960.

623   _____.   "Does Money Win Elections?"   The Ameri-
      can Party System, ed. John Robert Owens and P. J.
      Staudenraus.   New York: The Macmillan Co., 1965.

624   _____.   "Money and Politics."   New York: Public
      Affairs Committee, 1956, 28 pp.

625   Heckscher, August.   "The Spirit of a Presidential Cam-
      paign," Yale Review, 41 (1952), pp. 482-90.

626   "Help Keep Campaign Literature Fair," Christian Cen-
      tury, 81 (Aug. 12, 1964), p. 1004.

627   Hennessy, Bernard.   "Politicals and Apoliticals: Some
      Measurements of Personality Traits," Midwest
      Journal of Political Science, 3 (1959), pp. 336-55.

628   _____, and Hennessy, Erna R.   "The Prediction of
      Close Elections: Comments on Some 1960 Polls,"
      Public Opinion Quarterly, 25 (1961), pp. 405-10.

629   Hennessy, David.   "Political Communication: An
      Analysis," Wiseman Review, No. 494 (Winter, 1962-
      63), pp. 327-38.

630   Herbold, P.   "The Effects of Present Audience Re-
      actions on Remote Audiences in Political Persua-
      sion."   Unpublished Ph.D. dissertation, U. of
      Minnesota, 1958.

631   Hershey, Marjorie Susan Randon.   "The Making of Cam-
      paign Strategy: How Personality and Attitudes In-
      fluence Campaign Decision Making."   Unpublished
      Ph.D. dissertation, U. of Wisconsin, 1972.

632   Hesse, Michael, and Chaffee, Steven H.   "Coorienta-
      tion in Political Communication."   Paper presented
      at the International Communication Association Con-
      vention, Montreal, April 25-29, 1973.

633   Hetherington, E. Mavis, and Carlson, Mary.   "Effects
      of Candidate Support and Election Results upon Atti-
      tudes to the Presidency."   Journal of Social Psy-
      chology, 64 (1964), pp. 333-38.

634 Hickey, Neil. "They Love Oregon in the Springtime,"
     TV Guide, 20 (May 6, 1972), pp. 6-9.

635 _____. "What America Thinks of TV's Political
     Coverage," TV Guide, April 8, 1972, pp. 6-11.

636 Hiebert, Ray, et al. (eds.). The Political Image Mer-
     chants. Washington, D.C.: Acropolis Books, 1971.

636 Higbie, Charles E. "Wisconsin Dailies in the 1952
     Campaign: Space vs. Display," Journalism Quarterly,
     31 (1954), pp. 56-60.

637 Hill, Gladwin. Dancing Bear: An Inside Look at Cali-
     fornia Politics. Cleveland: World Publishers Co.,
     1968.

639 Hill, Ruane B. "Political Uses of Broadcasting in the
     U.S. in the Context of Public Opinion and the Po-
     litical Process, 1920-60." Unpublished Ph.D. dis-
     sertation, Northwestern U., 1964.

640 Himmelfarb, Gertrude. "The Hero as Politician,"
     Twentieth Century, 153, no. 915 (1953), pp. 356-61.

641 Hirsch, Robert O. "The Influence of Channel, Source,
     and Message Variables on Voting Behavior in the
     1972 Illinois Primary Election." Paper presented
     at the International Communication Association Con-
     vention, Montreal, April 25-29, 1973.

642 _____. "The Influence of Channel, Source, and
     Message Variables on Voting Behavior in the 1972
     Illinois Primary Election." Unpublished Ph.D. dis-
     sertation, Southern Illinois U., 1972.

643 _____. "The 1972 Illinois Primary: Did the Media
     Make a Difference?" Paper presented at the Illinois
     Speech and Theatre Association Convention, St. Louis,
     Nov., 1972.

644 "Hmm, Gosh, Yup," Reporter, 15 (Oct. 18, 1956), p. 4.

645 Hochstein, Rollie. "Campaign Sidelights," Contemporary
     Review, 198 (Oct., 1960), pp. 540-43.

646 Holland, Thomas Hayes.   "The Campaign Trail of Ten-
      nessee's 'Grey Fox': Senator Albert Gore's 1970
      Campaign Speaking." Unpublished Ph.D. disserta-
      tion, Southern Illinois U., 1971.

647 Hollis, Christopher. "The Reluctant Politician,"
      Spectator, no. 6798 (1958), p. 477.

648 Holloron, Jerry R.   "The Montana Daily Press and the
      1964 Gubernatorial Campaign." Unpublished M.A.
      thesis, U. of Montana, 1965.

649 Honan, William H. "The Men Behind Nixon's Speeches,"
      New York Times Magazine, Jan. 19, 1969, pp. 20-
      21+.

650 Hood, Stuart. "De arte Rhetorica: The TV Campaign,"
      Spectator, March 25, 1966, pp. 351-52.

651 Hooper, Michael. "Party and Newspaper Endorsement
      as Predictors of Voter Choice," Journalism Quarter-
      ly, 46 (1969), pp. 302-5.

652 Hovland, C. I. "Effects of the Mass Media of Com-
      munication," Handbook of Social Psychology, Vol.
      III, ed. Gardner Lindzey.   Cambridge, Mass.: Ad-
      dison-Wesley, 1954, pp. 1062-1103.

653 "How Election Coverage Rated on TV Networks,"
      Broadcasting, 55 (Nov. 10, 1958), p. 62.

654 "How Hannibal Did It," Newsweek, 71 (June 3, 1968),
      p. 30+.

655 "How Media Are Used in a National Political Campaign:
      A Report on: Advertising at the Conventions, Media
      Buying for Presidential Candidates, Republican and
      Democratic Agencies, the Issue of Free Time,"
      Media/Scope, 4 (July, 1960), pp. 62-63+.

656 "How Mr. Nixon Woos the Democrats," Newsweek, 80
      (Oct. 2, 1972), pp. 15-16.

657 "How Nixon Changed His TV Image: Interview with
      Roger Ailes, President's TV Advisor," United States
      News and World Report, 68 (Feb. 2, 1970), pp. 68-
      71.

658   "How to Get That Good Media Image," Newsweek, 74
       (Sept. 29, 1969), p. 69.

659   "How to Sell a Candidate: 1956," Sponsor, 10 (July 9,
       1956), p. 28.

660   Howell, R. G. "Fairness ... Fact or Fable?" Journal
       of Broadcasting, 8 (1964), pp. 321-30.

661   Huckshorn, Robert J., and Spencer, Robert C. The
       Politics of Defeat: Campaigning for Congress. Am-
       herst, Mass.: U. of Massachusetts Press, 1971.

662   Hunt, Albert R. "'Psst! Did You Hear--?' As Elec-
       tion Day Nears, The Mud Begins to Fly...," Wall
       Street Journal, 180 (Oct. 26, 1972), p. 1+.

663   Hurley, N. P. "Marshall McLuhan: Communications
       Explorer," America, 116 (Feb. 18, 1967), pp. 241-
       43.

664   Hy, Ronn. "Mass Media in Election Campaigns (Extent
       to Which Voters Are Affected by Political Advertise-
       ment in the Mass Media)," Public Administration
       Survey, 20 (Jan., 1973), pp. 1-6.

665   Hyman, Herbert, and Sheatsley, Paul. "The Political
       Appeal of President Eisenhower," Public Opinion
       Quarterly, 17 (Winter, 1953-54), pp. 443-60.

666   "I Say Tell the Truth: Pictures and Texts from GOP
       Campaign Document," New Republic, 135 (Oct. 8,
       1956), pp. 10-11.

667   "Illegal Election Practices in Philadelphia," University
       of Pennsylvania Law Review, 106 (Dec., 1957), p.
       279.

668   Irving, J. A. "Television Performance Unknown Factor
       in Winning Elections," Saturday Night, 72 (May 11,
       1957), pp. 9, 43.

669   Irwin, William P. "Peace Wins an Election," Nation,
       187 (Dec. 6, 1958), pp. 419-22.

670   "Is Blanket Convention Coverage an Audience Bust?"
       Sponsor, 10 (Sept. 17, 1956), p. 19.

671   "Is It Wise for Entertainers to Take Part in Political
       Campaigns?" Senior Scholastic, 84 (May 1, 1964),
       pp. 6-7.

672   "Is the Press Biased?" Newsweek, 72 (Sept. 16, 1968),
       pp. 66-67.

673   "Is TV Changing US Politics for Better or Worse?"
       Senior Scholastic, 87 (Oct. 7, 1965), pp. 10-11.

674   Isaacs, Jeremy. "Television and the Election," Lis-
       tener, 83 (June 18, 1970), p. 822.

675   Jackson, John S., III, and Miller, Roy E. "Campaign
       Issues, Candidate Images, and Party Identification
       at Multiple Electoral Levels." Paper presented at
       the Midwest Political Science Association Convention,
       Chicago, May 3-5, 1973.

676   Jacobson, Gary Charles. "The Impact of Radio and
       Television on American Election Campaigns." Un-
       published Ph.D. dissertation, Yale U., 1972.

677   Jacobson, Harvey K. "The Credibility of Three Mass
       Media as Information Sources." Unpublished Ph.D.
       dissertation, U. of Wisconsin, 1967.

678   _____. "Mass Media Believability: A Study of Re-
       ceiver Judgments," Journalism Quarterly, 46 (1969),
       pp. 20-28.

679   Jacoby, Jacob, and Aranoff, Daniel. "Political Polling
       and the Lost-Letter Technique," Journal of Social
       Psychology, 83 (1971), pp. 209-12.

680   Jaffe, Louis L. "The Editorial Responsibility of the
       Broadcaster: Reflections on Fairness and Access,"
       Harvard Law Review, 85 (1972), pp. 768-92.

681   Janowitz, Morris, and Marvick, Dwaine. "The Impact
       of the Mass Media," Competitive Pressure and Demo-
       cratic Consent: An Interpretation of the 1952 Presi-
       dential Election. Ann Arbor, Mich.: Institute of Public
       Administration, U. of Michigan, 1956.

682   Jeffries, Vincent, and Ransford, H. Edward. "Ideology,
      Social Structure, and the Yorty-Bradley Mayoralty
      Election," Social Problems, 19 (1972), pp. 358-72.

683   Jennings, M. Kent, and Niemi, R. G. "Patterns of
      Political Learning," Harvard Educational Review, 38
      (Summer, 1968), pp. 443-67.

684   _____, and Zeigler, L. Harmon (eds.).   The Elec-
      toral Process. Englewood Cliffs, N.J.: Prentice-
      Hall, 1966.

685   Jennings, Ralph. "Dramatic License in Political Broad-
      casts," Journal of Broadcasting, 12 (1968), pp. 229-
      46.

686   Johnson, Donald B. "The Congressional Campaign and
      the Off-Year Elections of 1962," American Govern-
      ment Annual, 1963.

687   Johnson, G. W. "In Search of Identity," New Republic,
      143 (Oct. 10, 1960), p. 20.

688   Jonas, F. H. "The Art of Political Dynamiting,"
      Western Political Quarterly, 10 (1957), pp. 374-91.

689   Jonas, Frank H. (ed.). "Western Politics and the
      1958 Elections," Western Political Quarterly, 12
      (1959), pp. 241-366.

690   Jones, Charles O. "The Role of the Campaign in
      Congressional Politics," The Electoral Process, ed.
      M. Kent Jennings and L. Harmon Zeigler. Engle-
      wood Cliffs, N.J.: Prentice-Hall, 1966, pp. 21-41.

691   Jones, Thomas M. "'56 Presidential Campaigns with
      a New York Advertising Look," Printers' Ink, Aug.
      10, 1956, pp. 21-24+.

692   Jordan, A. T. "Political Communication: The Third
      Dimension of Strategy," Orbis, 8 (1964), pp. 670-85.

693   Joyner, Conrad. The American Politician. Tucson,
      Ariz.: U. of Arizona Press, 1971.

694   _____. "The 1968 Election in the West," Western
      Political Quarterly, 22 (1969), pp. 451-551.

695 _____ . "Running a Congressional Campaign, "
Practical Politics in the United States, ed. Cornelius
P. Cotter. Boston: Allyn and Bacon, 1969, pp.
143-72.

696 Just, W. "Nixon Avoids the Dirt, " New Statesman, 84
(1972), pp. 495-96.

697 Kaid, Lynda Lee. "Public Speaking in the 1972 Illinois
Presidential Campaign: Did It Make a Difference? "
Paper presented at the Illinois Speech and Theatre
Association Convention, St. Louis, Nov., 1972.

698 _____ . "A Selected, Indexed Bibliography on Political Campaign Communication. " Unpublished M.S.
thesis, Southern Illinois U., 1972.

699 _____ , and Hirsch, Robert O. "Selective Exposure
and Candidate Image: A Field Study Over Time, "
Central States Speech Journal, 24 (Spring, 1973),
pp. 48-51.

700 Kaselow, J. "Necessity in Politics, " Saturday Review,
47 (Oct. 10, 1964), p. 106; Reply R. W. Cooley, 47
(Nov. 14, 1964), p. 77.

701 Katona, George. "How Right Are the Polls? " United
States News and World Report, 57 (Sept. 21, 1964),
pp. 33-36.

702 Katz, Daniel, and Eldersveld, Samuel J. "The Impact
of Local Party Activity upon the Electorate, " Public
Opinion Quarterly, 25 (1961), pp. 1-24.

703 Katz, Elihu. "On Reopening the Question of Selectivity
in Exposure to Mass Communications, " Theories of
Cognitive Consistency: A Sourcebook, ed. Robert
P. Abelson, et al. Chicago: Rand McNally, 1968.

704 _____ . "Platforms and Windows: Broadcasting's
Role in Election Campaigns, " Journalism Quarterly,
48 (1971), pp. 304-14.

705 _____ , and Feldman, Jacob J. "The Debates in
Light of Research: A Survey of Surveys, " The Great
Debates, ed. Sidney Kraus. Bloomington, Ind.:
Indiana U. Press, 1962.

706   _____, and _____. "The Kennedy-Nixon Debates:
       A Survey of Surveys," Studies in Public Communica-
       tion, 4 (1962), pp. 127-63.

707   _____, and _____. "Who Won the Kennedy-Nixon
       Debates," Speech Communication, eds. Howard Mar-
       tin and Kenneth Andersen. Boston: Allyn and Ba-
       con, Inc., 1968, pp. 297-311.

708   _____, and Lazarsfeld, Paul F. Personal Influences:
       The Part Played by People in the Flow of Mass
       Communications. Glencoe, Ill.: The Free Press,
       1955.

709   Kauffman, Charles. "The Rhetorical Visions of Two
       Professional Journalists," Moments in Contemporary
       Rhetoric and Communication (Temple U.), 2 (Fall,
       1972), pp. 28-33.

710   Kelleher, James F. "TV's Perennial Star: The Po-
       litical Candidate," Public Relations Journal, 12
       (April, 1956), pp. 6-7.

711   Kellerman, Richard. "Political Impact of TV," Nation,
       200 (Jan. 11, 1965), pp. 24-26.

712   Kelley, Douglas. "Press Coverage of Two Michigan
       Congressional Elections," Journalism Quarterly, 35
       (1959), pp. 447-49.

713   Kelley, Joseph. The Influence of Television on the
       Election of 1952. Miami: Miami U. Press, 1954.

714   _____. "A Study of the 1960 Primary and General
       Election Campaigns for U.S. House of Representa-
       tives in Montana's Second Congressional District."
       Unpublished Ph.D. dissertation, Washington U.,
       1963.

715   Kelley, Stanley. "Afterthoughts on Madison Avenue
       Politics," Antioch Review, 17 (1957), pp. 173-86.

716   _____. "Campaign Debates: Some Facts and Is-
       sues," Public Opinion Quarterly, 26 (1962), pp. 351-
       66.

717 _____. "Elections and the Mass Media," Law and Contemporary Problems, 27 (1962), pp. 307-26.

718 _____. "The 1960 Presidential Election," American Government Annual, 1961-1962, ed. K. Hinderaker. New York: Holt, Rinehart and Winston, 1961.

719 _____. Political Campaigning: Problems in Creating an Informed Electorate. Washington, D.C.: The Brookings Institute, 1960.

720 _____. "P.R. Man: Political Mastermind," New York Times Magazine, Sept. 2, 1956, pp. 10+.

721 _____. Professional Public Relations and Political Power. Baltimore: Johns Hopkins U. Press, 1956.

722 Kenworthy, E. W. "Campaign Special: TV or Train?" New York Times Magazine, April 29, 1956, pp. 13, 30, 32, 34, 36.

723 Keogh, James. President Nixon and the Press. New York: Funk and Wagnalls, 1972.

724 Kerle, Kenneth E. Campaign Management. Washington, D.C.: American U. Press, 1958.

725 Kerpelman, L. C. "Personality and Attitude Correlates of Political Candidate Preference," Journal of Social Psychology, 76 (1968), pp. 219-26.

726 Kerr, Harry P. "The Great Debates in a New Perspective," Today's Speech, 9 (Nov., 1961), pp. 9-11, 28.

727 Kessel, John H. "Cognitive Dimensions and Political Activity," Public Opinion Quarterly, 29 (Fall, 1965), pp. 377-89.

728 _____. "A Game Theory Analysis of Campaign Strategy," The Electoral Process, eds. M. Kent Jennings and L. Harmon Zeigler. Englewood Cliffs, N.J.: Prentice-Hall, 1966, pp. 290-305.

729 _____. The Goldwater Coalition. Indianapolis: Bobbs-Merrill Co., 1968.

730 _____ . "Road to the Mansion: A Study of the 1956
      Gubernatorial Campaign in Ohio." Unpublished
      Ph.D. dissertation, Columbia U., 1958.

731 Key, V. O., Jr. "Campaign Techniques," Politics
      1964, ed. Francis M. Carney and Frank Way.
      Belmont, Calif.: Wadsworth Publishing Co., 1964.

732 _____ . "Congressional Candidates and the Broad-
      cast Media in the 1968 Campaign," The Alfred I.
      DuPont-Columbia University Survey of Broadcast
      Journalism, 1968-69, ed. Marvin Barrett. New
      York: Grosset and Dunlap, pp. 83-104.

733 _____ . Politics, Parties, and Pressure Groups.
      5th edition. New York: Thomas Crowell Co., 1964.

734 _____ . Public Opinion and American Democracy.
      New York: Alfred Knopf Publishers, 1961.

735 _____ . The Responsible Electorate. New York:
      Vintage Books, 1966.

736 Kimball, Penn. Bobby Kennedy and the New Politics.
      Englewood Cliffs, N.J.: Prentice-Hall, 1968.

737 King, Andrew A., and Anderson, Floyd Douglas.
      "Nixon, Agnew, and the 'Silent Majority': A Case
      Study in the Rhetoric of Polarization," Western
      Speech, 35 (1971), pp. 243-55.

738 King, Robert, and Schnitzer, Martin. "Contemporary
      Use of Private Political Polling," Public Opinion
      Quarterly, 32 (1968), pp. 431-36.

739 Kingdon, John W. Candidates for Office: Beliefs and
      Strategies. New York: Random House, 1968.

740 _____ . "Opinion Leaders in the Electorate," Public
      Opinion Quarterly, 34 (1970), pp. 256-61.

741 _____ . "Politicians' Beliefs about Voters," Ameri-
      can Political Science Review, 61 (1967), pp. 137-45.

742 Kintner, Robert E. "Television and the World of Po-
      litics," Harper's Magazine, 230 (May, 1965), pp.
      121-32.

743 Kirkpatrick, S. "Political Attitude Structure and Component Change," Public Opinion Quarterly, 34 (1970), pp. 403-07.

744 Kirkpatrick, Samuel A. "Issue Orientation and Voter Choice in 1964," Social Science Quarterly, 49 (1968), pp. 87-102.

745 Kissel, Bernard C. "A Rhetorical Study of Selected Speeches Delivered by Vice-President Richard M. Nixon during the Convention and Presidential Campaign of 1956." Unpublished Ph.D. dissertation, U. of Michigan, 1959.

746 _____. "Richard M. Nixon: Definition of an Image," Quarterly Journal of Speech, 46 (1960), pp. 357-61.

747 Kitt, Alice S., and Gleicher, David B. "Determinants of Voting Behavior: A Progress Report on the Elmire Election Study," Public Opinion and Propaganda, ed. Daniel Katz, et al. New York: The Dryden Press, 1954.

748 Kjeldahl, Bill O. "Factors in a Presidential Candidate's Image." Unpublished Ph.D. dissertation, U. of Oregon, 1969.

749 _____; Carmichael, Carl W.; and Mertz, Robert J. "Factors in a Presidential Candidate's Image," Speech Monographs, 38 (June, 1971), pp. 129-31.

750 Klahr, D. "Computer Simulation of the Paradox of Voting," American Political Science Review, 60 (1966), pp. 384-90.

751 Klapper, Joseph T. The Effects of Mass Communication. Glencoe, Ill.: The Free Press, 1960.

752 _____. "Mass Communication, Attitude Stability and Change," Attitude, Ego-Involvement and Change, ed. Carolyn W. Sherif and Muzafer Sherif. New York: John Wiley and Sons, 1967.

753 Klein, Malcolm W., and Maccoby, Nathan. "Newspaper Objectivity in the 1952 Campaign," Journalism Quarterly, 31 (1954), pp. 285-96.

754   Klein, Rudolf. "Politicians and the Press," Observer,
      April 7, 1968, p. 10.

755   Kneier, C. M. "Misleading the Voters," National
      Municipal Review, 46 (Oct., 1957), pp. 450-55.

756   Knepprath, H. E. "The Elements of Persuasion in the
      National Broadcast Speeches of Eisenhower and
      Stevenson during the 1956 Presidential Campaign."
      Unpublished Ph.D. dissertation, U. of Wisconsin,
      1962.

757   Knight, Andrew. "Remembering George Wallace: The
      Anatomy of a Campaign," Interplay, 2 (Jan., 1969),
      pp. 25-28.

758   Knight, Robert P. "Polls, Sampling and the Voter."
      Columbia, Mo.: Freedom of Information Center,
      U. of Missouri, 1966.

759   Kobre, Sidney. "How Florida Dailies Handled the 1952
      Presidential Campaign," Journalism Quarterly, 30
      (1953), pp. 163-69.

760   Konrad, Evelyn. "What TV Did for Ike," Sponsor, 10
      (Nov. 10, 1956), pp. 36-39+.

761   Kornhauser, William. The Politics of Mass Society.
      Glencoe, Ill.: The Free Press, 1959.

762   Koslin, Bertram L.; Stoops, James W.; and Loh, Wal-
      lace D. "Source Characteristics and Communication
      Discrepancy as Determinants of Attitude Change and
      Conformity," Journal of Experimental Social Psy-
      chology, 3 (1967), pp. 230-42.

763   Kramer, Gerald H. "A Decision-Theoretic Analysis of
      a Problem in a Political Campaign," Mathematical
      Applications in Political Science, II, ed. Joseph L.
      Bernd. Dallas: Southern Methodist U. Press, 1966,
      pp. 137-60.

764   _____. "The Effects of Precinct-Level Canvassing
      on Voter Behavior," Public Opinion Quarterly, 34
      (1970-71), pp. 560-72.

765 Kraus, Sidney (ed.). The Great Debates. Bloomington,
     Ind.: Indiana U. Press, 1962.

766 _____. "The Political Use of TV," Journal of Broad-
     casting, 8 (1964), pp. 219-28.

767 _____. "Presidential Debates in 1964," Quarterly
     Journal of Speech, 50 (1964), pp. 19-23.

768 _____, and Smith, Raymond G. "Issues and Images,"
     The Great Debates, ed. Sidney Kraus. Bloomington,
     Ind.: Indiana U. Press, 1962, pp. 271-88.

769 Krebs, Albin. "Walter Cronkite: Do Politicians Fool
     the TV Camera--and You?" Good Housekeeping,
     175 (July, 1972), pp. 32, 34, 37-38, 40-42.

770 Krieghbaum, Hillier. "What about Editorials' Political
     Influence?" Masthead, 8 (Spring, 1956), p. 84+.

771 Krock, Arthur. "Is Honesty the Best Political Policy?"
     New York Times Magazine, Oct. 5, 1952, p. 9+.

772 _____. "'The Man Who'--Not 'the Issue Which,'"
     New York Times Magazine, Oct. 16, 1960, p. 19+.

773 Krugman, Herbert E. "The Measurement of Adver-
     tising Involvement," Public Opinion Quarterly, 30
     (1966-67), pp. 584-85.

774 Kugel, Peter. "Computers and Political Strategy,"
     Computers and Automation, 11 (May, 1962), pp. 17-
     22.

775 Kully, Robert D. "The 1962 California Gubernatorial
     Campaign: The 'New' Brown," Western Speech, 30
     (1966), pp. 111-22.

776 Kumar, Krishan. "The Political Consequences of Tele-
     vision," Listener, 82 (July 3, 1969), pp. 1-3.

777 Kushner, William. "The Role of Ethos in the Rhetoric
     of United States Congressman Charles A. Wolver-
     ton." Unpublished Ph.D. dissertation, Indiana U.,
     1972.

778   Lamb, Karl, and Smith, Paul. Campaign Decision-
         Making. Belmont, Calif.: Wadsworth Publishing
         Co., 1968.

779   Landauer, Jerry. "Political Fund-Raising: A Murky
         World," Wall Street Journal, 169 (June 28, 1967),
         p. 14.

780   Lane, Robert E. Political Life. Glencoe, Ill.: The
         Free Press, 1959.

781   _____, and Sears, David O. Public Opinion. Engle-
         wood Cliffs, N.J.: Prentice-Hall, 1964.

782   Lang, Gladys, and Lang, Kurt. "The Inferential
         Structure of Political Communications: A Study
         in Unwitting Bias," Public Opinion Quarterly, 19
         (1955), pp. 168-83.

783   Lang, Kurt, and Lang, Gladys Engel. "Ballots and
         Broadcasts: The Impact of Expectations and Election
         Day Perceptions on Voting Behavior." Paper pre-
         sented at the 1965 Annual Conference of the Ameri-
         can Association for Public Opinion Research, May
         14, 1965.

784   _____, and _____. "The Mass Media and Voting."
         American Voting Behavior, ed. Eugene Burdick and
         Arthur J. Brodbeck. Glencoe, Ill.: The Free
         Press, 1959.

785   _____, and _____. "Ordeal by Debate: Viewer
         Reactions," Public Opinion Quarterly, 25 (1961), pp.
         277-88.

786   _____, and _____. "Political Participation and
         the Television Perspective," Social Problems, 4
         (Oct., 1956), pp. 107-16.

787   _____, and _____. Politics and Television.
         Chicago: Quadrangle Books, 1968.

788   _____, and _____. "Television and the Intimate
         View of Politics," Journal of Broadcasting, 1 (1956-
         57), pp. 47-55.

789 _____, and _____. "The Television Personality
     in Politics: Some Considerations," Public Opinion
     Quarterly, 20 (1956), pp. 103-12.

790 _____, and _____. "The Unique Perspective of
     Television and Its Effect: A Pilot Study," American
     Sociological Review, 18 (1953), pp. 3-12.

791 _____, and _____. Voting and Non-Voting.
     Waltham, Mass.: Blaisdell Publishing Co.,
     1968.

792 Lang, Serge. The Sheer Campaign. New York: W. A.
     Benjamin, Inc., 1967.

793 Large, Arlen J. "Agnew's 'New' Presidential Style,"
     Wall Street Journal, 180 (Sept. 29, 1972), p. 10.

794 _____. "Political Debates: How to Keep Score,"
     Wall Street Journal, 179 (March 3, 1972), p. 8.

795 Larner, Jeremy. "NOBODY KNOWS ... Reflections on
     the McCarthy Campaign: Part I," Harper's Maga-
     zine, April, 1969, p. 66.

796 Larrabee, Eric. "The Imaginary Audience," Horizon,
     2 (March, 1960), pp. 46-51.

797 Larsen, O. N. "The Comparative Validity of Telephone
     and Face-to-Face Interviews in the Measurement of
     Message Diffusion from Leaflets," American Soci-
     ological Review, 17 (1952), pp. 471-76.

798 Larson, Barbara A. "The Election Eve Address of
     Edmund Muskie: A Case Study of the Televised
     Public Address," Central States Speech Journal,
     23 (1972), pp. 78-85.

799 "Last Blasts," Newsweek, 72 (Nov. 11, 1968), pp. 92-
     93.

800 "Later George, Not Now," New Republic, 164 (May 8,
     1971), pp. 5-6.

801 "Laughs-for Votes," New York Times Magazine, June
     17, 1956, p. 14.

802   Laurent, Lawrence (ed.). Equal Time, the Private
      Broadcaster and the Public Interest. New York:
      Atheneum, 1964.

803   Lawhorne, Clifton O. "Political Cartoons ... There
      Have Been Some Changes Made," Grassroots Editor,
      7 (April, 1966), pp. 8-12.

804   Lawrence, D. "Is There Such a Thing as Clean Po-
      litics?" United States News and World Report, 73
      (Sept. 25, 1972), p. 104.

805   _____ . "Issues Win Campaigns, Not Personalities,"
      United States News and World Report, 39 (Oct. 14,
      1955), p. 132+.

806   Lawrence, Gary Caldwell. "Media Effects in Congres-
      sional Election." Unpublished Ph.D. dissertation,
      Stanford U., 1972.

807   Lawrence, Morton B. "An Adman's Opinion of the 1956
      Political Contests: Effects of Advertising and the
      Role Played by Agencies," Printers' Ink, Dec. 14,
      1956, p. 62+.

808   _____ . "Political Campaigns--New Source of Agency
      Profits," Printers' Ink, 256 (Sept. 14, 1956), p. 44.

809   Lazarsfeld, Paul F.; Berelson, Bernard; and Gaudet,
      Hazel. The People's Choice. New York: Duell,
      Sloan and Pearce, 1944.

810   "LBJ TV Spot Draws First Political Blood," Broadcast-
      ing, 67 (Sept. 14, 1964), p. 10.

811   Lee, A. M. "What Will the Pall of Orthodoxy Do in
      the 1952 Campaign?" Oberlin College Publicity
      Bureau, Oberlin, Ohio, 1952, 10 pp.

812   Lee, Eugene C. "The Politics of Nonpartisan Elections
      in California Cities." Unpublished Ph.D. disserta-
      tion, U. of California at Berkeley, 1957.

813   Lee, Jae-Won. "Editorial Support and Campaign News:
      Content Analysis by Q-Methodology," Journalism
      Quarterly, 49 (1972), pp. 710-16.

814 Lees, John D. "Campaigns and Parties--The 1970 American Mid-Term Elections and Beyond," Parliamentary Affairs, 24 (Autumn, 1971), pp. 312-20.

815 Leiserson, A. "Notes on the Theory of Political Opinion Formation," American Political Science Review, 47 (1953), pp. 171-77.

816 Leuthold, David A. Electioneering in a Democracy. New York: John Wiley and Sons, 1968.

817 Leventhal, Howard; Jacobs, Robert L.; and Kudirka, Nijole Z. "Authoritarianism, Ideology, and Political Candidate Choice," Journal of Abnormal and Social Psychology, 69 (1964), pp. 539-49.

818 Levin, Murray B. The Alienated Voter: Politics in Boston. New York: Holt, Rinehart and Winston, 1960.

819 _____. Kennedy Campaigning. Boston: Beacon Press, 1966.

820 _____, with Blackwood, George. The Compleat Politician. Indianapolis, Inc.: Bobbs-Merrill, 1962.

821 Levine, R. A. "The Silent Majority: Neither Simple nor Simple-Minded." Santa Monica, Calif.: Rand Corp., July, 1971.

822 "The Levitation of Lodge," Nation, 198 (April 27, 1964), pp. 405-06.

823 Lewis, David L. "Postmark Public Relations, Another Medium for Your Over-All Campaign," Public Relations Journal, 18 (Oct., 1968), pp. 47-48.

824 Lewis, G. I. "Moneybags and Ballot Box," Time and Tide, 41 (1960), p. 762.

825 Lewis, Joseph. What Makes Reagan Run? New York: McGraw-Hill Book Company, 1968.

826 Lewis, L. S. "Political Heroes: 1936 and 1960," Journalism Quarterly, 42 (1965), pp. 116-18.

827 Lichty, Lawrence W.; Ripley, Joseph M.; and Sum-
     mers, Harrison B. "Political Programs on National
     Television Networks: 1960 and 1964," Journal of
     Broadcasting, 9 (1965), pp. 217-29.

828 Lieberman, Carl. "The 1966 Gubernatorial Campaign
     in Pennsylvania: A Study of the Strategies and
     Techniques of the Democratic Candidate." Unpub-
     lished Ph.D. dissertation, U. of Pittsburgh, 1969.

829 Liebling, A. J. "Wayward Press: When the Electorate
     Rocked," New Yorker, 26 (Nov. 25, 1950), p. 86+.

830 Lindsay, David S. "The Doctrine of Agency and Pub-
     licity in the Regulation of Campaign Finance." Un-
     published Ph.D. dissertation, Florida State U.,
     1969.

831 Ling, David. "Assessing Political Argument through
     Strategic Choice." Paper presented at the Central
     States Speech Association Convention, Chicago,
     April, 1972.

832 Lippmann, W. "Campaign Debating," Newsweek, 64
     (Aug. 31, 1964), p. 13.

833 Lipset, Seymour M. "The Political Animal: Genus
     Americana," Public Opinion Quarterly, 23 (1959-
     1960), pp. 554-62.

834 _____. Political Man: The Social Bases of Politics.
     Garden City, N.Y.: Doubleday, 1960.

835 _____, et al. "The Psychology of Voting: An
     Analysis of Political Behavior," Handbook of Social
     Psychology, Vol. VI, ed. Gardner Lindzey. Boston:
     Addison-Wesley, 1954, pp. 1124+.

836 Litfin, A. Duane. "Senator Edmund Muskie's 'Five
     Smooth Stones': An Analysis of Rhetorical Strategies
     and Tactics in His 1970 Election Eve Speech,"
     Central States Speech Journal, 23 (1972), pp. 5-10.

837 "Little Girls--Mushroom Clouds," Broadcasting, 67
     (Sept. 21, 1964), p. 30.

838   Little, Stuart W.   "TV, the Vote Maker," Saturday Review, 51 (Dec. 14, 1968), pp. 74-75.

839   Lobel, Martin.   "Federal Control of Campaign Contributions," Minnesota Law Review, 51 (1966), pp. 1-62.

840   Locher, Jack Snowden.   "Changing Media and Presidential Campaigns: 1900, 1948, 1956." Unpublished Ph.D. dissertation, U. of Pennsylvania, 1970.

841   Loeb, Marshall, and Safire, William.   Plunging into Politics. New York: David McKay Co., 1964.

842   Loevinger, Lee.   "The Ambiguous Mirror," ETC., 26 (1969), pp. 268-94.

843   _____ .   "Mass versus Media--Who Controls?" ETC., 26 (1969), pp. 295-317.

844   Lokos, Lionel.   Hysteria 1964: The Fear Campaign Against Barry Goldwater. New York: Arlington House, 1967.

845   Long, Norton E.   "Politicians for Hire--the Dilemma of Education and the Task of Research," Public Administration Review, 25 (June, 1965), pp. 115-20.

846   Lord, S.   "Repackaging Candidates for Television," Harper's Bazaar, 105 (Jan., 1972), pp. 48-49.

847   "The Los Angeles Mayoralty Race," Television Age, April 30, 1962, p. 30+.

848   "Love and Hisses," Time, 78 (Oct. 20, 1961), pp. 26-27.

849   Lowe, Francis E., and McCormick, Thomas C.   "A Study of the Influence of Formal and Informal Leaders in an Election Campaign," Public Opinion Quarterly, 20 (1956-57), pp. 651-62.

850   Lowenstein, Ralph L.   "The 1968 Campaign: TV Lost Its Cool." Columbia, Mo.: Freedom of Information Center, U. of Missouri, 1968.

      Lower, Elmer W.   See no. 896.

851   Lubell, Samuel.   "The New Technology of Election Reporting," Columbia Journalism Review, 3(Sum., '64),pp. 4-8.

852   Lucey, C. "Washington Front," America, 87 (Sept. 6, 1952), p. 533.

853   Ludlum, Thomas S. "Effects of Certain Techniques of Credibility upon Audience Attitude," Speech Monographs, 25 (1958), pp. 278-84.

854   Lupfer, Michael, and Price, David E. "On the Merits of Face-to-Face Campaigning," Social Science Quarterly, 53 (1972), pp. 534-43.

855   Lyle, J. "Four Days of Campaign News: Election Coverage in 20 Los Angeles Daily Newspapers October 28-31, 1964." Unpublished Ph.D. dissertation, U. of California at Los Angeles, 1965.

856   Lyons, Louis M. "The Conventions by Television," Nieman Reports, 10 (Oct., 1956), p. 2+.

857   Lyons, Robert A. "An Analysis of the Campaign Speaking of Chicago's Mayor Richard Daley in the 1964 Mayoral Campaign." Unpublished master's thesis, Michigan State U., 1967.

858   Maceda, E. M. "Television as a Political Advertising Medium." Unpublished master's thesis, U. of Illinois, 1961.

859   MacNeil, Robert. "Marketing the Candidates--The Use of Television in the American Election," Listener, 80 (Nov. 14, 1968), pp. 631-32.

860   _____. The People Machine. New York: Harper & Row, 1968.

861   _____. "Reporting the Results," The League of Women Voters of the United States Quarterly, 47 (Autumn, 1972), pp. 57-59.

862   "Magic Eye of Television; TV versus the Press," New Republic, 147 (Dec. 29, 1962), p. 2.

863   Mahaffey, Joseph H. "Do Campaigns Really Count," Speaker, 36 (Nov., 1953), pp. 1-5.

864 Maher, Terry. Effective Politics. London: Liberal
     Publications Department, n.d.

865 Makay, John J. "The Rhetoric of George C. Wallace, "
     Today's Speech, 18 (Fall, 1970), pp. 26-33.

866 _____. "The Rhetorical Strategies of Governor
     George Wallace in the 1964 Maryland Primary, "
     Southern Speech Journal, 36 (1970), pp. 164-75.

867 _____. "The Speaking of Governor George C. Wal-
     lace in the 1964 Maryland Presidential Primary."
     Unpublished Ph.D. dissertation, Purdue U., 1969.

868 _____, and Brown, William R. The Rhetorical
     Dialogue: Contemporary Concepts and Cases.
     Dubuque, Iowa: William C. Brown Co., 1972.

869 "The Making of a Candidate: A Look at the Reagan
     Boom, " United States News and World Report, 63
     (July 24, 1967), pp. 53-55.

870 "Making the Image: Presidential Candidates, " Time,
     92 (Sept. 20, 1968), pp. 85-86.

871 Mall, R. "Some Aspects of Political Broadcast Policies
     of Radio and Television Stations in the United States."
     Unpublished Ph.D. dissertation, Ohio State U., 1952.

872 "The Man Who Ran the Show, " Newsweek, 66 (Nov. 15,
     1965), p. 34.

873 Mandel, Jerry E. "A Critical Analysis of Three Forms
     of Oral Communication in Charles H. Percy's 1966
     Senatorial Campaign." Unpublished Ph.D. disserta-
     tion, Purdue U., 1968.

874 Manheim, Jarol B. "The Effects of Campaign Tech-
     niques on Voting Patterns in a Congressional Elec-
     tion." Unpublished Ph.D. dissertation, Northwestern
     U., 1971.

875 Mann, Leon, and Abels, Ronald. "Evaluation of Presi-
     dential Candidates as a Function of Time and Stage
     of Voting Decision, " Journal of Psychology, 74
     (1970), pp. 167-73.

876 Mannes, Marya. "Rabbit Punches on TV: The Gover-
     nor and the Lady, " Reporter, 7 (Nov. 25, 1952),
     pp. 12-13.

877 _____. "TV: Too Much of a Good Thing?" Re-
     porter, 15 (Sept. 6, 1956), pp. 21-22.

878 Margolis, Michael Stephen. "The Impact of Political
     Environment, Campaign Activity, and Party Organi-
     zation on the Outcomes of Congressional Elections."
     Unpublished Ph.D. dissertation, Michigan State U.,
     1968.

879 "Marketing the Candidates, " Newsweek, 71 (May 27,
     1968), p. 106+.

880 "Marketing the Issues, " America, 127 (Aug. 5, 1972),
     pp. 53-54.

881 Markham, J. "Press Coverage of the 1958 State Elec-
     tions in Pennsylvania: A Measure of Performance."
     Unpublished Ph.D. dissertation, Pennsylvania State
     U., 1959.

882 _____. "Press Treatment of the 1958 State Elec-
     tions in Pennsylvania, " Western Political Quarterly,
     14 (1961), pp. 912-24.

883 Markland, B. "Evasiveness in Political Discussion
     Broadcasts During the 1952 Election Campaign."
     Unpublished Ph.D. dissertation, U. of Michigan,
     1955.

884 Marr, Theodore J. "A New Method of Analysis for
     Panel Data on Political Candidate Image and Voter
     Communication Behavior." Paper presented at the
     Speech-Communication Association Convention, Chica-
     go, Dec. 27-30, 1972.

885 _____. "Q and R Analyses of Panel Data on Political
     Candidate Image and Voter Communication, " Speech
     Monographs, 40 (1973), pp. 56-65.

886 Marshall, Mac. "The Impact of Television on Politics."
     Columbia, Mo.: Freedom of Information Center, U.
     of Missouri, 1968.

887 Massmann, Sylvester H. "Dimensions of Myth in Political Thought," Western Political Quarterly, 19 (1966),
n. 3, suppl., p. 25.

888 Massoth, Clifford G. "That Speech-Writing Chore,"
Public Relations Journal, 16 (April, 1960), pp. 19-21.

889 Mauldin, B. "Cartoonist Goes Campaigning," Colliers,
138 (Sept. 28, 1956), pp. 38-39.

890 Mauser, Gary A. "Predicting Patterns of Competition
in Multiple Candidate Elections," Proceedings of the
77th Annual Convention of the American Psychological
Association, 4 (1969), pp. 435-36.

891 Mayer, Martin. "Recordings; Presidential Candidates'
Television Commercials," Esquire, 78 (Oct., 1972),
p. 42+.

892 _____. "What Did We Learn from the Polls this
Time? On the Biggest Decision of All--Eagleton--
George McGovern Went against the Polls and Suf-
fered Horribly by Doing So," New York Magazine, 5
(Nov. 6, 1972), pp. 55-59.

893 Mayo, Charles G. "The Mass Media and Campaign
Strategy in a Mayoralty Election," Journalism Quarterly, 41 (1964), pp. 353-59.

894 _____. "The 1961 Mayoralty Election in Los Angeles:
The Political Party in a Non-Partisan Election,"
Western Political Quarterly, 17 (June, 1964), pp.
325-37.

895 Mazo, Earl, et al. "Great Debates." Santa Barbara,
Calif.: Center for the Study of Democratic Institutions, 1962, 21 pp.

896 McAndrew, William R. "Broadcasting the Conventions";
Reinsch, Leonard. "Broadcasting the Political Conventions"; and Lower, Elmer W. "Broadcasting the
Conventions: A Choice," Journal of Broadcasting,
12 (1968), pp. 213-24.

897 McBath, J. H. "Debating on Television," Quarterly
Journal of Speech, 50 (1964), pp. 146-52.

898 McBath, James, and Fisher, Walter R. "Persuasion
      in Presidential Campaign Communication," Quarterly
      Journal of Speech, 55 (1969), pp. 17-25.

899 McCaffrey, Maurice. Advertising Wins Elections. Min-
      neapolis, Minn.: Gilbert Publishing Co., 1962.

900 McCain, Thomas A. "The Effect of Camera Treatment
      on Political Speakers' Credibility: Television Net-
      work Coverage of the Speeches of Ted Kennedy and
      George McGovern to the Democratic National Con-
      vention." Paper presented at the International Com-
      munication Association Convention, Montreal, April
      25-29, 1973.

901 McCarthy, Max. Elections for Sale. Boston: Houghton
      Mifflin Co., 1972.

902 McCartney, James. "What Really Happened in Man-
      chester?" Columbia Journalism Review, 11 (May/
      June, 1972), pp. 14-27.

903 McClosky, Herbert; Hoffman, P. J.; and O'Hara, Rose-
      mary. "Issue Conflict and Consensus Among Party
      Leaders and Followers," American Political Science
      Review, 54 (1960), pp. 406-27.

904 McCombs, Maxwell. "Editorial Endorsements: A
      Study of Influence," Journalism Quarterly, 44 (1967),
      pp. 545-48.

905 _____. "The Influence of Mass Communication in
      Politics," Today's Speech, 16, no. 4 (1968), p. 31+.

906 _____. "Negro Use of Television and Newspapers
      for Political Information. 1952-64," Journal of
      Broadcasting, 12 (1967-68), pp. 261-66.

907 _____, and Shaw, Donald L. "The Agenda-Setting
      Function of Mass Media," Public Opinion Quarterly,
      36 (1972), pp. 176-87.

908 _____; Shaw, Eugene; and Shaw, Donald. "The News
      and Public Response: Three Studies of the Agenda-
      Setting Power of the Press." Paper presented at
      the Association for Education in Journalism Conven-
      tion, Carbondale, Ill., Aug., 1972.

909 _____, and Weaver, David. "Voters' Need for Orientation and Use of Mass Communication." Paper
presented at the International Communication Association Convention, Montreal, April 25-29, 1973.

910 McCrone, Donald J., and Cnudde, Charles F. "Toward
a Communication Theory of Democratic Political Development: A Causal Model," American Political
Science Review, 61 (1967), pp. 72-79.

911 McCurtain, Marilyn E. "An Investigation of the
Voter's Decision Process and His Political Be-
havior." Unpublished Ph.D. dissertation, U. of
Washington, 1965.

912 McDougald, William. "Federal Regulation of Political
Broadcasting: A History and Analysis." Unpublished Ph.D. dissertation, Ohio State U., 1964.

913 McDowell, James L. "The Role of Newspapers in Illinois' At-Large Election," Journalism Quarterly,
42 (1965), pp. 281-84.

914 McGeachy, J. B. "They're Oiling up the Bandwagon,"
Financial Post (Toronto), 54 (July 9, 1960), p. 7.

915 _____. "Witty Politicians Don't Always Lose: Sir
Winston and JFK Scintillated," Financial Post (Toronto), 59 (Feb. 20, 1965), p. 7.

916 McGinnis, Joe. The Selling of the President 1968.
New York: Trident Press, 1969.

917 "The 'McGovern Phenomenon'--and How It Grew..."
United States News and World Report, 72 (June 12,
1972), pp. 29-32.

918 McGrath, Joseph E., and McGrath, Marion F. "Effects of Partisanship on Perceptions of Political
Figures," Public Opinion Quarterly, 26 (1962), pp.
236-48.

919 McGuckin, Henry E., Jr. "A Value Analysis of Richard
Nixon's 1952 Campaign-Fund Speech," Southern
Speech Journal, 33 (1968), pp. 259-69.

920 McGuire, William J. "The Nature of Attitudes and At-
       titude Change," Handbook of Social Psychology, Vol.
       III, eds. Gardner Lindzey and Elliot Aronson. Cam-
       bridge, Mass.: Addison-Wesley, 1969.

921 _____. "Selective Exposure: A Summing Up,"
       Theories of Cognitive Consistency: A Source Book,
       eds. Robert P. Abelson, et al. Chicago: Rand
       McNally, 1968.

922 McKesson, William B., and Derbey, John W. "Financing
       of Political Campaigns: Abuses and Suggested Con-
       trols," Southern California Law Review, 34 (Winter,
       1961), pp. 165-78.

923 McLaughlin, J. "Political Debates," America, 118
       (Jan. 15, 1968), pp. 778-80.

924 McLeod, Jack M., et al. "Political Conflict and Com-
       munication Behavior in the 1964 Political Campaign."
       Paper presented at the Association for Education in
       Journalism Convention, Syracuse, N.Y., Aug., 1965.

925 McLuhan, H. M. "Technology and Political Change,"
       International Journal, 7 (Summer, 1952), pp. 189-95.

926 McLuhan, Marshall. "Effects of the Improvements of
       Communication Media," Journal of Economic History,
       20 (1960), pp. 566-75.

927 _____. "New Media as Political Forms," Explora-
       tions, 3 (1954), pp. 6-13.

928 _____. "Parts of a Talk," Television Quarterly, 6
       (1967), pp. 39-44.

929 _____. "Report on Project in Understanding News
       Media." Unpublished Report Submitted to the United
       States Office of Education, 1960.

930 _____. Understanding Media. New York: New
       American Library, 1964.

931 McMillan, Edward Lee. "Texas and the Eisenhower
       Campaigns." Unpublished Ph.D. dissertation, U.
       of Texas Technological College, 1960.

932   McNaught, Kenneth W. "The Failure of Television in
      Politics," Canadian Forum, 38 (Aug., 1958), pp.
      104-05.

933   McPhee, William. "Note on a Campaign Simulator,"
      Public Opinion Quarterly, 25 (1961), pp. 184-93.

934   _____, and Ferguson, Jack. "Political Immuniza-
      tion," Public Opinion and Congressional Elections,
      eds. William McPhee and William Glaser. New York:
      The Free Press, 1962, pp. 155-79.

935   _____, and Smith, Robert B. "A Model for Analyz-
      ing Voting Systems," Public Opinion and Congres-
      sional Elections, eds. William McPhee and William
      Glaser. New York: The Free Press, 1962, pp.
      123-54.

936   McWilliams, Carey. "Campaign '72," Nation, 215
      (Nov. 13, 1972), pp. 450-52.

937   _____. "Government by Whitaker and Baxter III,"
      Nation, 172 (May 5, 1951), pp. 418-21.

938   _____. "Reagan versus Brown: How to Succeed with
      the Backlash," Nation, 203 (Oct. 31, 1966), pp. 438-
      42.

939   Meaney, J. W. "Propaganda as Psychical Coercion,"
      Review of Politics, 13 (1951), pp. 64-87.

940   "Meaning of the '70 Results--An Expert's Analysis: An
      Interview with John Kraft, Political Pollster,"
      United States News and World Report, 69 (Nov. 23,
      1970), pp. 28-29.

941   Melder, Keith. "American Parade of Politics, 1788-
      1960." Washington, D.C.: Smithsonian Press,
      1967, 24 pp.

942   Melich, Tanya. "Democratic Convention: Monitoring
      the TV Media," Ripon Forum, 8 (Aug., 1972), pp.
      17-18.

943   "Memo to Politicos," Time, 68, n. 15 (Oct. 8, 1956),
      p. 89.

944 Mendelsohn, Harold. "Behaviorism vs. Functionalism:
     Inadequacies in the Investigation of the Effects of
     Political Communications." Paper presented at the
     Speech-Communication Association Convention,
     Chicago, Dec. 27-30, 1972.

945 _____. "Election-Day Broadcasts and Terminal
     Voting Decisions," Public Opinion Quarterly, 30
     (1966), pp. 212-25.

946 _____. "Measuring the Process of Communication
     Effects," Public Opinion Quarterly, 26 (1962), pp.
     411-16.

947 _____. "Some Reasons Why Information Campaigns
     Can Succeed," Public Opinion Quarterly, 37 (1973),
     pp. 50-61.

948 _____. "TV and Youth: A New Style for Politics,"
     Nation, 202 (June 6, 1966), pp. 669-73.

949 _____, and Crespi, Irving. Polls, Television, and
     the New Politics. Scranton, Pa.: Chandler Pub-
     lishing Co., 1970.

950 "A Merciless Eye on Real Candidates," Life, 73 (July
     7, 1972), p. 22.

951 Merriam, Charles Edward. New Aspects of Politics.
     Chicago: University of Chicago Press, 1954.

952 Merriam, Robert, and Goetz, Rachel M. Going into
     Politics. New York: Harper, 1957.

953 Merrill, I. "Campaign Expenditures and their Control:
     A Study of Expenditures for Television Time in the
     1952 Federal Election." Unpublished Ph.D. disserta-
     tion, U. of Illinois, 1954.

954 Merrill, I. R., and Proctor, C. H. Political Per-
     suasion by Television: Partisan and Public Affairs
     Broadcasts in the 1956 General Election. East
     Lansing, Mich.: Michigan State U. Press, Oct.,
     1959.

955 Merritt, Richard L. "Political Science: An Approach
     to Human Communication," Approaches to Human
     Communication, eds. Richard W. Budd and Brent D.
     Ruben. New York: Spartan Books, 1972, pp. 313-
     33.

956 Mervin, David. "Parochialism and Professionalism in
     a Congressional Election," Political Studies, 20
     (Sept., 1972), pp. 277-86.

957 Metcalf, George R. "How to Be a Politician," National
     Civic Review, 48 (Oct., 1959), p. 454.

958 Meyer, D. Swing. The Winning Candidate. New York:
     James H. Heineman, Inc., 1966.

959 Meyer, Levin. "Politics on TV: Will It Ever Replace
     Baseball?" Reporter, 7 (Sept. 2, 1952), pp. 34-36.

960 Meyer, Philip. "Toward Responsibility in Reporting
     Opinion Surveys: The Journalist: Friend or Foe?"
     Public Opinion Quarterly, 35 (1971), pp. 347-49.

961 Meyer, Timothy P. "Evaluative Response Sets of 18-20
     Year Old Voters to Media Sources of Political In-
     formation: Some Inter-Media Comparisons." Paper
     presented at the Speech-Communication Association
     Convention, Chicago, Dec. 27-30, 1972.

962 _____. "News Reporter Bias: A Case Study in Se-
     lective Perception," Journal of Broadcasting, 16
     (1972), pp. 195-203.

963 Meyers, William. "Doorbells: Politics of Activism,"
     Nation, 202 (May 16, 1966), pp. 581-83.

964 Miami University, Department of Marketing. The In-
     fluence of Television on the Election of 1952. Ox-
     ford, Ohio: Oxford Research Associates, Dec., 1954.

965 Michaelson, Ronald D. "The Politics of Gubernatorial
     Endorsements in Cook County, Illinois: An Empirical
     Analysis." Unpublished Ph.D. dissertation, Southern
     Illinois U., 1970.

966 Mickelson, Sig. The Electric Mirror: Politics in an Age
     of Television. New York: Dodd, Mead and Co., 1972.

967 _____ . "TV and the Candidate," Saturday Review, April 16, 1960, pp. 13-15+.

968 _____ . "Two National Conventions Have Proved Television's News Role," Quill, 44 (Dec., 1956), pp. 15-16.

969 _____ . "The Use of Television," Politics U.S.A.: A Practical Guide to the Winning of Public Office, ed. James M. Cannon. Garden City, N.Y.: Doubleday, 1960, pp. 285-301.

970 _____ . "Why TV Has Become a Political Force," Broadcasting, 50 (March 5, 1956), p. 32+.

971 Middleton, R. "National TV Debates and Presidential Voting Decisions," Public Opinion Quarterly, 26 (1962), pp. 426-29.

972 Mikardo, Ian. "The Politician as Publicist," Tribune (London), no. 750 (1952), p. 7.

973 Milbrath, Lester W. Political Participation: How and Why Do People Get Involved in Politics? Chicago: Rand-McNally and Co., 1971.

974 Miller, Norman C. "John Tower's Battle with Barefoot," Wall Street Journal, 180 (Oct. 23, 1972), p. 8.

975 _____ . "Opinion Surveys Play an Ever-Widening Role in Political Campaigns," Wall Street Journal, March 8, 1968, p. 1.

976 _____ . "Scion of the Times: Jay Rockefeller Faces Tough West Virginia Bid Despite Charisma, Cash...." Wall Street Journal, 180 (Aug. 16, 1972), p. 1+.

977 _____ . "Smoothing the Way: Work by 'Advance Men' Can Be Key to Success when Candidates Travel," Wall Street Journal, 172 (July 3, 1968), p. 1+.

978 Miller, W. E. "Analysis of the Effect of Election Night Predictions on Voting Behavior." University of Michigan, Survey Research Center, Unpublished Report, Political Behavior Program, 1965.

979 Mills, C. Wright. Power, Politics and People. New York: Ballantine, 1963.

980 Millstein, G. "Political Hit, and Miss Parade," New York Times Magazine, Sept. 16, 1956, pp. 26-27+.

981 Minott, Rodney G. The Sinking of the Lollipop. San Francisco: Diablo Press, 1968.

982 Moley, R. "Politics Discovers Freud," Newsweek, 47 (Jan. 16, 1956), p. 84.

983 _____. "Raise the Sights," Newsweek, 58 (July 31, 1961), p. 84.

984 Monagan, John S. "Campaign for Short Campaigns," New York Times Magazine, May 8, 1960, pp. 30, 87-88.

985 Montgomery, Robert. "TV Can't Fool the Voters," This Week Magazine, Oct. 16, 1955, p. 7+.

986 Morgan, Edward P. "1956--How Television Could Help the Voter," New Republic, 134 (June 4, 1956), p. 15.

987 Moriarity, James. "Campaigns and the New Technology," Science News, 98 (Sept. 12, 1970), pp. 229-30.

988 Morris, R. B. "Hits on the Hustings," New York Times Magazine, April 24, 1960, p. 98+.

989 Morrison, Matthew C. "The Role of the Political Cartoonist in Image-making," Central States Speech Journal, 20 (1969), pp. 252-60.

990 Mortensen, C. David. "The Influence of Role Structure on Message Content in Political Telecast Campaigns," Central States Speech Journal, 19 (1968), p. 279+.

991 _____. "The Influence of Television on Policy Discussion," Quarterly Journal of Speech, 54 (1968), p. 277+.

992 _____. "Toward Theory Building in Campaign Persuasion." Paper presented at the Central States Speech Association Convention, Chicago, April, 1972.

993 _____, and Sereno, D. D. "Influence of Ego-Involvement and Discrepancy on Perceptions of Communication," Speech Monographs, 27 (1970), pp.
127-34.

994 Mortensen, Calvin. A Comparative Analysis of Political Persuasion on Four Telecast Program For-
mats in the 1960 and 1964 Presidential Campaigns.
Minneapolis: U. of Minnesota Press, 1967.

995 Moshman, Jack. "Computers in Elections: How Busi-
ness Benefits." Paper presented at the Business
Equipment Manufacturers Exposition, Los Angeles,
Oct. 22, 1964.

996 _____. "The Role of Computers in Election Night
Broadcasting," Advances in Computers, 5 (1965),
p. 3+.

997 Mueller, John. "Choosing Among 133 Candidates,"
Public Opinion Quarterly, 34 (1970), pp. 395-402.

998 Muggeridge, Malcolm. "Tele-Politics," New Statesman,
66 (Aug. 9, 1963), pp. 162-63.

999 Mullen, James J. "How Candidates for the Senate
Use Newspaper Advertising," Journalism Quarterly,
40 (1963), pp. 532-38.

1000 _____. "Newspaper Advertising in the Johnson-
Goldwater Campaign," Journalism Quarterly, 45
(1968), pp. 219-25.

1001 _____. "Newspaper Advertising in the Kennedy-
Nixon Campaign," Journalism Quarterly, 40 (1963),
pp. 3-11.

1002 Mumford, Manly. "The 'Blunt Truth' Technique,"
Public Relations Journal, 9 (March, 1953), p. 8.

1003 Murphy, Thomas P. "Strategies in the USA Presidential Election," Contemporary Review, 213, n.
1232 (Sept., 1968), pp. 113-20.

1004 Nadig, H. D. "New Orleans Believes TV May Change
Requirements for Age, Type of Officials," American
City, 65 (Oct., 1950), pp. 124-25.

1005   Napolitan, Joseph.   The Election Game and How to
       Win It.   Garden City, N.Y.:   Doubleday and Co.,
       Inc., 1972.

1006   Natchez, Peter B.   "Images of Voting: The Social
       Psychologists," Public Policy, 18 (1970), pp. 553-
       88.

1007   _____, and Bupp, Irvin C.   "Candidates, Issues
       and Voters," Public Policy, 17 (1968), pp. 409-37.

1008   Navasky, Victor S.   "Making of the Candidate," New
       York Times Magazine, May 7, 1972, p. 27+.

1009   Naylor, Thomas; Schauland, Horst; and Kornberg,
       Allan.   "A Campaign Simulator."   Paper presented
       at the American Political Science Association Con-
       vention, Chicago, Sept., 1971.

1010   "Nearly $10 Million in Radio-TV Spent in Political
       Campaigns," Broadcasting, 52 (Feb. 4, 1957), p.
       78+.

1011   Nelson, Bardin H.   "Seven Principles in Image
       Formation," Journal of Marketing, 26 (Jan., 1962),
       pp. 67-71.

1012   "Nelson Rockefeller's Last Hurrah: The Almost Per-
       fect Political Campaign," National Observer, Jan.
       9, 1967, p. 1.

1013   Neuberger, R. L.   "Isn't There a Better Way to Elect
       a President?" Saturday Review, Oct. 27, 1956,
       pp. 11-13.

1014   _____.   "The Professional Touch," New Republic,
       132 (May 9, 1955), p. 12.

1015   "New Political Qualifications," Commonweal, 52 (Oct.
       6, 1950), p. 622.

1016   "A New Survey Suggests Changes in Political TV,"
       Broadcasting, 44 (Feb. 23, 1953), p. 77.

1017   The Newspaper Information Committee.   A Study of
       the Opportunity for Exposure to National Newspaper
       Advertising.   New York: Bureau of Advertising,
       Newspaper Information Committee, 1966.

1018 Nicholas, H. G. "The 1968 Presidential Elections,"
      Journal of American Studies, 3 (1969), pp. 1-15.

1019 Nichols, Roger. "Voter Motivation in Two Florida
      Primary Elections." Unpublished Ph.D. disserta-
      tion, Florida State U., 1965.

1020 Niebuhr, Reinhold. "Personalities and Social Forces:
      Thoughts on the Recent Elections," New Leader,
      41 (Dec. 1, 1958), pp. 7-8.

1021 "Nielson Says 88% of TV Homes Saw at Least One Ses-
      sion of Conventions," Broadcasting, 51 (Sept. 24,
      1956), p. 88.

1022 Nimmo, Dan (ed.). Legislative Recruitment in Texas.
      Houston: Public Affairs Research Center, U. of
      Houston, 1967.

1023 _____. "News Sources and News Channels: A
      Study in Political Communication." Unpublished
      Ph.D. dissertation, Vanderbilt U., 1962.

1024 _____. The Political Persuaders. Englewood
      Cliffs, N.J.: Prentice-Hall, 1970.

1025 "The 1970 Elections in the West (Symposium),"
      Western Political Quarterly, 24 (1971), pp. 225+.

1026 "Nixon's the One; Choice of Editorial Pages," Time,
      92 (Oct. 18, 1968), pp. 69-70.

1027 "No, Madison Avenue Hasn't Taken over our Political
      Parties," Saturday Evening Post, 231 (Jan. 17,
      1959), p. 8.

1028 Nogee, Philip, and Levin, Murray B. "Some De-
      terminants of Political Attitudes Among College
      Voters," Public Opinion Quarterly, 22 (1958-59),
      pp. 449-63.

1029 Nolan, M. F. "Reselling the President," Atlantic,
      230 (Nov., 1972), pp. 79-81.

1030 Nollet, Monica. "The Boston Globe in Four Presi-
      dential Elections," Journalism Quarterly, 45 (1968),
      pp. 531-32.

1031 "Non-support," Commonweal, 97 (Nov. 3, 1972), pp.
      99-100.

1032 Nordvold, Robert O. "Rhetoric as Ritual: Hubert H.
      Humphrey's Acceptance Address at the 1968 Demo-
      cratic National Convention," Today's Speech, 18
      (Winter, 1970), pp. 34-38.

1033 North, R. C. "Communication as an Approach to
      Politics," American Behavioral Scientist, 10 (April,
      1967), p. 12+.

1034 Norton, Robert Wayne. "The Rhetorical Situation Is
      the Message: Muskie's Election Eve Television
      Broadcast," Central States Speech Journal, 22
      (1971), pp. 171-78.

1035 "November Songs," New York Times Magazine, Sept.
      13, 1964, pp. 150-51.

1036 "Now Is the Time for All Good Men," America, 123
      (July 11, 1970), pp. 6-7.

1037 "Now Is Time for TV Experts to Aid Their Favorite
      Party," Financial Post (Toronto), 56 (Dec. 12,
      1962), p. 15.

1038 Nunnery, Michael Y., and Kimbrough, Ralph B.
      Politics, Power, Polls, and School Elections.
      Berkeley, Calif.: McCutchan Publishing Corp.,
      1971.

1039 Ogden, Daniel M., Jr. "A Voting Behavior Approach
      to Split-Ticket Voting in 1952," Western Political
      Quarterly, 11 (1958), pp. 481-93.

1040 _____, and Peterson, Arthur L. Electing the
      President: 1964. San Francisco: Chandler Pub-
      lishing Co., 1964.

1041 Ogle, Marbury Bladen. Public Opinion and Political
      Dynamics. Boston: Houghton Mifflin, 1950.

1042 Oliphant, T. "Selling Out the Candidate: 1972,"
      Ramparts, 11 (Feb., 1973), pp. 25-28.

1043   Oliver, R. "Message on the Media," The Record, 70
       (Nov., 1968), pp. 139-42.

1044   Olson, David M. Nonpartisan Elections: A Case
       Analysis. Austin, Texas: Institute of Public Af-
       fairs, The U. of Texas at Austin, 1965.

1045   "On the Box," Economist, 244 (Aug. 19, 1972), pp.
       47-48.

1046   "On the Spot," Newsweek, 80 (Oct. 2, 1972), pp. 20-
       21.

1047   Orbell, John M.; Dawes, Robyn M.; and Collins,
       Nancy J. "Grass Roots Enthusiasm and the
       Primary Vote," Western Political Quarterly, 25
       (1972), pp. 249-59.

1048   Osborne, John. "Why Not Ban Paid Political Broad-
       casting?" New Republic, 158 (June 15, 1968), pp.
       13-15.

1049   Osgood, Charles E.; Suci, George J.; and Tannenbaum,
       Percy H. The Measurement of Meaning. Urbana,
       Ill.: U. of Illinois Press, 1957.

1050   Osten, Donald W. "How Media Planners Helped Percy
       Win in Illinois," Media/Scope, 11 (July, 1967), pp.
       45-50.

1051   Otten, Alan L. "Electronic Politics: Oregon Race
       Points up Mounting Stress on TV and Radio in
       Campaigns," Wall Street Journal, 171 (May 24,
       1968), p. 1+.

1052   "Out Damned Spot!" Time, 99 (April 24, 1972), pp.
       13-14.

1053   Overracker, Louise. "Dirty Money and Dirty Politics,"
       New Republic, 123 (Sept. 11, 1950), pp. 11-13.

1054   Owens, John R. Money and Politics in California:
       Democratic Senatorial Primary, 1964. Princeton,
       N.J.: Citizen's Research Foundation, 1966.

1055   Paletz, David L.   "Delegates' View of TV Coverage
       of the 1968 Democratic Convention," Journal of
       Broadcasting, 16 (1972), pp. 441-51.

1056   "Papert Hits His Ad Peers," Broadcasting, 74 (April
       1, 1968), p. 54.

1057   Parkinson, Hank.   Winning Your Campaign: A Nuts-
       and-Bolts Guide to Political Victory.   Englewood
       Cliffs, N.J.:   Prentice-Hall, 1970.

1058   Parks, Oral Eugene.   "An Analysis of Net Deviation
       Voting."   Unpublished Ph.D. dissertation, Michigan
       State U., 1972.

1059   Parsons, A. H., Jr.   "Button, Button; or How We
       Elected Eisenhower," Harper's Magazine, 211 (Oct.,
       1955), pp. 58-60.

1060   "The Partners," Time, 66 (Dec. 26, 1955), p. 11.

1061   Patch, B. W.   "Control of Campaign Abuses," Edi-
       torial Research Reports, Vol. 1, No. 16 (1952).

1062   "The Patrician and the Pol," Newsweek, 75 (May 4,
       1970), p. 30.

1063   Patton, Bonnie G. B.   "The 1968 Political Campaign
       of Senator Eugene J. McCarthy: A Study of Rhe-
       torical Choice."   Unpublished Ph.D. dissertation,
       U. of Kansas, 1969.

1064   Payne, D. E. (ed.).   The Obstinate Audience.   Ann
       Arbor, Mich.:   Foundation for Research on Human
       Behavior, 1965.

1065   Pearson, Kathy.   "Campaign '72: Politics and the
       Media," Washington University Magazine, 43, no.
       2 (Winter, 1973), pp. 34-35.

1066   Peirce, Neal R.   The People's President.   New York:
       Simon and Schuster, 1968.

1067   Penniman, Howard R., and Winter, Ralph K., Jr.
       "Campaign Finances: Two Views of the Political
       and Constitutional Implications."   Washington, D.C.:
       American Enterprise Institute for Public Policy Re-
       search, 1971.

1068 Perry, James M. "The Almost-Perfect Political
      Campaign," The National Observer, Jan. 9, 1967,
      p. 1+.

1069 _____. "A Genuine Exclusive on Image-Makers at
      Work," The National Observer, Sept. 19, 1969,
      p. 31.

1070 _____. The New Politics. New York: Clarkson
      N. Potter and Co., 1968.

1071 _____. "Noise, Involvement, and Political TV
      Blurbs," The National Observer, April 27, 1960,
      p. 10.

1072 _____. "Time Passes Some Notables By," The
      National Observer, May 11, 1970, p. 13.

1073 _____. "Wooing Voters with a Computer," Na-
      tional Observer, 6 (Sept. 11, 1967), p. 1.

1074 Perry, Paul. "A Comparison of Voting Preferences
      of Likely Voters and Likely Nonvoters," Public
      Opinion Quarterly, 37 (1973), pp. 99-109.

1075 Persico, Joseph E. "The Rockefeller Rhetoric:
      Writing Speeches for the 1970 Campaign," Today's
      Speech, 20 (Spring, 1971), pp. 57-62.

1076 Peterson, Donald C. "A Comparative Analysis of Two
      Junior College Elections in Northern Illinois Re-
      lating Mass Media Performance and Other Factors
      to Election Outcome." Unpublished Ph.D. disser-
      tation, Indiana U., 1967.

1077 Pettengill, D. B. "Regulation of Campaign Finance--
      The Maryland Experience," Maryland Law Review,
      19 (Spring, 1959), p. 91.

1078 Phillips, C. "Eisenhower as Campaigner," New York
      Times Magazine, Oct. 19, 1952, p. 10+.

1079 _____. "Torchlight, Train, Television," New York
      Times Magazine, Sept. 18, 1960, pp. 16-17+.

1080 Phillips, K. "Making of the GOP Candidate '76,"
      Newsweek, 80 (Sept. 4, 1972), pp. 28-29.

1081   Pickles, W.   "Political Attitudes in the Television
         Age," Political Quarterly, 30 (1959), pp. 54-66.

1082   Pierce, Neal R.   "Presidential Campaign Strategies
         Geared to Changing Electorate," National Journal,
         4 (Sept. 23, 1972), pp. 1504-13.

1083   Pilat, Oliver Ramsay.   Lindsay's Campaign: A Behind-
         the-Scenes Diary.   Boston: Beacon Press, 1968.

1084   Pincus, Walter.   "Nixon's Businesslike Campaign,"
         New Republic, 167 (Sept. 23, 1972), pp. 9-11.

1085   Pitchell, Robert J.   "The Influence of Professional
         Campaign Management Firms in Partisan Elections
         in California," Western Political Quarterly, 11
         (1958), pp. 278-300.

1086   "Plague on Both Houses," Time, 100 (Sept. 18, 1972),
         p. 47+.

1087   "Pointers on Using TV," Sponsor, 10 (July 23, 1956),
         p. 40.

1088   Polisky, Jerome B.   "The Kennedy-Nixon Debates:
         A Study in Political Persuasion." Unpublished
         Ph.D. dissertation, U. of Wisconsin, 1965.

1089   "Political Campaign Funds," Association of the Bar of
         the City of New York Record, 27 (May, 1972), pp.
         345-56.

1090   "The Political Pitch," Newsweek, 72 (Oct. 14, 1968),
         p. 74.

1091   "Political Polling 1968," Analyst, 1 (March, 1969),
         pp. 14-18.

1092   "Political Pulse-Taking: How the Pollsters Do It...,"
         United States News and World Report, 72 (Oct. 16,
         1972), pp. 26-28.

1093   "Political Soap Opera," Reporter, 14 (June 14, 1956),
         p. 2.

1094   "Political Television," Commonweal, 61 (Feb. 4, 1955),
         p. 469.

1095 "Politicians and Potshots," Newsweek, 39 (June 9, 1952), p. 84.

1096 "Politicians and Pros," Time and Tide, 40 (1959), N. 401, pp. 1068-69.

1097 "Politicians on the Air," Economist, July 16, 1955, p. 225.

1098 "Politicos Learn How to Act," Life, 32 (June 9, 1952), pp. 139-40+.

1099 "Politics, New Style," Nation, 206 (April 29, 1968), pp. 556-57.

1100 "Politics Pays Its Way on Television," Business Week, Feb. 9, 1952, p. 21.

1101 "Politics: TV's Latest Feature," Business Week, Sept. 23, 1950, pp. 24-25.

1102 Pollard, J. "Eisenhower and the Press: The Final Phase," Journalism Quarterly, 38 (1961), pp. 181-86.

1103 "Poll-Axed?" Newsweek, 74 (Nov. 17, 1969), p. 87.

1104 "Polling the Voters for Advice--and Votes," Business Week, March 13, 1954, pp. 30-31.

1105 "Polls as Election Guides," United States News and World Report, 33 (Nov. 14, 1952), p. 32.

1106 "Pollsters: The Voters Still Elude Them," Business Week, Nov. 15, 1952, pp. 43-44.

1107 Polsby, Nelson W., and Wildavsky, Aaron B. Presidential Elections. New York: Charles Scribner Sons, 1968.

1108 Pomper, Gerald M. Elections in America: Control and Influence in Democratic Politics. New York: Dodd, Mead and Co., 1971.

1109 _____. "The 1972 Presidential Election in the USA," International Problems, 11 (July, 1972), pp. 44-54.

1110   Pool, Ithiel de Sola.   "The Effect of Communication
          on Voting Behavior," The Science of Human Com-
          munication, ed. Wilbur Schramm.   New York:
          Basic Books, 1963.

1111   _____.   "The 'New Political Science' Re-Examined:
          A Symposium," Social Research, 29 (Summer,
          1962), pp. 127-56.

1112   _____.   The Prestige Press: A Comparative Study
          of Political Symbols.   Cambridge, Mass.:   The
          M.I.T. Press, 1970.

1113   _____.   "TV: A New Dimension in Politics,"
          American Voting Behavior, ed. Eugene Burdick and
          Arthur J. Brodbeck.   Glencoe, Ill.:   The Free
          Press, 1959.

1114   _____; Abelson, Robert P.; and Popkin, Samuel.
          Candidates, Issues and Strategies.   Cambridge:
          The M.I.T. Press, 1965 Revised Edition.

1115   Porter, Richard.   "Some Values to the Broadcaster of
          Election Campaign Broadcasting, Journal of Broad-
          casting, 7 (1963), pp. 145-56.

1116   Powell, James G.   "An Analytical and Comparative
          Study of the Persuasion of Kennedy and Nixon in
          the 1960 Campaign."   Unpublished Ph.D. disserta-
          tion, U. of Wisconsin, 1963.

1117   _____.   "Reactions to John F. Kennedy's Delivery
          Skills during the 1960 Campaign," Western Speech,
          32 (1968), pp. 59-68.

1118   "Power of the Polls," Trans-Action, 5 (June, 1968),
          pp. 4-5.

1119   "Presidential Campaign 1960: A Symposium: Part I:
          Contest for the Nomination," Quarterly Journal of
          Speech, 46 (1960), pp. 239-52.

1120   "Presidential Campaign 1960: A Symposium: Part II:
          Contest for the Presidency," Quarterly Journal of
          Speech, 46 (1960), pp. 355-64.

1121 "Presidential Campaign, 1964: A Political Symposium, "
      Quarterly Journal of Speech, 50 (1964), pp. 385-
      414.

1122 "Presidential Campaigns, " Economist, Nov. 9, 1957,
      pp. 491-92.

1123 President's Commission on Campaign Costs. "Fi-
      nancing Presidential Campaigns, " Report of the
      President's Commission on Campaign Costs, April,
      1962.

1124 "The Press as Mob, " New Republic, 167 (Aug. 19,
      1972), pp. 19-20.

1125 Preston, Peter. "Television's Hidden Qualities, "
      Guardian, July 28, 1964, p. 8.

1126 Prial, Frank J. "Politicking for Pay: Professional
      Managers Play an Expanding Role in Election Cam-
      paigns, " Wall Street Journal, 168 (Sept. 15, 1966),
      p. 1+.

1127 Price, G. "Analysis of Methods for Measuring News-
      papers' Coverage of Presidential Election Cam-
      paigns." Unpublished Ph.D. dissertation, U. of
      Missouri, 1954.

1128 _____. "A Method for Analyzing Newspaper Cam-
      paign Coverage, " Journalism Quarterly, 31 (1954),
      pp. 447-58.

1129 "Price of Victory, " Time, 88 (Aug. 19, 1966), p. 22.

1130 Priest, Robert F., and Abrahams, Joel. "Candidate
      Preference and Hostile Humor in the 1968 Elec-
      tions, " Psychological Reports, 26 (1970), pp. 779-
      83.

1131 Prisuta, Robert H. "Broadcasting by Candidates for
      the Michigan Legislature: 1970, " Journal of Broad-
      casting, 16 (1972), pp. 453-60.

1132 "Professional Managers, Consultants Play Major Roles
      in 1970 Political Races, " National Journal, 2 (1970),
      pp. 2007-87.

1133   "Professionals in the Saddle," Economist, 165 (Oct. 4,
        1952), pp. 21-22.

1134   "Propaganda for Parties," Economist, 171 (May 15,
        1954), pp. 516-17.

1135   Prosser, Michael. "Selected Sources on Contemporary
        Communication and Politics, 1948-64," Today's
        Speech, 16 (1968), pp. 95-118.

1136   "Pseudo-campaign," New Republic, 159 (Sept. 21, 1968),
        pp. 9-10.

1137   "Psychology in Politics," Science News Letter, 58
        (Sept. 9, 1950), p. 164.

1138   Pulse, Inc. "How Viewers Vote: A Special Pulse
        Study Checks Before and After Effects of TV on At-
        titudes Toward Candidates," Television Age, 3
        (1956), pp. 56-57+.

1139   Pulzer, Peter. "Voters, Polls, and Myths," Spectator,
        (March 4, 1966), pp. 251-52.

1140   "Punctured Image: Deflation of Television's Political
        Image-Makers," Newsweek, 76 (Nov. 16, 1970), p.
        77.

1141   Putnam, Linda L. "The Rhetorical Vision and Fantasy
        Themes of McGovern Campaign Planners," Moments
        in Contemporary Rhetoric and Communication (Tem-
        ple U.), 2 (Fall, 1972), pp. 13-20.

1142   Qualter, T. H. "Politics and Broadcasting: Case
        Studies of Political Interference in National Broad-
        casting Systems," Canadian Journal of Economics
        and Political Science, 28 (May, 1962), pp. 225-34.

1143   "Radio and Television Appearances of Candidates for
        Office: Amended Section 315 of the Communications
        Act," Yale Law Journal, 69 (1960), pp. 805-15.

1144   Radke, H. Theodore. "An Image of Ronald Reagan:
        The Role of Spencer-Roberts in the Campaign," New
        Scholar, 1 (April, 1969), pp. 122-23.

1145   Ranney, Austin. "The Representativeness of Primary
       Electorates," Midwest Journal of Political Science,
       12 (1968), pp. 224-38.

1146   Rapp, N. G. "The Political Speaking of Senator
       Robert A. Taft, 1939 to 1953." Unpublished Ph.D.
       dissertation, Purdue U., 1955, p. 530.

1147   Rarick, Galen R. Field Experiments in Newspaper
       Item Readership. Eugene, Ore.: Division of Com-
       munication Research, School of Journalism, U. of
       Oregon, 1967.

1148   _____ . "Political Persuasion: The Newspaper and
       the Sexes," Journalism Quarterly, 47 (1970), pp.
       360-64.

1149   Ratnam, K. J. "Charisma and Political Leadership,"
       Political Studies, 12 (Oct., 1964), pp. 341-54.

1150   Raucek, Joseph S. "The Influence of Television on
       American Politics," Politics, 28 (1963), pp. 124-34.

1151   Raven, B. H., and Gallo, P. S. "The Effects of
       Nominating Conventions, Elections and Reference
       Group Identification Upon the Perception of Political
       Figures," Human Relations, 18 (Aug., 1965), pp.
       217-29.

1152   Ray, Robert F. "Ghostwriting in Presidential Cam-
       paigns," Today's Speech, 4 (1956), pp. 13-15.

1153   Redish, M. H. "Campaign Spending Laws and the
       First Amendment," New York University Law Re-
       view, 46 (Nov., 1971), pp. 900-34.

1154   Rees, C. A. "Uncandid Candidates and the Oregon
       Corrupt Practices Act," Oregon Law Review, 50
       (Spring, 1971, pt. 1), p. 299.

1155   Rees, Matilda R., and Paisley, William J. Social
       and Psychological Predictors of Information Seeking
       and Media Use. Report of the Institute for Com-
       munication Research, Stanford U., Sept., 1967.

1156   Rege, G. M. "Poster As an Effective Medium of
       Communication," Social Bulletin, 12 (1963), pp. 34-
       39.

1157   Reid, Ronald F., and Beck, N. B. "The Campaign
       Speaking of Dwight D. Eisenhower," Speaker, 35
       (Jan., 1953), pp. 11-12, 17.

1158   Reinsch, J. Leonard. "Broadcasting the Political Con-
       ventions," Journal of Broadcasting, 12 (1968), pp.
       219-23. See also no. 896.

1159   RePass, David E. "Issue Salience and Party Choice,"
       American Political Science Review, 65 (1971), pp.
       389-400.

1160   _____. "Coverage by Eight Wisconsin Newspapers
       of the 1956 and 1964 Presidential Campaigns." Un-
       published master's thesis, U. of Wisconsin, 1968.

1161   _____, and Chaffee, Steven. "Administrative vs.
       Campaign Coverage of Two Presidents in Eight
       Partisan Dailies," Journalism Quarterly, 45 (1968),
       pp. 528-31.

1162   Report on Network News' Treatment of the 1972 Demo-
       cratic Presidential Candidates. Bloomington, Ind.:
       Alternative Education Foundation, 1972.

1163   "Report on Regulation, Limitation and Minimization of
       Campaign Finance," Georgia State Bar Journal, 8
       (Feb., 1972), p. 339.

1164   "Reporting Election Returns and Computer Predictions:
       Proposed Regulation," Iowa Law Review, 50 (Sum-
       mer, 1965), pp. 1173-93.

1165   Republican National Committee. Ways to Win. A
       Digest of Remarks from Campaign Management
       Seminars. Washington, D.C.: Republican Na-
       tional Committee, 1968.

1166   "Reshaping Teddy's Image: Advertisements Prepared
       by Three Advertising Agencies," Esquire, 73 (June,
       1970), pp. 87-99.

1167   Reston, James. "Our Campaign Techniques Re-
       examined," New York Times Magazine, Nov. 9,
       1952, p. 8+.

1168   "Returns Affect Few in Oregon," Broadcasting, 67
       (Nov. 16, 1964), p. 102.

1169   Rhine, Ramon J. "The 1964 Presidential Election
       and Curves of Information Seeking and Avoidance,"
       Journal of Personality and Social Psychology, 5
       (1967), pp. 416-23.

1170   Rickman, H. P. "Dramatization in Politics," Fort-
       nightly Review, 176 (Nov., 1954), pp. 328-32.

1171   Rider, J. R. "The Charleston Study: The Television
       Audience of the Nixon-Kennedy Debates." Unpub-
       lished Ph.D. dissertation, Michigan State U., 1963.

1172   Riedel, James A., and Dunne, James R. "When the
       Voter Decides," Public Opinion Quarterly, 33
       (1969-70), pp. 619-21.

1173   Rieselbach, Leroy N., and Balch, George (eds.).
       Psychology and Politics, an Introductory Reader.
       New York: Holt, Rinehart and Winston, 1969.

1174   Rigier, Hilda Mae. "A Content Analysis of Time's
       Coverage of the 1964 Presidential Campaign." Un-
       published master's thesis, U. of Iowa, 1965.

1175   Ritter, Kurt W. "Ronald Reagan and 'The Speech':
       The Rhetoric of Public Relations Politics,"
       Western Speech, 32 (1968), pp. 50-58.

1176   Rivers, William L. The Adversaries: Politics and
       the Press. Boston: Beacon Press, 1970.

1177   Roberts, C. "Brain-trust Race for '72," Newsweek,
       77 (March 15, 1971), p. 30+.

1178   Roberts, Churchill. "Voting Intentions and Attitude
       Change in a Congressional Election," Speech Mono-
       graphs, 40 (March, 1973), pp. 49-55.

1179   Roberts, S. V. "The Elections: Poor Guys Finish
       Last," Commonweal, 87 (Dec. 1, 1967), pp. 291-
       92.

1180   Robertson, Heather. "The Unmaking of an Image,"
       McLean's Magazine, 85 (Oct., 1972), p. 122.

1181 Robinson, David. "The Elusive Politicians," Contrast, 3 (Summer, 1964), pp. 218-20.

1182 Robinson, John P. "The Audience for National TV News Programs," Public Opinion Quarterly, 35 (1971), pp. 403-05.

1183 _____. "Perceived Media Bias and the 1968 Vote: Can the Media Affect Behavior After All?" Journalism Quarterly, 49 (1972), pp. 239-46.

1184 _____, and Shaver, Phillip R. Measures of Political Attitudes. Ann Arbor, Mich.: Survey Research Center, Institute for Social Research, U. of Michigan, 1968.

1185 Rochester, G. W. "High Cost of Politics," Trial, 4 (Dec., 1967-Jan., 1968), p. 32.

1186 Rogers, Everett M., and Shoemaker, F. Floyd. Communication of Innovations: A Cross-Cultural Approach. New York: The Free Press, 1971.

1187 Rogers, W. E. "Campaign Techniques," Social Education, 20 (1956), pp. 264-66.

1188 Roll, Charles W., Jr. "Straws in the Wind: The Record of the Daily News Poll," Public Opinion Quarterly, 32 (1968), pp. 251-60.

1189 _____, and Cantril, Albert H. Polls: Their Use and Misuse in Politics. New York: Basic Books, 1972.

1190 "Romance," Time, 77 (Jan. 13, 1961), p. 36.

1191 "Ronald Reagan, Star," Commonweal, 84 (June 24, 1966), p. 383.

1192 Roper, Burns W. A Ten-Year View of Public Attitudes Toward Television and Other Mass Media, 1959-1968. New York: Television Information Office, 1969.

1193 Roper, Elmo. Emerging Profiles of Television and Other Mass Media: Public Attitudes 1959-67. New York: Television Information Office, April, 1967.

1194 _____ . The Public's View of Television and Other
      Media: 1959-1964. New York: Television In-
      formation Office, 1967.

1195 Roper Organization. An Extended View of Public Atti-
      tudes Toward Television and Other Mass Media,
      1959-1971. New York: Television Information Of-
      fice, 1971.

1196 Rose, Ernest D., and Fuchs, Douglas. "Reagan vs.
      Brown: A TV Image Playback," Journal of Broad-
      casting, 12 (1968), pp. 247-60.

1197 Rose, R. "Political Decision-Making and the Polls,"
      Parliamentary Affairs, 15 (1962), pp. 188-202.

1198 Rose, Richard. Influencing Voters. New York: St.
      Martin's Press, 1967.

1199 _____ . "The Professionals in Politics," New Soci-
      ety, Aug. 8, 1963, pp. 10-12.

1200 Roseman, Cyril; Mayo, Charles G.; and Collinge, F.
      B. (eds.). Dimensions of Political Analysis.
      Englewood Cliffs, N.J.: Prentice-Hall, 1966.

1201 Rosen, Benson, and Einhorn, Hillel J. "Attractiveness
      of the 'Middle of the Road' Political Candidate,"
      Journal of Applied Social Psychology, 2 (1972), pp.
      157-65.

1202 Rosenbaum, Leonard L., and McGinnies, Elliott. "A
      Semantic Differential Analysis of Concepts Associ-
      ated with the 1964 Presidential Election," Journal
      of Social Psychology, 78 (1969), pp. 227-35.

1203 Rosenthal, Paul I. "Ethos in the Presidential Cam-
      paign of 1960: A Study of the Basic Persuasive
      Process of the Kennedy-Nixon Debates." Unpub-
      lished Ph.D. dissertation, U.C.L.A., 1963.

1204 Roshwalb, I., and Resnicoff, L. "Impact of Endorse-
      ments and Published Polls on the 1970 New York
      Senatorial Election," Public Opinion Quarterly, 35
      (1971), pp. 410-14.

1205   Rosnow, Ralph L.   "Bias in Evaluating the Presidential
       Debates: A 'Splinter' Effect, " Journal of Social
       Psychology, 67 (1965), pp. 211-19.

1206   Ross, Irwin.   "Supersalesmen of California Politics:
       Whitaker and Baxter, " Harper's Magazine, 219
       (July, 1959), pp. 55-61.

1207   Rossman, Jules.   "Meet the Press and the National
       Elections: The Candidates and the Issues, 1952-
       64. " Unpublished Ph.D. dissertation, Michigan
       State U., 1968.

1208   Rotter, George S., and Rotter, Naomi G.   "The In-
       fluence of Anchors in the Choice of Political Candi-
       dates, " Journal of Social Psychology, 70 (1966),
       pp. 275-80.

1209   Roucek, J. S.   "Influence of Television on American
       Politics. " Bridgeport, Conn.: U. of Bridgeport,
       1963, 9 pp.

1210   Rowse, A. E.   "Political Polls, " Editorial Research
       Reports, Vol. 2, No. 14 (1960), 18 pp.

1211   Rubin, Bernard.   Political Television.   Belmont,
       Calif.: Wadsworth Publishing Co., 1967.

1212   Rucker, Bryce W.   "News Services' Crowd Reporting
       in the 1956 Presidential Campaign, " Journalism
       Quarterly, 37 (1960), pp. 195-98.

1213   _____.   "A Study of Associated Press, International
       News Service, and United Press Reports of At-
       tendance and Reactions of Crowds at Appearances
       of Eisenhower, Stevenson, Nixon, and Kefauver in
       the 1956 Presidential Campaign. " Unpublished
       Ph.D. dissertation, U. of Missouri, 1959.

1214   Runyon, John H., et al. (eds.).   Source Book of
       American Presidential Campaign and Election
       Statistics, 1948-68.   New York: Ungar Publishing
       Co., 1971.

1215   Rush, C.   "The Analysis of Political Campaign News, "
       Journalism Quarterly, 28 (1951), pp. 250-52.

1216   Rusk, Jerrold G., and Weisberg, Herbert F. "Per-
       ceptions of Political Candidates: Implications for
       Electoral Change," Midwest Journal of Political
       Science, 16 (1972), pp. 388-410.

1217   _____, and _____. "Perceptions of Presidential
       Candidates: A Midterm Report." Paper presented
       at the American Political Science Association Con-
       vention, Chicago, Sept., 1971.

1218   Russell, Charles. "A Multi-Variate Descriptive Field
       Study of Media and Non Media Influences on Voting
       Behavior in the 1970 Texas Gubernatorial Elec-
       tion." Unpublished Ph.D. dissertation, Southern
       Illinois U., 1971.

1219   Safire, William. "All-purpose Political Speech,
       1968," New York Times Magazine, June 9, 1968,
       p. 39+.

1220   _____. "It's Time for a Change of Political Slo-
       gans," New York Times Magazine, Dec. 26, 1971,
       pp. 8-9.

1221   _____. The New Language of Politics: An Anec-
       dotal Dictionary of Catch Words, Slogans, and Po-
       litical Usage. New York: Random House, 1968.

1222   Salant, R. "The 1960 Campaigns and Television."
       Unpublished Ph.D. dissertation, U. of Missouri,
       1961.

1223   _____. "Political Campaigns and the Broadcaster,"
       Public Policy, 8 (1958), pp. 336-67.

1224   Salinger, Pierre. With Kennedy. New York: Double-
       day, 1966.

1225   Samovar, Larry A. "Ambiguity and Unequivocation in
       the Kennedy-Nixon Television Debates: A Rhe-
       torical Analysis," Western Speech, 29 (1965), pp.
       211-18.

1226   Samuelson, Merrill; Carter, Richard F.; and Ruggels,
       Lee. "Education, Available Time, and Use of
       Mass Media," Journalism Quarterly, 40 (1963), pp.
       491-96.

1227   Sanders, Keith R., and Kraus, Sidney. "Presidential
       Campaign Communication 1972: Trends in Strategy
       and Tactics." Paper presented at the Speech-Com-
       munication Association Convention, Chicago, Dec.
       27-30, 1972.

1228   _____; Hirsch, Robert; and Pace, Thomas. Poli-
       tical Communication: A Bibliography. Carbondale,
       Ill.: Center for Communications Research, South-
       ern Illinois U., 1972.

1229   _____, and Pace, Thomas J. "The 'Natural Ex-
       periment' as a Research Methodology for the Study
       of Speech-Communication," Proceedings of the 1969
       SAA Summer Conference on Research and Action,
       ed. James Roeaver. New York: Speech Association
       of America, 1970, pp. 80-87.

1230   "Saturation of Radio and TV Spots Seems to Have Paid
       Off for GOP," Advertising Age, 23 (Nov. 10, 1952),
       p. 3.

1231   Sawyer, Thomas C. "A Technique of Mass Communi-
       cation Used by Republican State Organizations."
       Unpublished Ph.D. dissertation, Ohio State U.,
       1968.

1232   Scammon, R. M. "Electoral Participation," Annals
       of the American Academy, 371 (May, 1967), pp.
       59-71.

1233   Scammon, Richard M., and Wattenberg, Ben J. The
       Real Majority. New York: Coward-McCann,
       Inc., 1970.

1234   "Scandals in Practical Politics," United States News
       and World Report, 35 (Aug. 14, 1953), pp. 24-25.

1235   "Scandals of '68," Nation, 207 (Oct. 14, 1968), pp.
       354-55.

1236   Scheele, Henry. "Evaluations by Experts and Laymen
       of Selected Political Speakers," Southern Speech
       Journal, 33 (1968), pp. 270-78.

1237 _____. "The Rhetoric of the Incumbent--Richard Nixon." Paper presented at the Central States Speech Association Convention, Minneapolis, April, 1973.

1238 Scheff, Edward A. "The Application of the Semantic Differential to the Study of Voter Behavior in the 1964 Political Campaigns." Unpublished Ph.D. dissertation, U. of Kansas, 1965.

1239 Schiller, H. I. "Mind Management: Mass Media in the Advanced Industrial State," Quarterly Review of Economics and Business, 11 (1971), pp. 39-52.

1240 Schlesinger, Arthur M., Jr. (ed.). History of American Presidential Elections, 1789-1968. New York: Chelsea House, 1971.

1241 Schnare, Helen T. "A Rhetorical Analysis of Selected Speeches of Stuart Symington in the Senatorial Campaign of 1952." Unpublished Ph.D. dissertation, U. of Wisconsin, 1966.

1242 Schneider, John G. "'56: Show-biz Flop," Nation, 183 (Nov. 24, 1956), pp. 449-52.

1243 _____. "The Worst that Television Could Do in a Campaign," New Republic, 134 (June 4, 1956), pp. 14-16.

1244 Schneidman, Edwin S. "The Logic of Politics," Television and Human Behavior: Tomorrow's Research in Mass Communications, ed. Leon Arons and Mark May. New York: Appleton-Century-Crofts, 1963, pp. 178-99.

1245 Schoenberger, Robert A. "Campaign Strategy and Party Loyalty: The Electoral Relevance of Candidate Decision-Making in the 1964 Congressional Elections," American Political Science Review, 63 (1969), pp. 515-20.

1246 Schonfeld, Maurice. "Seeing Is Not Believing," Reporter, June 25, 1959, pp. 37-38.

1247 "School for Candidates," Time, 100 (July 3, 1972), pp. 13-14.

1248   Schrag, Peter. "The Failure of Political Language,"
       Saturday Review, 55 (March 25, 1972), pp. 30-31.

1249   Schramm, Wilbur, and Carter, R. F. "Effectiveness
       of a Political Telethon," Public Opinion Quarterly,
       23 (1959), pp. 121-27.

1250   Schulz, W. "Buttoning-Up the Campaigns," Readers'
       Digest, 101 (Oct., 1972), pp. 156-60.

1251   Schuman, H., and Harding, J. "Sympathetic Identifi-
       cation with the Underdog," Public Opinion Quarterly,
       27 (1963), pp. 230-41.

1252   Schwartz, Alan J. "An Analysis of Selected Television
       Political Debates Produced in New York by WCBS-
       TV and Transmitted Locally during the Elections
       of 1962 and 1966." Unpublished Ph.D. disserta-
       tion, New York U., 1970.

1253   Scott, George. "Television Politics and the Need for
       Inquisitors," Time, May 4, 1968, p. 9.

1254   Seabury, Paul. "Television, a New Campaign Weapon,"
       New Republic, 127 (Dec. 1, 1952), pp. 12-14.

1255   Sears, David O. "Opinion Formation and Information
       Preferences in an Adversary Situation," Journal
       of Experimental Social Psychology, 2 (1966), pp.
       130-42.

1256   _____. "The Paradox of De Facto Selective Ex-
       posure without Preference for Supportive Informa-
       tion," Theories of Cognitive Consistency: A
       Source Book, ed. Robert P. Abelson, et al.
       Chicago: Rand McNally, 1968.

1257   _____. "Political Behavior," Handbook of Social
       Psychology, Vol. 5, ed. Gardner Lindzey and
       Elliott Aronson. Cambridge, Mass.: Addison-
       Wesley, 1969.

1258   _____, and Freedman, J. L. "Selective Exposure
       to Information: A Critical Review," Public Opin-
       ion Quarterly, 31 (1967), pp. 194-213.

1259   Sebald, Hans. "Limitations of Communication:
          Mechanisms of Image Maintenance in the Form of
          Selective Perception, Selective Memory, and Se-
          lective Distortion," Journal of Communication, 12
          (Sept., 1962), pp. 142-49.

1260   Sebring, Jay. "Making Up of a President; Suggested
          Images," Esquire, 69 (May, 1968), pp. 91-94.

1261   Seddon, William G. "A Content Analysis of News
          Coverage of the 1968 Presidential Campaign by
          Florida Daily Newspapers." Unpublished M.A.
          thesis, U. of Florida, 1969.

1262   "Seeing Spots," Newsweek, 68 (Nov. 7, 1966), p. 34+.

1263   Segal, M. W. "Selective Processes Operating in the
          Defense of Consonance," Psychology, 7 (May,
          1970), pp. 14-37.

1264   Seldes, Gilbert. "The More the Media," Saturday
          Review, Nov. 27, 1954, pp. 29-30.

1265   _____. "Politics, Freedom and Madison Avenue,"
          Saturday Review, Sept. 8, 1956, p. 36.

1266   _____. "Politics--Televised and Sponsored,"
          Saturday Review, 35 (March 15, 1952), pp. 30-31.

1267   _____. "TV and the Voter," Saturday Review, 35
          (Dec. 6, 1952), pp. 17-19+.

1268   Seldin, J. J. "Selling Presidents Like Soap," Ameri-
          can Mercury, 83 (Sept., 1956), pp. 5-10.

1269   "Selling of the Candidates 1970," Newsweek, 76 (Oct.
          19, 1970), pp. 34-38+.

1270   "Selling of the Candidates: 1972," Economist, 240
          (Aug. 14, 1971), pp. 30-40.

1271   Sevareid, Eric. "Making Friends with the Robots,"
          Reporter, Nov. 1, 1956, p. 15.

1272   "'72 Campaign Trends: More Computers, Fewer TV
          Spots," Congressional Quarterly Weekly Report,
          30 (April 15, 1972), pp. 856-59.

1273 Shabecoff, Phillip B. "Press and Television Coverage of the 1956 National Political Conventions," Studies in Public Communication, 2 (1959), pp. 40-46.

1274 Shadegg, Stephen C. What Happened to Goldwater. New York: Holt, Rinehart and Winston, 1965.

1275 Shaffer, H. B. "Campaign Smearing," Editorial Research Reports, Vol. 1, No. 1 (1956), 20 pp.

1276 _____. "Television and the 1956 Campaign," Editorial Research Reports, Vol. 2, No. 1 (1955), pp. 615-32.

1277 Shaffer, S. "How to Campaign," Newsweek, 42 (Oct. 12, 1953), p. 32.

1278 Shaffer, William R. Computer Simulation of Voting Behavior. New York: Oxford University Press, 1972.

1279 _____. "Partisan Loyalty and the Perceptions of Party, Candidates and Issues," Western Political Quarterly, 25 (1972), pp. 424-33.

1280 Shannon, J. B. Money and Politics. New York: Random House, 1959.

1281 Shanor, Donald. "The Columnists Look at Lindsay," Journalism Quarterly, 43 (1966), pp. 287-90.

1282 Sharkey, Samuel N., Jr. "Visual Coverage of National News Has Come of Age Says NBC Executive," Quill, 44 (Dec., 1956), p. 14+.

1283 Shayon, Robert Lewis. "Campaigning before the Cameras," Saturday Review of Literature, 34 (Oct. 6, 1951), p. 37.

1284 _____. "Elections by Electronics," Saturday Review, 47 (March 14, 1964), p. 22.

1285 _____. "How to Look Like a Winner," New Republic, 166 (March 25, 1972), p. 18.

1286 _____. "Pavlov and Politics," Saturday Review, 43 (Jan. 23, 1960), p. 28.

1287   Skeinkopf, Kenneth G. "Electronic Political Adver-
       tising: Marketing Facts or Images?--A Content
       Analysis of the 1952 Eisenhower Campaign."
       Paper presented at the Association for Education
       in Journalism Convention, Columbia, S.C., Aug.,
       1971.

1288   _____. "Political Advertising and Dirty Politics:
       What to Expect in '72." Paper presented at the
       Association for Education in Journalism Convention,
       Carbondale, Ill., Aug., 1972.

1289   _____; Atkin, Charles K.; and Bowen, Lawrence.
       "The Functions of Political Advertising for Cam-
       paign Organizations," Journal of Marketing Re-
       search, 9 (Nov., 1972), pp. 401-05.

1290   _____; _____; and _____. "How Political
       Party Workers Respond to Political Advertising,"
       Journalism Quarterly, 50 (Spring, 1973).

1291   _____; _____; and _____. "Political Adver-
       tising and Campaign Workers: Prompting the Po-
       litical Persuaders." Paper presented at the As-
       sociation for Education in Journalism, Columbia,
       S.C., Aug., 1971.

1292   _____, and O'Keefe, M. Timothy. "The Eagleton
       Affair: A Study of News Diffusion." Paper
       presented at the International Communication
       Association Convention, Montreal, April 25-29,
       1973.

1293   _____, and _____. "Political Advertising and
       the 1972 Campaign: A Communication Failure."
       Paper presented at the International Communica-
       tion Association Convention, Montreal, April 25-
       29, 1973.

1294   Shepard, William Bruce. "Political Preferences, Par-
       ticipation, and Local Policy-Making: A Study of
       Referendum Voting Behavior in American Cities."
       Unpublished Ph.D. dissertation, U. of California-
       Riverside, 1972.

1295 Shepsle, Kenneth A. "The Strategy of Ambiguity: Uncertainty and Electoral Competition," American Political Science Review, 66 (1972), pp. 555-68.

1296 Sherif, Carolyn W.; Sherif, Muzafer; and Nebergall, Roger. Attitude and Attitude Change. Philadelphia: W. B. Saunders Co., 1965.

1297 Sherrill, Robert. "Nixon's Man in Dixie," New York Times Magazine, Sept. 15, 1968, pp. 32-33+.

1298 Sherrod, Drury R. "Selective Perception of Political Candidates," Public Opinion Quarterly, 35 (1971-72), pp. 554-62.

1299 "Show-biz in Politics," Newsweek, 80 (Sept. 25, 1972), pp. 34-38.

1300 Shubik, Martin. Readings in Game Theory and Political Behavior. New York: Doubleday Short Studies in Political Science, No. 9, Doubleday and Co., 1954, 74 pp.

1301 Sidey, H. "After all that Fuss, U.S. Voters Ignored the Slogans," Life, 69 (Nov. 13, 1970), pp. 38-39.

1302 _____. "How to Watch Nixon on the Tube," Life, 67 (July 11, 1969), p. 2.

1303 _____. "Myth of Splendid Misery," Life, 62 (Feb. 24, 1967), p. 32B.

1304 _____. "Some Advantages and Disadvantages of Being In," Life, 65 (Aug. 9, 1968), p. 2.

1305 _____. " 'Tis the Season to be Nasty," Life, 71 (Dec. 3, 1971), p. 4.

1306 Siebert, J. C., et al. The Influence of Television on the Election of 1952. Oxford: Oxford Research Associates, 1954.

1307 Siepmann, Charles A. "TV and the Campaign," Nation, 182 (March 17, 1956), pp. 218-20.

1308 _____. "Were They 'Great'?" The Great Debates, ed. Sidney Kraus. Bloomington, Ind.: Indiana U. Press, 1962.

1309   Sievers, H. J. "Updating Campaign Procedures,"
       America, 120 (Jan. 18, 1969), p. 57.

1310   Sigel, Roberta A. "Effect of Partisanship on the Per-
       ception of Political Candidates," Public Opinion
       Quarterly, 28 (1964), pp. 483-96.

1311   Silber, Irwin. Songs America Voted By. Harrisburg,
       Pa.: Stackpole Books, 1971.

1312   "Silent Vote, the Debates," Newsweek, 56 (Oct. 17,
       1960), pp. 27-28.

1313   Sillers, Malcolm O. "The Presidential Campaign of
       1952," Western Speech, 22 (1958), pp. 94-99.

1314   Simon, Herbert A. "Bandwagon and Underdog Effects
       and the Possibility of Election Predications," Public
       Opinion Quarterly, 18 (1954), pp. 245-53.

1315   _____, and Stern, Frederick. "The Effect of Tele-
       vision upon Voting Behavior in Iowa in the 1952
       Presidential Election," American Political Science
       Review, 49 (1955), pp. 470-77.

1316   Simons, Herbert W.; Chesebro, James W.; and Orr,
       C. Jack. "A Movement Perspective on the 1972
       Presidential Campaign," Quarterly Journal of
       Speech, 59 (1973), pp. 168-79.

1317   Simpson, Dick. Winning Elections: A Handbook in
       Participatory Politics. Chicago: Swallow Press,
       1972.

1318   Sisk, J. P. "Politics and Style," America, 102 (Oct.
       10, 1959), pp. 38-41.

1319   Sizemore, Afton A. "Television and Presidential
       Politics, 1952-1970." Unpublished master's
       thesis, U. of Kansas, 1970.

1320   "Small Screen, Super Weapon," Newsweek, 62 (Aug.
       19, 1963), pp. 76-77.

1321   Smith, C. R. "Richard Nixon's 1968 Acceptance
       Speech as a Model of Dual Audience Adaptation,"
       Today's Speech, 19 (Fall, 1971), pp. 15-22.

1322   Smith, C. W., Jr.   "Measurement of Voter Attitudes,"
       Annals of the American Academy, 283 (Sept.,
       1952), pp. 148-55.

1323   Smith, Denys.   "The American Elections," National
       and English Review, 151, no. 910 (1958), pp. 239-
       41.

1324   _____.   "The Coming Presidential Election," Na-
       tional and English Review, 153, no. 920 (1959),
       pp. 119-20.

1325   _____.   "The Last Lap," National and English Re-
       view, 139, no. 837 (1952), pp. 279-83.

1326   _____.   "The New Face of U.S. Politics," National
       and English Review, 152, no. 911 (1959), pp. 24-
       25.

1327   Smith, Donald K.   "The Speech Writing Team in a
       State Political Campaign," Today's Speech, 4
       (1956), pp. 16-19.

1328   Smith, H.   "The Campaign and Television," Saturday
       Review, 39 (Nov. 17, 1956), p. 26.

1329   Smith, T. V.   "The Serious Problem of Campaign
       Humor," New York Times Magazine, Sept. 28,
       1952, p. 11+.

1330   Smith, Terry.   "Bobby's Image," Esquire, 63 (April,
       1965), pp. 62-63, 132.

1331   Soloveytchik, George.   "The American Elections,"
       Contemporary Review, 182, no. 1042 (1952), pp.
       193-98.

1332   _____.   "The American Elections and After,"
       Contemporary Review, 194 (1958), pp. 309-12.

1333   "Speaking of Pictures ... The Democrats Make US
       Political History--and Rewrite It--with Comic
       Books," Life, 29 (Sept. 25, 1950), pp. 14-16.

1334   Spector, J. J.   "The Impact of the Editorial Page on
       a Municipal Referendum," Journalism Quarterly,
       47 (1970), pp. 762-66.

1335   "Speechless in New Jersey," Time, 69, no. 12 (March
       25, 1957), p. 80.

1336   Spencer, Walter. "Cranked Up for the Year's Top
       Story," Television, 25 (April, 1968), pp. 45-57.

1337   "Spotting the Candidates," Newsweek, 64 (Sept. 21,
       1964), pp. 76-77.

1338   Sprague, John D., and Hinich, Melvin. "Some Prob-
       lems for Economic Theories of Political Behavior."
       Paper presented at the American Political Science
       Association Convention, Chicago, Sept., 1971.

1339   Squier, Robert D., and Squier, Jane M. "TV in
       Election Campaigns--a Call for Changes," United
       States News and World Report, 73 (Nov. 27, 1972),
       pp. 84-85.

1340   Stano, Michael. "The 1970 Presidential Contenders:
       Visions, Dramas and Fantasy Themes of Radio
       Commentators," Moments in Contemporary Rhetoric
       and Communication (Temple U.), 2 (Fall, 1972),
       pp. 21-27.

1341   Stanton, Frank. "Case for Political Debates on TV,"
       New York Times Magazine, Jan. 19, 1964, p. 16+.

1342   Staples, John Harvey. "Style and Position Issues: A
       Field Experiment Employing Systematically Selected
       Members of the Oahu City and County of Honolulu
       Electorate." Unpublished Ph.D. dissertation, U.
       of Hawaii, 1969.

1343   Stearns, Joseph G. "An Analysis of Selected Speech
       and Relevant Newspaper Coverage of the Political
       Campaign Communication of Paul Eggers, Texas
       Republican Gubernatorial Candidate, 1968." Unpub-
       lished Ph.D. dissertation, Southern Illinois U.,
       1969.

1344   Steele, E. D. "The Rhetorical Use of the 'American
       Value System' in the 1952 Presidential Campaign
       Addresses." Unpublished Ph.D. dissertation,
       Stanford U., 1957.

1345   Steinbeck, John. "Madison Avenue and the Election,"
       Saturday Review, 39 (March 31, 1956), p. 11.

1346   Stempel, G. H. "The Prestige Press Covers the
       1960 Presidential Campaign," Journalism Quarterly,
       38 (1961), pp. 157-63.

1347   _____. "The Prestige Press in Two Presidential
       Elections," Journalism Quarterly, 42 (1965), pp.
       15-21.

1348   _____. "Selectivity in Readership of Political
       News," Public Opinion Quarterly, 25 (1961), pp.
       400-04.

1349   Stempel, Guido. "Content Patterns in Presidential
       Campaign Coverage." Paper presented at the As-
       sociation for Education in Journalism Convention,
       Syracuse, N.Y., Aug., 1965.

1350   Stephenson, William. "Operational Study of an Oc-
       casional Paper on the Kennedy-Nixon Television
       Debates," Psychological Record, 14 (1964), pp.
       475-88.

1351   Stern, Philip M. "The Debates in Retrospect," New
       Republic, 143 (Nov. 21, 1960), pp. 18-19.

1352   Sternthal, Brian. "Persuasion and the Mass Com-
       munication Process." Unpublished Ph.D. dis-
       sertation, Ohio State U., 1972.

1353   Stevenson, J. A. "The Presidential Election in the
       USA," Quarterly Review, 290 (1952), pp. 512-27.

1354   _____. "Press and the Election," Saturday Night,
       72 (March 30, 1957), p. 21.

1355   Stratmann, William Craig. "A Concept of Voter Ra-
       tionality." Unpublished Ph.D. dissertation, U. of
       Rochester, 1972.

1356   Street, Warren R. "Cognitive Dissonance in Sup-
       porters of a Losing Candidate," Journal of Social
       Psychology, 70 (1966), pp. 213-19.

1357   Stricker, George. "The Operation of Cognitive Dis-
       sonance on Pre- and Post-Election Attitudes, "
       Journal of Social Psychology, 63 (1964), pp. 111-
       19.

1358   _____. "The Use of the Semantic Differential to
       Predict Voting Behavior, " Journal of Social Psy-
       chology, 59 (1963), pp. 159-67.

1359   Stuart, I. R. "Primary and Secondary Process as
       Reflections of Catastrophe: The Political Cartoon
       as an Instrument of Group Emotional Dynamics, "
       Journal of Social Psychology, 64 (1964), pp. 231-
       39.

1360   "Studies in Political Communication, " Public Opinion
       Quarterly, 20 (1956), pp. 5-345.

1361   Stylites, S. "What Did He Say? " Christian Century,
       69 (July 9, 1952), p. 799.

1362   Suchman, Edw. A. "Socio-psychological Factors Af-
       fecting Predictions of Elections, " Public Opinion
       Quarterly, 16 (Fall, 1952), pp. 436-38.

1363   Sullivan, Denis G. "Psychological Balance and Re-
       actions to the Presidential Nominations of 1960, "
       The Electoral Process; ed. M. Kent Jennings and
       L. Harmon Zeigler. Englewood Cliffs, N.J.:
       Prentice-Hall, 1966.

1364   Sussmann, L. "Mass Political Letter Writing in
       America: The Growth of an Institution, " Public
       Opinion Quarterly, 23 (1959), pp. 203-12.

1365   _____. "Voices of the People. A Study of Political
       Mass Mail. " Unpublished Ph.D. dissertation,
       Columbia U., 1957.

1366   Swanson, David. "The New Politics Meets the Old
       Rhetoric: New Directions in Campaign Communica-
       tion Research, " Quarterly Journal of Speech, 58
       (1972), pp. 31-40.

1367   _____. "Persuasion and the New Politics: Founda-
       tions for a Strategy of Communication in the Modern
       Presidential Campaign. " Unpublished Ph.D. disser-
       tation, U. of Kansas, 1971.

1368   _____ . "Political Information, Influence, and Judg-
         ment, " Quarterly Journal of Speech, 59 (1973), pp.
         130-42.

1369   _____ . "Political Information, Influence and Judg-
         ment in the 1972 Presidential Campaign." Paper
         presented at the International Communication As-
         sociation Convention, Montreal, April 25-29, 1973.

1370   "The Tailored Press, " Nation, 205 (Dec. 25, 1967),
         p. 676.

1371   "Taking a Stand, " Newsweek, 66 (Nov. 8, 1965), p. 71.

1372   Tannenbaum, Percy H.; Greenberg, Bradley S.; and
         Silverman, Fred R.   "Candidate Images, " The
         Great Debates, ed. Sidney Kraus.   Bloomington,
         Ind.:   Indiana U. Press, 1962.

1373   Taylor, A. H.   "The Effect of Party Organization:
         Correlation Between Campaign Expenditure and
         Voting in the 1970 Election, " Political Studies, 20
         (Sept., 1972), pp. 329-31.

1374   Taylor, James S.   "An Analysis of the Effect of John
         Malcolm Patterson's Campaign Speaking in the 1958
         Alabama Democratic Primary." Unpublished Ph.D.
         dissertation, Florida State U., 1968.

1375   "The Telelection, " Sunday London Times, March 6,
         1966, p. 9.

1376   "Television and Politics, " Television, 17 (July, 1960),
         p. 47.

1377   "Television for Campaigns: Politicians' Friend or
         Foe?"   United States News and World Report, 28
         (June 23, 1950), p. 14.

1378   "Television in US Politics, " London Times, Feb. 14,
         1956.

1379   Television Information Office.   Television in Govern-
         ment and Politics: A Bibliography.   New York:
         Television Information Office, 1964.

1380　"The Thirty-second Spot Commercial," Nation, 211
　　　　(Nov. 2, 1970), p. 421.

1381　Thompson, Alan.　"The Vigour of American Election-
　　　　eering," London Times, Nov. 6, 1962, p. 13.

1382　Thompson, J. W. M.　"The Entertainers:　Election
　　　　Television," Spectator, #7110, Oct. 2, 1964, p.
　　　　426+.

1383　_____.　"The Old Soapbox," Spectator, #7111, Oct.
　　　　9, 1964, pp. 467-68.

1384　_____.　"The Soloists:　Election TV," Spectator,
　　　　#7112, Oct. 16, 1964, p. 499.

1385　Thomson, Charles A. H.　"Mass Media Performance,"
　　　　The National Election of 1964, ed. Milton C. Cum-
　　　　mings, Jr.　Washington, D.C.:　The Brookings In-
　　　　stitution, 1966.

1386　_____.　Television and Presidential Politics.　Wash-
　　　　ington, D.C.:　The Brookings Institution, 1956.

1387　_____.　"Television, Politics and Public Policy,"
　　　　Public Policy, 8 (1958), pp. 368-406.

1388　Toffler, A.　"Artists of the Political Smear," Coro-
　　　　net, 45 (Nov., 1958), pp. 88-92.

1389　Topping, Malachi C., and Lichty, Lawrence W.　"Po-
　　　　litical Programs on National TV Networks:　1968,"
　　　　Journal of Broadcasting, 15 (1971), pp. 161-79.

1390　Totaro, Ronald.　How to Conduct a Political Campaign
　　　　with the Systematic Analysis Study System.　New
　　　　York:　Vantage Press, 1970.

1391　Treneman, J., and McQuail, D.　Television and the
　　　　Political Image.　London:　Methuen, 1961.

1392　Trent, Judith S.　"An Examination and Comparison of
　　　　the Rhetorical Style of Richard Milhous Nixon in
　　　　the Presidential Campaigns of 1960 and 1968:　A
　　　　Content Analysis."　Unpublished Ph.D. disserta-
　　　　tion, U. of Michigan, 1970.

1393 _____ . "An Exploration and Explanation of Richard
        Nixon's Use of Ethos and Evidence." Paper pre-
        sented at the Speech-Communication Association
        Convention, San Francisco, Dec. 27-30, 1971.

1394 _____ . "The Rhetoric of the Challenger--George
        McGovern." Paper presented at the Central States
        Speech Association Convention, Minneapolis, April,
        1973.

1395 _____ . "Richard Nixon's Methods of Identification
        in the Presidential Campaigns of 1960 and 1968:
        A Content Analysis," Today's Speech, 19 (Fall,
        1971), pp. 23-30.

1396 Tuchman, S., and Coffin, T. E. "Influence of Elec-
        tion Night Television Broadcasts in a Close Elec-
        tion," Public Opinion Quarterly, 35 (1971), pp. 315-
        26.

1397 Tucker, Duane E. "Broadcasting in the 1956 Oregon
        Senatorial Campaign," Journal of Broadcasting, 3
        (1959), pp. 225-43.

1398 _____ . "Radio and Television Speaking of Douglas
        McKay and Wayne Morse in the 1956 Oregon Sena-
        torial Campaign." Unpublished Ph.D. dissertation,
        U. of Wisconsin, 1959.

1399 "The Tumult and the Shouting," American Heritage,
        15 (Aug., 1964), pp. 88-89.

1400 "TV and the Ballot Box," Television Age, June 27,
        1960, pp. 30-31.

1401 "TV as a Political Weapon," Sponsor, 19 (Jan. 18,
        1965), p. 33.

1402 "TV Debate Backstage; Did the Cameras Lie?" News-
        week, 56 (Oct. 10, 1960), p. 25.

1403 "TV in a Presidential Election," Media/Scope, May,
        1964, p. 110.

1404 "TV-Made Man," Newsweek, 38 (Oct. 1, 1951), p. 79.

1405 "TV Politics: Too High a Price," Life, 69 (Sept. 11,
      1970), p. 2.

1406 "TV-Radio Spending: Nixon Broadcast Costs Are
      Twice Those for Humphrey," Congressional Quar-
      terly Weekly Report, 27 (Sept. 12, 1969), pp.
      1701-03.

1407 "TV Still Isn't Everything," Business Week, Sept. 8,
      1956, pp. 32-33.

1408 "TV's Political Dollar," Newsweek, 71 (May 20, 1968),
      p. 92.

1409 "TV's School for Candidates," Business Week, May
      24, 1952, pp. 120-22, 124.

1410 United States. Congress. House. Committee on
      Campaign Expenditures. Special Committee to In-
      vestigate Campaign Expenditures, 1956. "Cam-
      paign Expenditures, 1956." 84th Cong., 2d sess.,
      1956. Dec. 17-18, 1956, 1957.

1411 _____. Congress. House. Committee on Cam-
      paign Expenditures. Special Committee to In-
      vestigate Campaign Expenditures, 1952. Hearings
      on Campaign Expenditures. 82d Cong., 2d sess.,
      1952. Dec. 1-5, 1952.

1412 _____. Congress. House. Committee on Cam-
      paign Expenditures. Special Committee to In-
      vestigate Campaign Expenditures, 1964. "Investi-
      gation of Campaign Expenditures, 1964." Report
      of the Special Committee to Investigate Campaign
      Expenditures, 1964. 88th Cong., 2d sess., 1965.
      House Report 1946. Jan. 2, 1965.

1413 _____. Congress. House. Committee on Cam-
      paign Expenditures. Special Committee to In-
      vestigate Campaign Expenditures, 1960. "Report
      and Hearings of the Special Committee to Investi-
      gate Campaign Expenditures, 1960." 86th Cong.,
      2d sess., 1960. House Report 2236.

1414   . Congress. House. Committee on Campaign Expenditures. Special Committee to Investigate Campaign Expenditures, 1952. "Report of the Special Committee to Investigate Campaign Expenditures, 1952." 83d Cong., 1953. House Report 2517.

1415   . Congress. House. Committee on Campaign Expenditures. Special Committee to Investigate Campaign Expenditures, 1962. "Report of the Special Committee to Investigate Campaign Expenditures, 1962." 87th Cong., 2d sess., 1963. House Report 2570.

1416   . Congress. House. Committee on Campaign Expenditures. Special Committee to Investigate Campaign Expenditures, 1966. "Report of the Special Committee to Investigate Campaign Expenditures, 1966." 89th Cong., 2d sess., 1967. House Report 2348.

1417   . Congress. House. Committee on Campaign Expenditures. Special Committee to Investigate Campaign Expenditures, 1968. "Report of the Special Committee to Investigate Campaign Expenditures, 1968." 90th Cong., 2d sess., 1969. House Report 2 pursuant to House Resolution 1239.

1418   . Congress. House. Committee on House Administration. Subcommittee on Elections. Hearings on H.R. 8284, To Limit Campaign Expenditures. 92d Cong., 1st sess., 1971.

1419   . Congress. House. Committee on Interstate and Foreign Commerce. Subcommittee on Communications and Power. Hearings on H.R. 5389, Political Broadcasts, Equal Time. 86th Cong., 1st sess., 1959.

1420   . Congress. House. Committee on Interstate and Foreign Commerce. Subcommittee on Communications and Power. Hearings on H.R. 8627, H.R. 8628, Political Broadcasting. 92d Cong., 1st sess., 1971.

1421 _____. Congress. House. Committee on Interstate and Foreign Commerce. Subcommittee on
Communications and Power. Hearings on H.R.
13721, Political Broadcasting, 1970. 91st Cong.,
2d sess., 1970.

1422 _____. Congress. House. Committee on Interstate and Foreign Commerce. Subcommittee on
Communications and Power. "Political Broadcasting." 91st Cong., 1st sess., 1970. House Report
1347 to accompany H.R. 18434.

1423 _____. Congress. House. Committee on Standards
of Office Conduct. Hearings on House Resolution
1031, Campaign Finances. 91st Cong., 2d sess.,
1971.

1424 _____. Congress. Senate. Committee on Commerce, Subcommittee on Communications. Hearings
on S. 2876, Campaign Broadcasts Reform Act of
1969. 91st Cong., 1st sess., 1969.

1425 _____. Congress. Senate. Committee on Finance.
Hearings on Political Campaign Financing Proposals.
90th Cong., 1st sess., 1967.

1426 _____. Congress. Senate. Committee on Finance.
Hearings on S. 3496, amendment 732, S. 2006, S.
2965, S. 3014, Financing Political Campaigns.
89th Cong., 2d sess., 1966.

1427 _____. Congress. Senate. Committee on Inter-
state and Foreign Commerce, Subcommittee on
Communications. Hearings on S. 1585, S. 1604,
S. 1858, S. 1929, Political Broadcasting. 86th
Cong., 1st sess., 1959.

1428 _____. Congress. Senate. Committee on Inter-
state and Foreign Commerce. Hearings on S. 3171,
Presidential Campaign Broadcasting Act. 86th
Cong., 2d sess., 1960.

1429 _____. Congress. Senate. Committee on Rules
and Administration. "Legislative Recommendations
of the President's Commission on Campaign Costs."
87th Cong., 2d sess., 1962. Committee Print.

1430 _____. Congress. Senate. "Federal Election Campaign Act of 1971, Conference Report to Accompany S. 382." 92d Cong., Dec. 14, 1971.

1431 "The U.S. Election Gathers Pace," Time and Tide, 42 (1960), pp. 1207-08.

1432 The United States Law Week. "Federal Election Campaign Act." (Text of Public Law 92-225) Washington, D.C.: The Bureau of National Affairs, Inc., Vol. 40 (Feb. 15, 1972).

1433 "The United States Presidential Election," World Today (London), 8, no. 7 (July, 1952), pp. 278-87.

1434 Universal Reference System. Public Opinion, Mass Behavior and Political Psychology: An Annotated and Extensively Indexed Compilation of Significant Books, Pamphlets and Articles, Selected and Processed by the System. Political Science, Government and Public Policy Series, Vol. 6. Princeton Research Publishing Co., 1969.

1435 "The Use of Radio in Political Campaigns," County Officer, 29 (1964), pp. 77-84.

1436 Van Riper, Paul. Handbook of Practical Politics. New York: Harper and Row, 1967.

1437 Vasilew, E. "The New Style in Political Campaigns: Lodge in New Hampshire, 1964," Review of Politics, 30 (1968), pp. 131-52.

1438 Vebler, Eric P. "Newspaper Impact in Election Campaigns: The Case of Two New England States." Unpublished Ph.D. dissertation, Yale U., 1969.

1439 "Vice-President Humphrey," New Yorker, 44 (Sept. 14, 1968), p. 43.

1440 "Victory through TV," America, 122 (May 23, 1970), p. 546.

1441 Vinyard, Dale, and Sigel, Roberta S. "Newspapers and Urban Voters," Journalism Quarterly, 48 (1971), pp. 486-93.

1442   Voegelin, Eric. The New Science of Politics. Chica-
       go: University of Chicago Press, 1952.

1443   "Voices over Illinois," Time, 56 (Oct. 9, 1950), pp.
       22-23.

1444   "Vote for Me on TV," Newsweek, 44 (Nov. 1, 1954),
       p. 58.

1445   "Vote No on 'Yes': Post Election Post Mortem on
       Political Advertising by a Group of Agency Men,"
       Western Advertising, 72 (Dec., 1958), pp. 30-32.

1446   "Voters' Time: Reports of the Twentieth Century
       Fund Commission on Campaign Costs in the Elec-
       tronic Era." New York: Twentieth Century Fund,
       1969, 72 pp.

1447   Wade, Richard C. "Backlash in the Percy Campaign,"
       Reporter, 36 (Jan. 12, 1967), pp. 37-40.

1448   Wade, Serena. "A California Pre-Election Telephone
       Poll," Journalism Quarterly, 49 (1972), pp. 129-33.

1449   _____, and Schramm, Wilbur. "The Mass Media
       as Sources of Public Affairs, Science and Health
       Knowledge," Public Opinion Quarterly, 33 (1969),
       pp. 197-209.

1450   Waisanen, F. B., and Durlak, J. T. "Mass Media
       Use, Information Source Evaluation and Perception
       of Self and Nation," Public Opinion Quarterly, 31
       (1967), pp. 399-406.

1451   Walker, D. "McLuhan Explains the Media," Executive,
       6 (Aug., 1964), pp. 22-27.

1452   Waltzer, H. "In the Magic Lantern: TV Coverage of
       the 1964 National Conventions," Public Opinion
       Quarterly, 30 (1966), pp. 33-53.

1453   Wanger, B. "Writing for Political Candidates,"
       Writers' Digest, 52 (Nov., 1972), pp. 34-35.

1454 Wasby, Stephen L. "Rhetoricians and Political Sci-
      entists: Some Lines of Converging Interest,"
      Southern Speech Journal, 36 (1971), pp. 231-42.

1455 Washburn, Frank. "The Television Panel as a Vehicle
      of Political Persuasion," Western Speech, 16
      (1952), pp. 245-53.

1456 Washburn, Wilcomb E. "Speech Communication and
      Politics," Today's Speech, 16 (1968), pp. 3-16.

1457 Watkins, Alan. "The Language of Politicians," New
      Statesman, 76 (Oct. 25, 1968), p. 518.

1458 _____. "Politicians and the Box," New Statesman,
      79 (Jan. 30, 1970), p. 135.

1459 Wearin, Otha D. Political Americana. Hastings,
      Iowa: Nishna Vale Shop, 1967.

1460 Weatherby, W. J. "American Election on Television,"
      Guardian, Oct. 15, 1960, p. 6.

1461 Weaver, Paul H. "Is Television News Biased?"
      Public Interest, Winter, 1962, pp. 57-74.

1462 Weaver, Warren, Jr. "Nixon Gain Found from His
      TV Ads," New York Times, Nov. 25, 1972, Sec.
      1, p. 39.

1463 Weber, Ronald E., et al. "Computer Simulation of
      State Electorates," Public Opinion Quarterly, 36
      (1972-73), pp. 549-65.

1464 Webking, Edwin W., Jr. "The 1968 Gruening Write-
      In Campaign." Unpublished Ph.D. dissertation,
      Claremont Graduate School, 1972.

1465 "Weeklies Support Ike, Survey Shows," National Pub-
      lisher, Oct., 1952, p. 5.

1466 Weisberg, Herbert F., and Rusk, Jerrold C. "Dimen-
      sions of Candidate Evaluation," American Political
      Science Review, 64 (1970), pp. 1167-85.

1467   Weisbord, Marvin. Campaigning for President: A
        New Look at the Road to the White House. Wash-
        ington, D.C.: Public Affairs Press, 1964.

1468   Weiss, E. B. "Political Advertising Blackens the
        Other Eye of the Ad Business," Advertising Age,
        Feb. 12, 1973, pp. 35+.

1469   Weiss, Walter. "Effects of the Mass Media of Com-
        munication," Handbook of Social Psychology, Vol.
        5, ed. Gardner Lindzey and Elliot Aronson. Cam-
        bridge, Mass.: Addison-Wesley, 1969.

1470   _____. "Mass Communication," Annual Review of
        Psychology, 22 (1971), pp. 309-36.

1471   _____, and Steenbock, Sandra. "The Influence of
        Communication Effectiveness of Explicitly Urging
        Action and Policy Consequences," Journal of Ex-
        perimental Social Psychology, 1 (1965), pp. 396-
        406.

1472   Weitzel, Al. "Candidate and Electorate Perceptions
        of the Nature and Function of Media Messages:
        A Case Study Approach." Paper presented at the
        International Communication Association Convention,
        Montreal, April 25-29, 1973.

1473   _____. "Goldwater's 1964 Acceptance Address: A
        Case Study in the Rhetoric of Polarization." Paper
        presented at the Speech-Communication Association
        Convention, San Francisco, Dec. 27-30, 1971.

1474   Wernick, Robert. "The Perfect Candidate," Life, 60
        (June 3, 1966), pp. 41-42, 44, 46.

1475   West, A. P. "US Campaign: Deliberate Mediocrity,"
        Saturday Night, 71 (Oct. 27, 1956), pp. 15-16, 18.

1476   _____. "U.S. Carnival of Mediocrity," Saturday
        Night, 75 (July 23, 1960), pp. 30-31.

1477   Westley, Bruce H., and Severin, Werner J. "Some
        Correlates of Media Credibility," Journalism Quar-
        terly, 41 (1964), pp. 325-35.

1478   _____, et al.   "The News Magazines and the 1960
        Conventions," Journalism Quarterly, 40 (1963), pp.
        525-31.

1479   Weyr, T.   "Political Books 1972," Publishers Weekly,
        202 (Oct. 30, 1972), pp. 31-33.

1480   Whale, John.   Half-Shut Eye: Television and Politics
        in Britain and America.   New York: St. Martin's
        Press, 1969.

1481   "What Air Media Did to Swing the Vote," Sponsor, 6
        (Nov. 3, 1952), p. 25.

1482   "What TV Is Doing to America," United States News
        and World Report, 39 (Sept. 2, 1955), pp. 36+.

1483   "What TV Is Doing to Politics," United States News
        and World Report, 39 (Sept. 2, 1955), p. 44.

1484   "What Wins Elections Today?" Senior Scholastic, 97
        (Oct. 12, 1970), pp. 15-17.

1485   Whatenore, R. W.   "Who's for President?"   Time and
        Tide, 40 (1959), p. 1150.

1486   Whitaker, Clem, and Baxter, Leone.   "Election Year
        Coming Up," Public Relations Journal, 11 (Oct.,
        1955), p. 11+.

1487   White, Howard B.   "The Processed Voter and the New
        Political Science," Social Research, 28 (Summer,
        1961), pp. 127-50.

1488   White, J. P.   "The Role of Public Opinion Polls in
        the Study of Political Parties."   Ann Arbor, Mich.:
        U. of Michigan Bureau of Government, Institute of
        Public Administration, 1956.

1489   White, Theodore.   The Making of the President: 1960.
        New York: Atheneum Publishers, 1961.

1490   _____.   The Making of the President: 1964.   New
        York: Atheneum Publishers, 1965.

1491   _____.   The Making of the President: 1968.   New
        York: Atheneum Publishers, 1969.

1492   White, W. J. "An Index for Determining the Relative
       Importance of Information Sources, " Public Opinion
       Quarterly, 33 (1969-70), pp. 607-10.

1493   Whiteside, Thomas. "Corridor of Mirrors: The Tele-
       vision Editorial Process, Chicago, " Columbia
       Journalism Review, 7 (Winter, 1968-69), pp. 35-54.

1494   Whittaker, James O.   "Perception and Judgment in the
       Political Extremist, " Journal of Communication,
       17 (1967), pp. 136-41.

1495   "Whiz Kids, Old Pros; George McGovern's Top-Most
       Aides, " Newsweek, 80 (July 17, 1972), pp. 20-21.

1496   "Who Backed Whom, " Newsweek, 64 (Nov. 2, 1964),
       p. 64.

1497   "Who's for Whom, " Time, 84 (Sept. 11, 1964), pp.
       97-98.

1498   Wicker, Tom.   "Kennedy as a Public Speakah, " New
       York Times Magazine, Feb. 25, 1962, p. 14+.

1499   _____ ; O'Donnell, Kenneth P.; and Evans, Rowland.
       "TV in the Political Campaign, " Television Quar-
       terly, 5 (Winter, 1966), pp. 13-26.

1500   Wigg, G. "Politicians and the Press, " Listener, 78
       N. 2008 (1967), pp. 363-66.

1501   Wilhelmsen, Frederick D., and Bret, Jane. Tele-
       politics. New York: Tundra Books, 1972.

1502   "Will TV--or Events--Swing It? " Newsweek, 56 (Oct.
       3, 1960), p. 37.

1503   Williams, Dwight A., Jr. "Mass Media Preference
       Patterns: A Cross-Media Study." Unpublished
       Ph.D. dissertation, Ohio State U., 1971.

1504   Williams, R. L. "The Advance Men, " Life, 33 (Oct.
       6, 1952), pp. 135-36+.

1505   Willis, E. E. "McLuhanism, Television, and Politics, "
       Quarterly Journal of Speech, 54 (1968), pp. 404-
       09.

1506   Willis, Edgar E.   "Radio and Presidential Campaign-
           ing," Central States Speech Journal, 20 (1969), pp.
           187-93.

1507   Wilson, David.   "Campaign and Communications,"
           New Society, 17 (April 1, 1971), pp. 531-33.

1508   Wilson, Will.   "The Adversary Process in Political
           Programming," Journal of Broadcasting, 1 (1957),
           pp. 232-40.

1509   Wimmer, Roger.   " 'Trust Me' Is Not for a Winner:
           Muskie's Decline--A Burkeian Perspective,"
           Moments in Contemporary Rhetoric and Communi-
           cation (Temple U.), 2 (Fall, 1972), pp. 53-56.

1510   "Windbreak," Time, 72, no. 1 (July 7, 1958), p. 52.

1511   Windes, Russel, Jr.   "Adlai E. Stevenson's Speech
           Staff in the 1956 Campaign," Quarterly Journal of
           Speech, 46 (1960), pp. 32-43.

1512   _____.   "The Speech-Making of Adlai E. Stevenson
           in the 1956 Presidential Campaign." Unpublished
           Ph.D. dissertation, Northwestern U., 1959.

1513   _____.   "A Study of Effective and Ineffective Presi-
           dential Campaign Speaking," Speech Monographs,
           28 (1961), pp. 39-49.

1514   Windlesham, Lord.   "Television as an Influence on
           Political Opinion," Political Quarterly, 35 (1964),
           pp. 375-85.

1515   Winstanley, Michael.   "Political Stage Shows,"
           Guardian, Sept. 18, 1969, p. 12.

1516   Witcover, Jules.   Eighty-Five Days: The Last Cam-
           paign of Robert Kennedy.   New York: G. P. Put-
           nam's Sons, 1969.

1517   _____.   "The Indiana Primary and the Indianapolis
           Newspapers--A Report in Detail," Columbia Jour-
           nalism Review, 7 (Summer, 1968), pp. 11-17.

1518 _____ . "William Loeb and the New Hampshire
       Primary: A Question of Ethics...," Columbia
       Journalism Review, 11 (May/June, 1972), pp. 14-
       27.

1519 Wolfe, Alan P. "The Senatorial Campaign." Unpub-
       lished Ph.D. dissertation, U. of Pennsylvania,
       1967.

1520 Wolfe, G. Joseph. "Some Reactions to the Advent of
       Campaigning by Radio," Journal of Broadcasting,
       13 (Summer, 1969), pp. 305-14.

1521 Wolff, Robert Paul (ed.). Styles of Political Action in
       America. New York: Random House, 1972.

1522 Wolfinger, R. E. "The Influence of Precinct Work on
       Voting Behavior," Public Opinion Quarterly, 27
       (1963), pp. 387-98.

1523 Wolfson, Richard Martin. "The Nonpartisan Per-
       spective on Municipal Voting: The Cases of Min-
       neapolis and Los Angeles." Unpublished Ph.D.
       dissertation, U. of Minnesota, 1972.

1524 Woodside, C. W. "It Is Magnificent, But Is It
       Politics?" Saturday Night, 67 (Oct. 4, 1952), pp.
       14-16.

1525 Worsnop, R. I. "Television and Politics," Editorial
       Research Reports, Vol. 1, No. 19 (1968).

1526 Wright, C. R., and Cantor, M. "The Opinion Seeker
       and Avoider: Steps Beyond the Opinion Leader
       Concept," Pacific Sociological Review, 10 (Spring,
       1967), pp. 33-43.

1527 Wrong, Dennis H. "The American Congressional
       Campaign," Canadian Forum, 38 (Nov., 1958), p.
       170.

1528 Wuerthner, J. J., Jr. "What Will Politics Be Like
       in 2059?" Petroleum Engineer, 31, no. 9 (1959),
       pp. A32-A33.

1529 Wyckoff, Gene. The Image Candidates. New York:
       The Macmillan Co., 1968.

1530   Wyden, P.   "Television in Politics, " Newsweek, 46
       (Sept. 19, 1955), pp. 39-40.

1531   Yeager, R.   "A Rhetorical Analysis of the 1952 Presi-
       dential Campaign Speeches of Adlai Ewing Steven-
       son. "   Unpublished Ph. D. dissertation, Ohio State
       U. , 1957.

1532   Yeager, Raymond.   "Stevenson: The 1956 Campaign, "
       Central States Speech Journal, 12 (1960), pp. 9-15.

1533   Youman, Roger J.   "What Does America Think Now? "
       TV Guide, Sept. 23, 1972, pp. 1-4.

1534   Zajonc, R. B.   "The Additudinal Effects of Mere Ex-
       posure, " Journal of Personality and Social Psy-
       chology, Monograph Supplement, part 2, 1968, pp.
       1-27.

1535   Zannes, Estelle.   "Cleveland's Eloquent Hour: The
       1967 Mayoral Campaign. "   Unpublished Ph. D. dis-
       sertation, Case Western Reserve U. , 1969.

1536   Zeidenstein, H.   "Presidential Primaries--Reflections
       of the 'People's Choice'? "   Journal of Politics, 32
       (1970), pp. 856-74.

1537   Zimmerman, Fred L.   "A Message from the Media:
       Contrary to Theory, More than Just a Pretty Ad
       Is Needed to Win in Politics, the Candidates Find, "
       Wall Street Journal, 179 (May 10, 1972), p. 34.

1538   _____.   "A Political Consultant Gets to Point:
       'How are Tennis Courts? '   A Rich Puerto Rico
       Election Lures U. S. Political Experts, But What
       Are They Doing? "   Wall Street Journal, 180 (Sept.
       7, 1972), p. 1+.

1539   _____.   "Private Eyeing: How Political Pollster
       Influences Candidates, Stays in Background, " Wall
       Street Journal, 180 (Oct. 5, 1972), p. 1+.

3. GERMAN AND FRENCH SUPPLEMENT

This division of the bibliography is intended primarily to aid the scholar who might be interested in identifying foreign perspectives on political communication. Books and periodical articles in French and German are included.

The original goal of the supplement was to provide material which would conform to the definition provided for the bibliography as a whole. However, in practice it was necessary to adjust the definition. For instance, it was not always possible to determine from entry titles in indexes whether or not an entry concerned the United States. In addition, some works of a more general nature were included because they seemed to offer some relevant views on communication theory, especially in regard to mass media and information theory. As in the original definition, articles or books on particular political campaigns or candidates which did not appear (either because of title or index heading) to relate to communication variables were excluded.

Some problems were encountered in obtaining complete citations. German bibliographic form does not always include publishing companies, and in some cases, other missing information and validation of accuracy could not be provided because the work itself was not available to the authors. An attempt has been made to provide as much information as was available. Consequently, a somewhat Americanized style has been adopted for the entries.

The citations were drawn from the following indexes:

1. Verzeichnis liefbarer Bücher, 1972-73 (under Fernsehen, Kommunikation, Massenmedien, Massenkommunikation, Partei, Politik, politische(n), Vereinigte Staaten, Wahl, and Wahlkampf).

2. Le Catalogue de l'Edition Française, 1970 (under

communications, information, media, politique, and télévision).

3. Bibliographie der Fremdsprachigen Zeitschriften-
literatur, 1950-1964; Bibliographie der Deutschen Zeitschriften-
literatur, 1950-1964; and Internationale Bibliographie der
Zeitschriftenliteratur aus allen Gebieten des Wissens, 1965-
1972 (under Fernsehen, Fernsehprogramm, Fernsehtechnik,
Kommunikation, Journalismus, Massenmedien, Nachrichten-
theorie, Partei, Politik, Politiker, politische Bildung, Public
Relations, Rundfunk, Rundfunkprogramm, Stimmrecht,
Sprechen, Vereingte Staaten von Amerika, Wahl, Werbung,
Werbefernsehen, Zeitung, and Zeitschrift).

4. Public Affairs Information Service Foreign Language Index, Vol. II, 1972 (under advertising; campaigns,
political; candidates; elections; communication; and mass
media).

The researcher who is interested in this area should
take special note of the last index listed, as this is a relatively new service offered by the P.A.I.S. indexes. It is a
selective index of books and articles on public and economic
affairs in German, French, Italian, Portuguese and Spanish,
with subject headings in English. The first volume included
the years 1968-1971. The Quarterly Checklist of Economics
and Political Science: An International Index of Current
Books, Monographs, Brochures and Separates might also
prove useful for specialized topics, but it provides no subject
index.

Because of the specialized interest of this division of
the bibliography, no attempt has been made to provide trans-
lations. The following are the abbreviations commonly used
in the entries, and they appear exactly as used in the indexes.

                    N.------Nummer, Number
                    H.------Hefte
                    J.------Jahre
                    B., Bd.--Band, Bind
                    T.------Tome
                    Vol.----Volume

142   Political Campaign Communication

Adam, Robert. "Hörfunk und Fernsehen in den USA" in
    Frankfurter Hefte (Frankfurt/M), J. 21 (1966), n. 5,
    S. 320, 328; II, N. 6, S. 403-412.

Aftmann, Rüdiger. "Der Politiker und ihr Stil" in Der
    Volkswirtschaft, J. 19 (1965), N. 51-52, S. 65-66.

Amelung, E. "Amerikanische Wahlen" in Civis (Bonn),
    J. 5 (1958-59), S. 182-83.

Annett, Betty G. "Die Präsidentschaftswahlen in den USA"
    in Marxistische Blätter, J. 7 (1969), H. 2, S. 57-62.

Aptheker, Herbert. "Avant les élections présidentielle aux
    Etats-Unis" in La nouvelle revue internationale
    (Paris), Vol. 11 (1968), no. 10-11, p. 112-21.

_____. "Was Zeigen die Wahlen in den Vereinigten
    Staaten?" in Einheit, J. 20 (1965), H. 1, S. 73-77.

Arndt, Adolf. "Wahlrechtsgleichheit in USA" in Neue juris-
    tische Wochenschrift, J. 17 (1964), S. 856.

Baukloh, Friedhelm. "Propaganda, Manipulation oder
    politische Bildung?" in Volkshochschule im Westen
    (Dortmund), J. 20 (1968), H. 3, S. 116-17.

Bausch, H. "Der Kampf um das neue Medium in Zwanzig
    Jahre danach" in Eine deutsche Bilanz 1945-1965,
    hrsg. von Helmut Hammerschmidt. München: 1965,
    S. 360-74.

_____. "Politik im Rundfunk" in Die politische Meinung
    (Köln), J. 3 (1958), H. 23, S. 9-24.

Beaupain, Gh. "Mass-media et communication" in La foi
    et le temps, a. 2 (1969), n. 4, p. 397-406.

Becker, Jürgen. Modell eines möglichen Politikers in
    Plädoyer für eine Regierung oder Keine Alternative,
    hrsg. von Hans Werner Richter. Reinbek: 1965,
    S. 121-25.

Bedel, Maurice. "Parties de campagnes aux USA" in
    Revue des deux mondes, 1952, N. 18, p. 277-86.

"Die Bedeutung des Fernsehens für die amerikanischen Präsidentschaftswahlen" in Fernseh-Informationen (München), J. 7 (1956), S. 153-54.

Behrendt, E. "Wirtschaft und Wahlen in den USA" in Technische Rundschau (Bern), J. 52 (1960), N. 45, S. 1-2.

Bell, Daniel. "Es tut zu weh, um zu lachen! Betrachtungen zu den Wahlen in den USA" in Geist und Tat, J. 7 (1952), N. 12, S. 364.

Besser, Klaus. "Politik und Werbung im Wahlkampf" in Die neue Gesellschaft, J. 3 (1956), S. 433-38.

"Bibliographie (zur politischen Forschung)" in Politische Forschung. Köln: 1960, S. 212-59.

Biehle, Herbert. "Der Politiker als Redner" in Zeitschrift für Politik (Berlin, Zürich, Wien), J. 4 (1957), H. 1, S. 71-81.

Bilger, Emma Priska. "Politische Erziehung als psychologisches Problem" in Unser Weg, J. 23 (1968), H. 5, S. 178-81.

Böhler, Eugen. "Unser lebender Mythus" in Schweizer Monatshefte, J. 46 (1966-67), H. 7, S. 621-33.

Böllinger, Klaus. "Die Präsidentschaftswahlen in den USA 1968" in Deutsche Aussenpolitik, J. 14 (1969), N. 2, S. 162-74.

Brocher, Tobias. "Die Unterhaltungssendung als Instrument gesselschaftspolitischer Bewusstseinsbildung" in Fernsehen in Deutschland. Mainz: 1967, S. 283-95.

Browder, Earl. "Kandidaturkämpfe und--dilemmas in den USA" in Internationale Politik (Belgrad und Bonn), J. 11 (1960), N. 246-47, S. 17-20.

Brown. "Der Wahlkampf in den Vereinigten Staaten" in Neue Zeit (Moskau), 1952, N. 24, S. 11-14.

Brown, Esther. "Der Wahlkampf in den Vereinigten Staaten" in Neue Zeit (Moskau), 1952, N. 18, S. 7-10.

Buddingh, Bertus. "Politik und Massenkommunikation" in
    Medium, J. 4 (1967), H. 2, S. 73-90.

Budzislawski, H. "Wahlen in den USA" in Heute und Morgen
    (Schwerin), 1950, N. 10, S. 585-87.

"La Campagne électorale" in Chronique étrangères (Paris),
    1950, N. 148, p. 2-5.

La campagne présidentielle de 1965. Paris: Schwartzenberg
    Presses, Universitaires de France.

Capek, Abe. "Der Elefant, der Esel und der arme ameri-
    kanische Wähler" in Deutsche Aussenpolitik (Berlin),
    J. 5 (1960), S. 1265-71.

Cayrol, Roland. "A propos de télévision et politique, "
    Revue Française de Science Politique, 21 (Dec.,
    1971), p. 1317-28.

César, Jaroslav. "Über die Parteiensysteme und die bürger-
    liche Presse" in Wissenschaftliche Zeitschrift der
    Friedrich Schiller-Universität Jena/Thüringer, 14
    (1965), 2, p. 291-93.

Charlot, Monica und Cotta, Michele. La campagne électorale
    (octobre-novembre 1962). Centre d'Etude le la Vie
    Politique Française 1963.

Chatelain, Nicolas. "Les élections américaines" in Revue
    de Paris, A. 67 (1960), N. 9, p. 33-42.

Courtade, Pierre. "Quelques aspects de la campagne
    présidentielle aux Etats-Unis" in Pensée (Paris),
    1952, N. 44, p. 8-15.

Czerney, Wilhelm F. "Was Heisst und wozu braucht man
    Parteien?" in Forum (Wien), J. 12 (1965), H. 142,
    S. 429-32.

Davies. "Gedanken am Wahltag 1960" in Deutsches Pfarrer-
    blatt (Essen), J. 61 (1961), S. 251.

Davis, Thurston N. "L'élection du trente-sixieme président aux Etats-Unis" in Etudes (Paris), T. 305 (1960), p. 200-208.

"Demokratische USA--Präsidentschaftskandidaten" in Industriekurier (Düsseldorf), J. 5 (1952), N. 109, S. 3.

de Molènes, Charles Melchior. "Le triomphe démocrate aux élections américaines" in Revue politique des idées et des Institutions (Paris), an. 53 (1964), n. 20-21, p. 423-32.

de Thassy, Eugene. "La campagne electorale aux U.S.A." in Revue, 1968, n. 14, p. 210.

Diederich, Nils. "Empirische Wahlforschung," Band 8, von Staat und Politik, Köln und Opladen, 1965.

Dietrich, Wolf. "Die kritische Funktion politischer Fernsehsendunger" in Fernsehen und Bildung, J. 4 (1970), H. 4, S. 229-33.

Dill, Richard W. "Staat und Fernsehen. Eine Literatureübersicht für den Politiker" in Fernseh-Informationen, J. 16 (1965), H. 24-25, S. 428-31.

Domenach, M. La Propagande Politique. Paris: 1956.

Dröge, Franz. Politische Werbung und die Wähler von morgen. Regensberg Buchhandlung und Buchdruckerei 1968.

Dzelepy, E. N. "Le drame de la politique américaine" in Temps modernes (Paris), 6.A. (1950), N. 60, p. 603-32.

Eberhard, Fritz. "Macht durch Massenmedien" in Publizistik (Bremen), J. 10 (1965), H. 4, S. 477-94.

_____. "Politische Sendung des Rundfunks" in Welt der Arbeit (Köln), 1 (1950), N. 11, S. 9.

_____. "Die Rolle der Massenkommunikationsmittel beim Zustandekommen politischer Entscheidungen" in Interdependenzen von Politik und Wirtschaft. 1967, S. 507.

_____. "Wie informiert das Fernsehen? Eine Unter-
suchung über moderne Massenmedien" in Die Zeit
(Hamburg), J. 21 (1966), N. 39, Beil., S. 29.

Eckstein, Gunther. "Präsidentenwahl in USA" in Gewerk-
schaftliche Monatshefte, J. 19 (1968), H. 12, S. 705-
08.

Eichler, Willi. "Zur Aufgabe und Finanzierung der Parteien"
in Geist und Tat, J. 20 (1965), N. 1, S. 1-4.

Ellwein, Thomas. "Vom Wählen" in Die bayrische Schule
(München), J. 18 (1965), S. 409-11.

Ensthaler, Jürgen D. "Fernsehen und Präsidentschaftswahlen.
Erfahrungen und Methoden in USA" in Fernsehen
(Heidelberg), J. 5 (1957), S. 16-24.

Epstein, Klaus. "Die amerikanischen Präsidentschaftswahlen
von 1964" in Das Parlament (Hamburg), J. 14 (1964),
Beil. 51, S. 3-22.

"Evolution de la politique américaine en 1961" in Chronique
de politique étrangère (Brussels), Vol. 15 (1962), p.
277-96.

Fechter, Heinrich. "Die Sprache der Politik" in Der Quell,
J. 6 (1954), S. 419-24.

Die Finanzpolitik in der Wahlperiode 1953-1957. Bonn:
Verlag Wilhelm Stollfluss.

Foerster, O. "Fernsehen und politische Bildung" in
Gesellschaft, Staat, Erziehung (Frankfurt/M), J. 6
(1961), N. 5, S. 218-25.

Fraser, Geoffrey. "Les élections américaines et la situation
mondiale" in Année politique et économique (Paris),
A. 25 (1952), N. 109, p. 395-99.

Frede, E. A. "Element politischer Propaganda" in
Politische Studien (München), 11 (1960), S. 641 ff.

Freund, Ludwig. "How to become a President? Die Methode
der amerikanischen Präsidentenwahl" in Ut omnes
unum (Paderborn), J. 7 (1952), N. 20, S. 8-9.

Friedrich-Ebert-Stiftung (hrsg.). Die politische urteils-
    bildung in der Demokratie. Hannover: Verlag für
    Literatur und Zeitgeschehen 1960.

Gather, Gernot. "Ein neuer politscher Stil--ein neues
    Verantwortungsbewusstsein" in Offene Welt, 1963, S.
    453-59.

Gayer, Kurt. Wie man Minister macht, Politik und Werbung.
    Stuttgart: 1963.

Gerhardt, P. "Phrasen in der Politik" in Volkshochschule
    im Westen (Dortmund), J. 12 (1960-61), H. 1, S. 15-
    16.

"Gesellschaft. Wahlpropaganda: Die Tute" in Der Spiegel
    (Hamburg), J. 10 (1956), N. 42, S. 56.

Les grands problèmes de la politique des Etats-Unis. Paris:
    Roz, Firmin/Armand Colin 1956.

Green, Gil. "Signification des élections américaines" in
    La nouvelle revue internationale (Paris), 10 (1967),
    n. 3, p. 18-36.

Gross, Rolf. "Zur Frage der staatlichen Finanzierung
    politischen Parteien" in Gewerkschaftliche Monatshefte,
    J. 16 (1965), H. 5, S. 274-75.

Guggenheim, Willy. "Die USA nach den Wahlen: Zwang fur
    Reife" in Weltwoche (Zürich), J. 36 (1968), N. 1827,
    S. 3.

Gütt, Dieter. "Über Erfolg und Misserfolg politischer
    Sendungen im Fernsehen" in Fernsehen und Bildung,
    J. 4 (1970), H. 4, S. 233-36.

Hartmann, K. D. "Zur Psychologie der Wahlpropaganda" in
    Praktische Psychologie, J. 23 (1969), H. 7-8, S. 181-
    88.

Haseloff, Otto W. "Uber Wirkungsbedingungen politischer
    und werblicher Kommunikation" in Kommunikation.
    Berlin: 1969, S. 151, 87.

148

Political Campaign Communication

Heidland, Hans W. Die politischen Wirkungen von Funk und Rundfunk. Stuttgart: RADIUS-Verlag 1970.

Hermens, Ferdinand A. "Medien der Massenkommunikation und Rationalität der politischer Entscheidung" in Wissenschaft und Praxis. Köln: 1967, S. 65-91.

_____, und Unkelbach, Helmut. "Die Wissenschaft und das Wahlrecht" in Politische Vierteljahresschrift (Köln), J. 8 (1967), H. 1, S. 2-22.

Hoffmann, Stanley. "La campagna présidentielle et la vie politique aux Etats-Unis en 1956" in Revue française de science politique, Vol. 7 (1957), p. 346-77.

Hoffmann, W. "Politische Erziehung als psychologisches Problem" in Praktische Psychologie, J. 20 (1966), H. 10, S. 243-44.

Holzamer, Karl. "Fernsehen--Mittel der Meinungsverbreitung oder Forum der Meinungsbildung?" in Publizistik (Bremen), J. 11 (1966), H. 3-4, S. 248.

_____. "Politik im Fernsehen" in Areopag (Mainz), J. 3 (1968), H. 2, S. 97-112.

Hufen, Fritz (Hrsg.). Politik und Massenmedien. S. Band 1. Mainz: von Hase und Koehler Verlag 1970.

Hüther, Jürgen. "Jugend--Fernsehen--Politik. Zur Informations-funktion des Fernsehens im Vergleich mit anderen Medien" in Recht der Jugend, J. 17 (1969), H. 5, S. 136-40.

"Im Vorfeld der amerikanischen Präsidentschaftswahlen" in Presse--Forum (Stuttgart), J. 5 (1951), N. 17, S. 7-12.

Ischeyt, Heinz. "Sprache der Politik" in Deutsche Studien, J. 8 (1970), N. 30, S. 193-200.

"Ist das nun Persönlichkeitswahl?" in Die freie Stadt (Hamburg), J. 6 (1952), N. 6, S. 4.

Jänicke, Martin. "Politische Sprache--politischer Konflikt--
politische Bildung" in Gesellschaft, Staat, Erziehung,
J. 15 (1970), H. 6, S. 361-70.

Kaase, Max. "Politiker und Wählerschaft" in Zeitwende, J.
36 (1965), H. 8, S. 537-50.

Kandt, Josef. "Politiker und Journalisten" in Zukunft
(Wien), 1965, H. 8, S. 17-19.

Kaspi, André. La vie politique aux Etats-Unis. Paris:
Librairie Hachette 1969.

Kitzinger, Uwe. Walkampf in Westdeutschland. Eine
Analyse der Bundestagswahl 1957. Göttingen: 1960.

Klein, Julius. "Public Relations and Image-Building" in
Der Volkswirt, J. 20 (1966), N. 43, Beil., S. 52-58.

Kohl, Helmut. "Politik im Fernsehen--Kritik und Kritikemp-
findlichkeit" in Fernsehen und Bildung, J. 4 (1970),
H. 4, S. 240-41.

Kossitsch, Mirko M. "Politische Soziologie" in Soziologische
Forschung in unserer Zeit. Koln: 1951, S. 171-86.

Kovacević, Stojan. "Die USA zwischen Johnson und Goldwater" in Internationale Politik, J. 15 (1964), N. 347,
S. 11-13.

Kramer, Helmut. "Die Kosten der Politik in den USA"
in Zukunft (Wien), 1967, H. 23-24, S. 21-24.

Kraschutzki, Heniz. "Neuer Wein in alten Schläuchen?
Präsidentenwahl in USA" in Das andere Deutschland
(Hannover), 1960, N. 23, S. 1-2.

Krivine, A. La farce électorale. Paris: Editions du Seuil.

Krüger, Ernst. "USA--Wahlen im Schatten Koreas" in Die
Zeit (Hamburg), 5 (1950), N. 44, S. 3.

Kuby, Erich. "Der Mystizismus im deutschen Wahlkampf"
in Süddeutsche Zeitung, 9. Jahrgang, Nr. 198 vom
29, 8 (1953).

Lanius, Gerhard. "Fernsehaktualität und Wirklichkeit.
    Zur Rolle des Fernsehens" in Der politischen Bildung
    in Deutsche Jugend (München), J. 9 (1961), S. 549-54.

_____. "Psychologie der Massenkommunikation" in Film--
    Bild--Ton, J. 14 (1964), N. 6, S. 42-44.

Lehner, Gunther. "Die Problematik meinungsbildender
    politischer Sendungen im Fernsehen" in Fernsehen und
    Bildung, J. 4 (1970), H. 4, S. 221-29.

Leichter, Otto. "Was veränderten die amerikanischen
    Wahlen?" in Zukunft, 1965, H. 1, S. 6-9.

Leistikow, Gunnar. "Wahltag in den Vereinigten Staaten"
    in Das Parlament (Hamburg), J. 8 (1958), N. 44, S.
    13.

Lingenberg, Jörg. "Politische Propaganda im Fernsehspiel"
    in Rundfunk und Fernsehen (Hamburg), J. 9 (1961),
    S. 241-49.

Löffler, Martin. "Die Rolle der Massenmedien in der
    Demokratie" in Die Öffentliche Verwaltung, J. 18
    (1965), H. 15, S. 523-24.

Lohr. George. "Die Kandidaten für die amerikanischen
    Präsidentschaftswahlen" in Deutsche Aussenpolitik
    (Berlin), J. 5 (1960), S. 646-53.

_____. "Wahlkampfdebatten in den USA" in Die Wirtschaft
    (Berlin), J. 15 (1960), N. 34, S. 16.

Lüders, Peter Jürgen. "Trotz Wahlkampf: Mehr Stil in der
    Politik!" in Junge Wirtschaft, J. 5 (1957), S. 2-5.

Mackenthun, W. "Präsidentenwahl und Energiepolitik in
    den V. St. A." in Elektrizitätswirtschaft (Frankfurt/
    M), 1951-52, H. 24, S. 661.

Maletzke, Gerhard. Psychologie der Massenkommunikation.
    Hans Bredlow-Institut für Rundfunk und Fernsehen.

Marcuse, Ludwig. "L'art politique pour l'art politique"
    in Club Voltaire, Bd. 3 (1967), S. 225.

Marlo, Hans und Neuburger, Edgar. "Über gerichte Grössen in der Informationstheorie. Untersuchungen zur Theorie der bidirektionalen Kommunikation" in Archiv der elecktrischen Übertragung, Bd. 21 (1967), S. 61-69.

"Massenmedien und Meinungsbildung" in Die neue Vertrieb, J. 17 (1965), N. 384, S. 251-58.

Mauer, Heinrich J. "Die Politiker und die Massenmedien" in Politische Studien (München), J. 16 (1965), S. 411-18.

Mehnert, Klaus. "Der Hut im Ring. Wahlkampf" in Christ und Welt (Stuttgart), 4 (1951), N. 45, S. 5.

Meynaud, Jean, et Coulombe, Françoise. La télévision américaine et l'information sur la politique. Montreal: Editions Nouvelle Frontiere, Inc., 1971.

Michelat, Guy. "Télévision. Moyens d'information et comportement electoral" in Revue française de science politique, 14 (1964), p. 877-905.

Molnar, Th. "Elections américaines--réactions françaises" in Le table ronde (Paris), 1960, N. 153, p. 112-16.

Mommsen, Konrad. "Die amerikanische Wählergesellschaft" in Mitteilungen, Deutsche Wählergessellschaft (Heidelberg), 1951, N. 2, S. 42-45.

Morkel, Arnd. "Über den politischen Stil" in Politische Vierteljahresschrift, J. 7 (1966), H. 1, S. 119-37.

Müller, Detlef. "Das Klischee--ein dramaturgisches Erfordernis? Zur Technik politischen Meinungsbildung" in Fernsehen in Deutschland. Mainz: 1967, S. 203.

"Neuer Stil im Wahlkampf--moderne Werbemethoden für den grossen Wettlauf im Herbst" in Die Aussprache (Bonn), J. 7 (1957), S. 107-08.

Nordenstreng, Kaarle. "Communication Research in the U.S.: A Critical Perspective" in Gazette (Leiden), Vol. 14 (1968), n. 3, p. 207-16.

Norman, Loyd. "Die amerikanische Präsidentschaftskampagne 1960" in Monatshefte (Hannover), J. 49 (1960-61), H. 2, S. 169-73.

Oeckl, Albert. Handbuch der PR. München: 1964.

Osthold, Paul. "Die Kräfte im amerikanischen Wahlkampf" in Der Arbeitgeber, 1962, S. 647-50.

Oudenne, Philippe. "La politique commerciale des Etats-Unis" in Problemes économiques, 1953, N. 276, p. 11-15.

Paetel, K. O. "Der amerikanische Wahlkampf" in Geist und Tat, J. 15 (1960), S. 299-301.

Pellissier, Edouard. "La plus grande élection du monde" in Revue de Paris, s. 75 (1968), n. 11, p. 77-84.

Pfizer, Th. "Politische Erziehung und Politik" in Der Burger im Staat, J. 17 (1967), H. 1, S. 4.

"Politische Parteien versuche verstärkten Einfluss auf Runkfunk und Fernsehen zu erlangen" in Fernseh-Informationen, J. 11 (1960), S. 494-95.

Pontius, Dale. "Die amerikanischen Wahlen. Über die Technik der Demokratie" in Ut omnes unum (Paderborn), J. 11 (1956), N. 22, S. 11-13.

"Die Quittung für die Politik der vollendeten Tatsachen" in Zeitungs-Verlag und Zeitschriften-Verlag (Bad Godesberg), J. 58 (1961), S. 269.

Ranney, Austin. "Les élections américaines de 1960. Analyse géographique et sociologique" in Revue française de science politique, 11 (1961), H. 4, p. 841-61.

Raskin, Heinrich. "Der Politiker als Persönlichkeit" in Kommunalpolitische Blätter (Recklinghausen), J. 15 (1963), S. 1.

Reithinger, Anton. "Die Verhexung der Politik durch die
    Sprache" in Blätter für deutsche und internationale
    Politik, J. 10 (1965), H. 8, S. 654-62.

Robertson, Edwin H. "Die Möglichkeiten von Rundfunk und
    Fernsehen in der modernen Kommunikation" in
    Medium, J. 4 (1967), H. 3, S. 172-94.

Rohlinger, Rudolf. "Der Einfluss der Massenmedien auf
    Wahlen in der Bundesrepublik" in Fernsehen und
    Bildung, J. 4 (1970), H. 1-2, S. 24-27.

Die Rolle der Massenmedien in der Demokratie. München:
    C. H. Beck'sche 1966.

Ronneberger, Franz. "Die politische Bedeutung der
    Tagezeitung heute und ihre Funktion in der Demo-
    kratie" in Zeitungs-Verlag und Zeitschriften-Verlag,
    J. 62 (1965), N. 25, S. 1163-67.

_____. "Die politischen Funktionen der Massenkommunka-
    tionsmittel" in Publizistik, J. 9 (1964), H. 4, S. 291-
    304.

_____. "Ziel und Formen der Kommunikationspolitik" in
    Publizistik (Bremen), J. 11 (1966), H. 3-4, S. 399-
    406.

Rooij, M., Heering, M. J. und Elfferich, P. "Massen-
    medien" in Kriminalistik, J. 20 (1966), 10, S. 545.

Rose, Arnold M. "The study of the influence of the mass
    media on public opinion" in Kyklos (Bern), Bd. 15
    (1962), S. 465-84.

Rössner, Lutz. Fernsehen in der politischen Bildung.
    Frankfurt: Mortiz Diesterweg 1971.

Sauer, W. "Zum Kausalitätsprinzip in der Nachrichten-
    theorie" in Wissenschaftliche Welt, Bd. 9 (1968), H.
    2, S. 108-19.

Schäfer, M. "Massenmedien und Meinungsbildung" in
    Wirtschaft und Erziehung, J. 15 (1963), 8, S, 358-63.

Schmid, Carlo. "Politiker und Journalist" in Die neue
Gesellschaft, J. 11 (1964), S. 318-20.

_____. "Die Rolle der Urteilskräfte für die moderne
Gesellschaft" in Der Mensch und seiner Meinung.
Darmstädter Gespräch 1960, Darmstadt, 1961.

Schneider, Franz. Politik und Kommunikation. Mainz: von
Hase und Koehler Verlag 1967.

Schoeck, Helmut. "Nixons Amerika wird anders sein.
Wider die Spekulation auf das Führer-Charisma" in
Die politische Meinung, J. 13 (1968), 4 (125), S. 21-
28.

Schütte, Manfred. Politische Werbung und totalitäre Propaganda. Düsseldorf: Econ Verlag 1968.

Schwab-Felisch, Hans. "Zur Sprache der Politiker" in
Die neue Rundschau, J. 77 (1966), H. 2, S. 230-39.

Schweilen, Joachim. "Kanditur als Opfergang. Senator
McCarthy: Der Mann, der Johnson in die Shranken
fordert" in Die Zeit (Hamburg), J. 22 (1967), N. 50,
S. 2.

Seehof, A. "USA--Politiker" in Weltbühne (Berlin), J. 6
(1951), N. 16, S. 490.

Setzen, Karl M. Fernsehen--Objektivität oder Manipulation?
Heidenheimer Verlagsanstalt 1971.

Smythe, Dallas W. "Das Bild des Politikers in den Massenmedien" in Rundfunk und Fernsehen (Hamburg), J. 9
(1961), S. 250-61.

Spiess, Volker. Bibliographie zu Rundfunk und Fernsehen.
Hans Bredow-Institut für Rundfunk und Fernsehen.

Stammler, Eberhard. "Die Wirkung der Massenmedien auf
das politische Bewusstsein" in Sozialpädagogik
(Gütersloh), J. 5 (1962), S. 16-21.

Steigner, Walter. "Politik im Rundfunk" in Ut omnes unum
(Paderborn), J. 10 (1955), N. 9, S. 3-6.

Steiner, J. "Überprufüng von Interviewergebnissen über die Stimm--und Wahl--beteiligung durch amtliche Angabe" in Kölner Zeitschrift für Soziologie, J. 17 (1965), N. 2, S. 234-45.

Steinmann, Matthias F. Massenmedien und Werbung. Freiburg: Rombach 1971.

Stosberg, Manfred und Gerber, Klaus P. Die Massenmedien und die Organization politische Interessen: Presse, Fernsehen, Rundfunk und die Parteien und Verbände im Selbstbild der Bonner Journalisten. Düsseldorf: Bertelsmann Universitäts-verlag 1971.

Sturminger, Alfred. 3000 Jahre politische Propaganda. Wien/München: 1960.

Tank, K. L. "Manipulation durch Massenmedien" in Zeitschrift für praktische Psychologie, J. 8 (1968), Bd. 4, H. 5-6, S. 284-96.

Teubner, H. "Über die Rolle des Propagandisten in der Partei" in Einheit, 1950, S. 519 ff.

Tillich, Ernst. "Über die Notwendigkeit und die psychologische Basis politischer Propaganda," in Politische Studien, 9, 1958.

Tschäppät, R. "Amerika vor den Präsidentschaftswahlen" in Schweizerisches kaufmännisches Zentralblatt (Zürich), J. 72 (1968), N. 12, S. 1-2.

_____. "Die Vereinigten Staaten vor den Wahlen" in Schweizerisches kaufmännisches Zentralblatt (Zürich), J. 72 (1968), N. 4, S. 1-2.

"US--Wahlen: Stimme aus dem Hinterland" in Der Spiegel (Hamburg), J. 6 (1952), N. 22, S. 20-23.

"US--Wahlkampf: Diese Burschen" in Der Spiegel (Hamburg), J. 14 (1960), N. 22, S. 53-54.

"US--Wahlkampf: Schnellgang im Getriebe" in Der Spiegel (Hamburg), J. 6 (1952), N. 32, S. 14.

"US--Werbung für die Präsidentschaftswahlen" in Wirtschaft
    und Werbung (Essen), J. 6 (1952), N. 10, S. 274-75.

"USA: Ein Mythos wurde gewählt" in Der Spiegel (Hamburg),
    J. 6 (1952), N. 46, S. 20-22.

"USA--Wahlen: Alte Wunden" in Der Spiegel, J. 20 (1966),
    N. 47, S. 119-20.

"USA--Wahlen: Der Kartoffelsack--Tip" in Der Spiegel
    (Hamburg), J. 6 (1952), N. 43, S. 20-21.

"USA--Wahlkampf: Ostküste absägen" in Der Spiegel (Ham-
    burg), J. 17 (1963), N. 47, S. 84.

"USA: Wahlkampf: Was für ein Sieg!" in Der Spiegel (Ham-
    burg), J. 9 (1955), N. 32, S. 30-31.

Vardin, Heinz-Josef. "Parteien und Wähler" in Wahlhandbuch
    1965, Fritz Sänger und Klaus Liepelt, ed. Frankfurt:
    1965.

v. Gleichen. "Politik und Werbung" in Zeitungs-Verlag und
    Zeitschriften-Verlag (Bad Godesberg), J. 58 (1961),
    S. 582-88.

v. Hentig. "Der ungleiche Wahlkampf" in Rundschau (Wangen/
    Allgäu), J. 4 (1952), N. 26, S. 2.

von Hagen, Volker. "Das Verhältnis von Wort und Bild in
    politischen Fernsehsendung" in Fernsehen in Deutsch-
    land. Mainz: 1967, S. 95-98.

von Wechmar, Rüdiger. "Politik im Fernsehen--Idee und
    Wirklichkeit" in Fernsehen und Bildung, J. 4 (1970),
    H. 4, S. 237-39.

"Votum zum Werbefernsehen" in Fernsehen (Heidelburg), J.
    4 (1956), S. 210-212.

"Wahlen und Skandale. USA--Kongresswahlen im November"
    in Deutsche Zeitung und Wirtschaftszeitung (Stuttgart),
    1950, N. 82, S. 1.

"Wahlkampf. Das Millionärs-Duell" in Der Spiegel (Hamburg), J. 12 (1958), N. 42, S. 38-40.

"Wahltechnik in USA" in Die Zeit (Hamburg), J. 7 (1952), N. 27, S. 2.

Wangermee, R. "Une dimension politique nouvelle: La télégénie" in Res publica (Brussels), Vol. 10 (1968), n. spec., p. 111-29.

Wasem, E. "Massenmedien und öffentliche politische Meinung" in Jugend und Film (München), J. 4 (1960), H. 4, S. 6-14.

Wasem, Erich. "Massenmedien und öffentliche politische Meinung" in Schule und Leben (München), J. 12 (1960-61), H. 10-11, S. 261-69.

Weber, Werner. "Sendezeiten für Wahlpropaganda der politischen Parteien im Rundfunk" in Die öffentliche Verwaltung (Stuttgart), J. 15 (1962), S. 241-46.

Weil, Gordon L. "La crise des partis politiques américains" in Res publica (Brussels), Vol. 11 (1969), N. 2, p. 351-71.

"Werbe--Fernsehen im politischen Blickfield" in Fernseh-Informationen (München), J. 7 (1956), S. 29-30.

"Wie haben die Zuschauer auf die Wahlsendungen im Fernsehen reagiert?" in Fernseh-Informationen, J. 16 (1965), H. 28, S. 485-87.

"Wie man in den Vereinigten Staaten Präsident wird" in Der Spiegel (Hamburg), J. 6 (1952), N. 28, S. 18-19.

Wildenmann, Rudolf. "Das Fernsehen und die Wahlen" in Fernsehen in Deutschland. Mainz: 1967, S. 135-42.

Winn, Ira J. "Dimensions of political unconsciousness" in Internationales Jahrbuch für Geschichts- und Geographieunterricht, Bd. 11 (1967), S. 35-53.

Zimmerman, Hans D. Die politische Rede. Stuttgart: W. Kohlhammer 1969.

Zundel, Rolf. "Barry Goldwaters trauriges Erbe. Die
     Republikanische Partei sammelt sich in den Trümmern
     der Niederlage" in <u>Die Zeit</u> (Hamburg), J. 19 (1964),
     N. 46, S. 7.

4. ANNOTATED LIST OF SELECTED BOOKS

We have included below annotations of 50 books which we believe to be seminal to the study of political campaign communication. Although we selected them subjectively, we have annotated books which are broadly representative of the wide range of those which have been written on the subject, including "classics," experientially based works, historical accounts, and behaviorally oriented analyses. We have also tended to include books published in the past 10 years, to the exclusion of equally representative ones published earlier. In any event, we hope that the annotations, though brief, will provide anyone with newly acquired interests in campaigning with a brief overview of the field and will provide sufficient information about each book to allow him to make intelligent decisions about those entries which he would like to read.

Agranoff, Robert. The New Style in Election Campaigns.
    Boston: Holbrook Press, 1972.
    This book is primarily a collection of readings on professional campaign management, the use of information systems in political campaigns, and the role of mass media in campaigning. In an extensive introduction, the author discusses the declining emphasis on party professionals and party organizations in the campaign process. Although the vote-mobilizing power of the party is seldom shunned by a political candidate, the candidate's personal style and image have taken precedence. This result is partially attributable to the increased use of professional managers, sophisticated research, and extensive use of television with its emphasis on the image of the candidate. Agranoff sees present electoral strategy as one which seeks "re-inforcement of the committed, activation of the indifferent, and conversion of the doubtful."

American Institute for Political Communication. The 1968
   Campaign: Anatomy of a Crucial Election. Washington, D.C.: American Institute for Political Communication, 1970.
      Supported by survey data gathered in the 1968 presi-
dential campaign in Milwaukee, Wisconsin, this book "is concerned primarily with general and 'elite' attitudes toward the
presidential contenders and toward state-level candidates running for the U.S. Senate, House of Representatives, and
Governor. It is concerned with attitudes toward issues.
And it is concerned with the manner in which attitudes toward
candidates and issues change with time." Panel interviewing
was utilized but results are reported only in terms of mean
scores and percentages, with no statistical testing of significance. From these descriptive results, the study concludes:
(1) issues cannot be greatly modified or obscured by campaign propaganda; (2) the media are politically influential as
channels of communication but their degree of influence
varies with time and is limited by many factors; (3) primary
forces such as the immediate family, close friends and political advisers are less influential on voting behavior than
are major issues and the manner in which the voter per-
ceives the personal attributes of the candidates; (4) the influ-
entials' attitudes toward candidates and the mass media dif-
fer in some important respects from those of the man on the
street but are very similar in respect to major issues; (5)
age, education level, and political party affiliation are important in determining media dependence; and (6) the campaign environment affects attitudes toward the mass media.

Anderson, Walt. Campaigns: Cases in Political Conflict.
   Pacific Palisades, California: Goodyear Publishing
   Company, Inc., 1970.
      Ranging from the campaigns of Lincoln and Douglas
in 1853 to the 1968 New Hampshire primary, this book
examines fourteen American campaigns for public office.
From the point of view of an historian, it discusses the
combatants, their strategy and tactics, and the factors which
influenced the results. Three themes predominate: the political status of Blacks, radicalism, and the influence of the
mass media. The campaigns covered occurred in widely
different regions of the country and range from mayoral
through presidential.

Archibald, Samuel J. (ed.). The Pollution of Politics. Washington, D.C.: Public Affairs Press, 1971.
      This book draws its basic data from the complaints

filed with the Fair Campaign Practices Committee, of which Archibald was executive director. These complaints are summarized for three campaigns prior to 1970 and numerous case studies are presented from the 1970 election year. The conclusions of the case studies indicate that voters are not as susceptible to political distortion and manipulation as political advertisers sometimes think.

Berelson, Bernard; Lazarsfeld, Paul; and McPhee, William. Voting: A Study of Opinion Formation in a Presidential Campaign. Chicago: University of Chicago Press, 1954.

The authors conducted an extensive survey in Elmira, New York, during the 1948 presidential campaign in an attempt to assess the voters' perceptions of politics, their reaction to the issues, their attention to the mass media, their influence on one another's political preferences, the role of class and religious affiliation in politics and the institutional leadership of the local community. The results reported in the book are based upon over a thousand interviews. While no statistical testing was reported, the book contains considerable information in percentage and category form. In discussing the impact of personal contact, the authors conclude from their data that voting change is correlated with personal contact. In addition, a major section is provided which focuses upon the influence of the mass media. The authors conclude (1) "the more exposure to the campaign in the mass media, the more interested voters become and the more strongly they come to feel about their candidate"; (2) "the more exposure to the campaign in the mass media, the less voters change their positions and the more they carry through on election day"; and (3) "the more exposure to the campaign in the mass media, the more correct information the voters have about the campaign and the more correct their perception of where the candidates stand on the issues."

Blumler, Jay G., and McQuail, Denis. Television in Politics: Its Uses and Influence. Chicago: The University of Chicago Press, 1969.

This volume presents the questions, research methodologies, research techniques, and conclusions of an investigation of the role of television in the British General Election of 1964. A three-stage panel survey was conducted utilizing as respondents 750 voters residing in two parliamentary constituencies in Yorkshire. The study was designed to answer two general questions: How do voters use political programs during a political campaign, and how does

television political communication influence voters' political
outlooks?   Until this study was conducted, there was, according to the authors, only one research-supported general-
ization which could be drawn about the political impact of
British television: It "... had helped to increase the store
of political information available to voters at the General
Election of 1959...." Through its major finding that television had helped increase the popularity of the Liberal Party
in the General Election of 1964, the inquiry reported in this
book doubled, according to the authors, the number of de-
fensible generalizations which could be drawn about the political impact of television. The book contains a foreword
to the American edition which provides the American reader
with a brief introduction to elections and broadcasting in
Britain and concludes with a general bibliography on British
political communication.

Bogart, Leo.   Silent Politics: Polls and the Awareness of
        Public Opinion. New York: Wiley Interscience, John
        Wiley and Sons, 1972.
        Although a great deal of the discussion in this book
concentrates on polls and public opinion in regard to policy
issues, considerable attention is given to the use of polls in
political campaigns. Polls are credited not only with the
obvious usefulness of predicting who will win an election or
what issues are important in the campaign but also with fund-
raising potential and impact on campaign workers. While
the author believes election-related polls provide more accurate predictions than do most other forms of public opinion
research because the opinions solicited (choice between two
candidates) are more concrete, he does not believe that reported polls per se directly influence the outcome of elections.

Campbell, Angus; Converse, Philip E.; Miller, Warren E.;
        and Stokes, Donald E. The American Voter. New
        York: John Wiley & Sons, 1960.
        This classic work on American voting behavior de-
velops the Survey Research Center's six-component model of
voting behavior drawing data from survey research conducted
during the period 1948 to 1956 on a probability sample of the
national electorate. The six elements in the model are:
perceptions of the Democratic candidate, perceptions of the
Republican candidate, group related perceptions, foreign
policy perceptions, domestic issues perceptions, and government management perceptions. As this model would suggest,
the volume is not directly concerned with the role of political
communication in the political process, but its findings and

theorizing are relevant to much of the research which has
been done on political communication, particularly the studies
which have sought to relate communication variables and
candidate image.

Chartrand, Robert L. Computers and Political Campaigning.
    New York: Spartan Books, 1972.
    Computers can now aid the political candidate in
numerous ways--maintaining voter and fund-raising files,
keeping track of research files, aiding in the conduct of
polling, and simulating election results. A descriptive and
practical discussion of the growing uses of computers and
information technology in political campaigns, this book provides many examples of computer applications including appendices on data processing costs and lists of political consultants.

Chester, Edward W. Radio, Television and American Politics.
    New York: Sheed and Ward, 1969.
    Writing from the perspective of an historian, Chester
develops the role played by radio and television in American
politics, with particular emphasis placed on the campaign setting. While the discussions are primarily descriptive, they
nonetheless provide an interesting perspective on the political
importance of the media. Detailed analyses of presidential
contenders' campaigns are provided which tend to support the
thesis that radio, in the past, and television, in the present,
are influential forces in American politics.

Chester, Lewis; Hodgson, Godfrey; and Page, Bruce. An
    American Melodrama: The Presidential Campaign of
    1968. New York: The Viking Press, 1969.
    Written by three British journalists, this book pro-
vides a unique opportunity for the American reader to view a
major election year through British eyes. The authors spent
considerable time following the candidates, both in person and
through the media. They place the campaigns of 1968 in historical perspective, find humor where American writers might
have found none, and, in general, wonder if American campaigns are not more illusory than substantive.

DeVries, Walter, and Tarrance, V. Lance. The Ticket-
    Splitter: A New Force in American Politics. Grand
    Rapids, Mich.: William B. Eerdmans Publishing Co.,
    1972.
    This book is based primarily on survey research con-
ducted by the authors in Michigan and Texas during the 1968

election. The authors (DeVries, a political science professor and campaign consultant, and Tarrance, former Research
Director for the Republican National Committee) argue that
the critical balance of electoral power is held by those who
vote for the candidates of more than one party in a single
election. These "ticket-splitters" are informed citizens who
rely heavily on the mass media for political information.
In the past most political scientists have argued that the potential voter who says he is an "Independent" is generally
less informed, less likely to be exposed to the mass media
and less likely to vote. DeVries and Tarrance wish to define
independence in behavioral terms rather than in attitudinal
(self-classification) terms. The data reported detail the relative importance to the ticket-splitter of various communication
channels, sources, and message types. The authors conclude
from their·descriptive data that some communication variables are more important than others in the decision-making
process of the ticket-splitter.

Downs, Anthony. An Economic Theory of Democracy. New
    York: Harper and Row, 1957.
        Although written several years ago, this book continues
to be a provocative and comprehensive theoretical statement
on voting behavior. Downs' theory is based on the assumption that voters (and non-voters) behave in a rational manner
in the pursuit of clearly envisioned political and economic
goals. Approximately one-fourth of the book is devoted to a
discussion of the process through which voters become informed, reduce "information costs," and in general determine
the personal utility of certain kinds, types, and amounts of
political information. Downs argues that "in general, it is
irrational to be politically well-informed because the low returns from data simply do not justify the cost in time and
other scarce resources."

Dunn, Delmar D. Financing Presidential Campaigns. Wash-
    ington, D.C.: Brookings Institution, 1972.
        While working as a research associate in governmental
studies at the Brookings Institution, Dunn completed this book
which is concerned principally with the rising costs of presidential campaigns. The data for the book consist of sixty-one
personal interviews with political consultants and advertising
agency personnel who had raised money for such candidates
as Richard Nixon, Hubert Humphrey and George Wallace, as
well as those involved in senatorial and congressional campaigns throughout the nation. After providing detailed discussions on such topics as (1) the impact of money on presi-

dential campaigns, (2) the cost of modern campaigning, (3) analysis of the 1970 Campaign Finance Reform Bill, (4) political and public participation in campaigns, (5) the importance of political parties as fund raisers, and (6) which candidates should be covered in campaign funding reform, the author provides his own suggestion for reforming campaign finance. The communications scholar will be interested in several charts depicting the impact of the media in political campaigning.

Edelman, Murray. The Symbolic Uses of Politics. Urbana, Illinois: University of Illinois Press, 1964.
Regarded by some as the classic statement of its kind, this book "... explores the meanings for large publics of the acts and gestures of leaders, of the settings in which political acts occur, of the language styles and the phrases that permeate political discussion and action. ... it tries to highlight the interplay in politics among acts, actors, settings, language, and masses...." The book owes its uniqueness to the fact that it tends to concentrate on the expressive, rather than the instrumental, aspects of political activity.

Felknor, Bruce L. Dirty Politics. New York: Norton Publication, 1966.
Written by a former director of the Committee for Fair Campaign Practices, this book details dirty campaign practices from the days of Washington to the present. With chapters on mudslinging by presidential contenders, the theft and purchase of votes, and political spying, the book discusses almost every known form of political chicanery. One section discusses the prominent use, in the campaign of 1964, of the "dirty book," a relatively new form of political sophistry made possible by the modern high speed printing press. While acknowledging the difficulty of legislating morality, the author calls for several new legislative initiatives which he believes will discourage questionable campaign practices.

Heard, Alexander. The Costs of Democracy. Chapel Hill, North Carolina: The University of North Carolina Press, 1960.
Despite the fact that it has become somewhat dated by changing patterns in campaign finance and by new legislation, this book should be read by everyone interested in political fundraising, for whatever reason. It discusses every aspect of its subject matter ranging from the influence

of money on electoral outcomes to the motivations behind
political contributions. There are also recommendations for
action at several levels which could be taken to correct
abuses. The author draws heavily from historical and empirical research and from formal and informal discussions
with over 600 politicians.

Huckshorn, Robert J., and Spencer, Robert C. The Politics
    of Defeat: Campaigning for Congress. Amherst,
    Mass.: The University of Massachusetts Press, 1971.
        This book is based upon a detailed empirical study of
the Congressional elections of 1962. The authors took as
their population to be studied some 800 candidates represent-
ing the two major parties in all contested congressional dis-
tricts. A lengthy questionnaire was sent to defeated candidates and a shorter version to winners. Paying particular
attention to those aspects of congressional candidacy which
appear to contribute to defeat, the authors report data and
offer conclusions on the social characteristics and career
patterns of the candidates, recruitment of candidates, campaign organization and management, the relationship between
the candidates and their parties, the value to the candidates
of various services offered by the national and state parties,
and the role of issues in the congressional campaign. In a
concluding chapter they make suggestions for change in state
party organizations, field work, staffing, and fund raising.

Joyner, Conrad. The American Politician. Tucson, Ari-
    zona: The University of Arizona Press, 1971.
        Essentially an essay about politicians, this book is
concerned with the broad environmental forces--physical,
social, economic, institutional, and ideological--which provide the framework within which politicians operate and
which in turn influence their behavior. While the author is
currently a professor of government, he also writes from
the perspective of someone who has had extensive experience
in politics, both as a campaign manager and a political office holder. Joyner argues that, through an analysis of
political socialization, citizen participation in politics and
motivations, it is possible to understand better how candidates are recruited, the campaign process, and the conduct
of elected officials.

Kelley, Stanley, Jr. Political Campaigning: Problems in
    Creating an Informed Electorate. Washington, D.C.:
    The Brookings Institution, 1960.
        This book has come to be regarded as the classic

modern statement on rational campaigning. It defines and
defends a set of standards for evaluating campaign communication, identifies deviations from these standards in contemporary campaigning, examines the causes of these deviations, and prescribes changes in the financing of campaign
communication, the expectations of the electorate, the legal
framework in which campaign communication takes place,
and the character of the audience-candidate relationship.
The philosophy and supportive logic underlying many of the
campaign reforms enacted in the past few years can be
found in this book.

Kelley, Stanley, Jr. Professional Public Relations and
        Political Power. Baltimore: The Johns Hopkins
        Press, 1956.
        This book is principally a review of "case studies of
recent political campaigns in which public relations men
have played significant parts." It provides the reader with
insight into several large public relations firms who handle
political campaigns while also pointing out the contribution
of professionals in the political campaign process.

Key, V. O., Jr. The Responsible Electorate. New York:
        Vintage Books, 1966.
        Key wrote this classic book to illustrate that voters
do not behave as "irrationally" as many political scientists
have come to assume. By re-examining and re-interpreting
presidential election data and Gallup Poll results from 1936
through 1960, Key rejects the idea that "switchers" are less
interested and less intelligent than other voters or that
"personality" of the candidate accounts for election victory.
Although admitting that campaigns can sway voters, Key
maintains that a voting decision is the rational result of the
voter's cumulative evaluation of past party/candidate per-
formances and events.

Klapper, Joseph T. The Effects of Mass Communication.
        New York: The Free Press, 1960.
        Although somewhat dated, this volume is still widely
regarded as the most complete and authoritative summary
of speculation and empirical research on the effects of mass
communication. Over 1000 studies, essays, and reports
were identified and investigated, of which more than 270
made a contribution to the book and are listed in the bibliography. Part I discusses the effects of specific kinds of
media content which have been alleged to produce socially
and psychologically important consequences. Included are

such topics as the persuasive value of reinforcement, the
differential persuasive power of each communication medium,
and the influence of the situation in which communication
takes place.   Part II addresses itself to the effects of
specific types of media material including the effects of
crime and violence, the effects of escapist material, and
the effects of adult TV fare on younger audiences.   Although
political communication is not treated as a separate topic,
several references are made to the classic voting behavior
studies, and the book provides a set of generalizations which
may apply, in one degree or another, to all forms and types
of mass communication.

Kraus, Sidney, ed.   The Great Debates.   Bloomington,
     Indiana: Indiana University Press, 1962.
     This collection of essays and research reports was
published in response to the four debates between Nixon and
Kennedy held during the 1960 presidential campaign.   Part I
contains a diversity of background material ranging
from an essay tracing the history of broadcasting in presidential campaigns, to a critical article entitled "The Counter-
feit Debates."   Part II presents the results of several
studies conducted before, during, and after the debates, in-
vestigating their effects on such dependent variables as voting
intentions and candidate image.   Part III contains the most
accurate texts of the debates available.

Lamb, Karl, and Smith, Paul.   Campaign Decision Making.
     Belmont, Calif.:   Wadsworth Publishing Co., 1968.
     These two authors are political scientists who have
used decision-making theory (developed by Lindblom and applied extensively throughout industry) to analyze the campaigns of Lyndon Johnson and Barry Goldwater in 1964.
Through the use of direct observation, informal discussions,
and systematic interviews, the authors noted that not only
were the campaigns significantly different from each other
in terms of their decision-making process, but different from
those of previous presidential campaigns of their respective
political parties.   The authors noted that both campaigns
initially operated from the "Comprehensive" Decision-Making
Model.   This particular model "combines classic forms of
rational choice and hierarchical authority.   The decision-
maker knows his goals and ranks them in a coherent, transi-
tive order.   Choosing between conflicting or competing goals
is then a simple matter of picking those of higher rank.
The means for achieving the chosen goals, together with all
their attendant consequences, are exhaustively surveyed, and

the best means selected." The authors noted that while both camps began with the model, the Democratic decision-makers abandoned it in the face of campaign realities, while the Republicans adhered to it. The Democrats shifted to an "Incremental" Decision-Making Model which posits that there is great uncertainty, and absolute knowledge is impossible to obtain. Thus a decision-maker operating from this model does not conduct an exhaustive study of every alternative course of action before he makes a decision but rather reacts on the basis of the information he currently has. The authors indicate that this latter model is more successful in political campaigns and is a principal reason for Johnson's victory.

Lang, Kurt, and Lang, Gladys Engel. Politics and Television. Chicago: Quadrangle Books, 1968.
    After studying the impact of television in politics for nearly twenty years, the Langs compiled from their previous writings this book which summarizes many of their findings. They are concerned about the shaping of public images of politics and politicians by television's presentation of events. Results reported were based on sociological studies of televised political events. Material is discussed which relates to financing television costs, the debates between Kennedy and Nixon, and other individual campaigns. Some distinct conclusions are drawn about the cumulative and long-range effects of television on politics, including the "... main conclusion, ... that communication systems are human systems, no matter how powerful the means of visual and audio communication." Television has no inherent capacity to convey reality since the appearance of anything on television depends upon the way those employing the technology make use of it.

Lazarsfeld, Paul F.; Berelson, Bernard; and Gaudet, Hazel. The People's Choice. New York: Duell, Sloan and Pearce, 1944.
    In 1940, these Columbia University sociologists conducted a landmark study of the decision-making process of the voter in a presidential campaign. It was the first major political study employing the panel interview technique, which attempts to determine shifts in opinions and attitudes. A sample of 600 potential voters in Erie County, Ohio, were interviewed once a month from May to November. The major results include: (1) opinion leaders occupy a special role in the influence network; (2) those highly interested in the election have more opinions on issues, participate more actively

in the campaign, are exposed to more campaign propaganda
(especially propaganda from the preferred political party), and
tend to make their final voting decision earlier than less interested people; and (3) those who have not decided for whom
to vote tend to expose themselves more to propaganda of the
party for which they are predisposed by background.

Leuthold, David A. Electioneering in a Democracy: Cam-
     paigns for Congress. New York: John Wiley and
     Sons, 1968.
     Leuthold is interested in comparing campaigns at dif-
ferent levels of government, and most of the data for this
book comes from ten 1962 congressional campaigns in California. The acquisition and use of campaign resources are
primarily determined by political party, incumbency, and
competitiveness of the race, he maintains. The specific use
of resources is discussed in various ways, including the percentage of expenditures on personnel, outdoor advertising,
mailings, newspaper, radio and television ads, etc. The
author notes a heavy emphasis on pictures and personal information in the advertising of the candidates (especially of
nonincumbents). The conclusions provide considerable validation of the common assumption that incumbents possess
tremendous advantages in political campaigns.

Levin, Murray B. Kennedy Campaigning. Boston: Beacon
     Press, 1966.
     The subject of this book is the successful 1962 pre-
primary, primary, and general election campaigns of Edward
Kennedy, who was, at that time, a thirty-year-old political
novice seeking the Massachusetts Senate seat previously held
by John Kennedy. Although the book treats in detail such
subjects as the Kennedy style of approaching convention delegates, allocating time, money and manpower, and the solicit-
ing and reporting of campaign finances, two chapters will be
of particular interest to students of political communication.
One chapter entitled "If His Name was Edward Moore" analyzes the Kennedy-McCormack debates held in South Boston.
Much of the text, the setting in which the debates occurred,
the response of the audience, newspaper response, comments
from staff members, and assessments of the author are provided. A final brief chapter quotes extensively from Boorstin's The Image and analyzes Kennedy and McCormack campaigns in the context of the "pseudo event." The author, a
professor of government, concludes with the comment that
"The Kennedy brothers and the men who help manage their
careers and campaigns have mastered the art of creating

shadows and taking advantage of substance. "

Levin, Murray, with Blackwood, George. The Compleat
     Politician. Indianapolis, Ind.: Bobbs-Merrill, 1962.
     Two professors of government collaborated to write
this book about candidates, campaign managers, public relations men, pollsters, and fund raisers. During the summer
and fall of 1960 they interviewed the Democratic and Republican candidates for Governor of Massachusetts and their
political advisers "in an attempt to discover how they formulated political strategy for the primary and general election
campaigns." In addition, the authors interviewed a sample
of voters before the primary and after the general election
in order "to determine the political attitudes of certain
groups in the electorate and their reactions to the strategies
designed by the politicians." Consequently, they spend considerable time discussing various strategies and assessing
their viability when compared with the perceptions of those
for whom the strategies were designed.

MacNeil, Robert. The People Machine. New York: Harper
     and Row, 1968.
     Writing from the point of view of a former NBC
news correspondent, the author discusses the "exploitation"
of television by office seekers and office holders. He ex-
presses particular concern regarding the "sophisticated"
and "extensive" use of political advertising on television,
though he admits that the real impact of television on American politics has not yet been adequately assessed.

McCarthy, Max. Elections for Sale. Boston: Houghton
     Mifflin Co., 1972.
     Max McCarthy lost a bid for the U.S. Senate nomina-
tion, after having served three terms in the House of Representatives, a background heavily reflected in this book. His
style is basically anecdotal. The stated purpose of the book
is to stimulate significant reform in campaign financing.
The book discusses the rapid rise in the cost of political
campaigns and traces a major part of the rise to increased
necessity for mass media spending, particularly on television. The compelling necessity to raise large sums of
money for re-election forces politicians to seek out the
moneyed special interests in order to maintain themselves
in office. McCarthy discusses the impact of "image-makers"
on campaigning and the unsavory hidden funds of money
necessary to hire them. The "walking" campaign for the

U.S. Senate by Lawton Chiles of Florida is cited as a hope-
ful sign that politicians are actively seeking ways to get into
office without spending vast amounts of money. After de-
lineating the many loopholes in current laws and discussing
provisions of the 1972 Federal campaign spending act and
the Florida spending law, McCarthy concludes by outlining
and justifying an extensive program of election finance reform.

McGinniss, Joe.   The Selling of the President 1968.   New
        York: Trident Press, 1969.
        An "inside" account of the 1968 Nixon campaign, this
book is a somewhat gossipy and dramatized report of the in-
tentional remolding of Nixon's image for television--of carefully selected panels for television question-answer shows,
of meticulous care given to the television spot commercials
and to all television exposure.   McGinniss attributes much
of the approach of the Nixon image-makers to a strong belief
in McLuhan's views.   According to McGinniss, the Nixon
campaigners believed that logical persuasion was insufficient
and issues unimportant, but that television and image were
supreme persuaders.

McLuhan, Marshall.   Understanding Media.   New York: New
        American Library, 1964.
        This book, whether one does or does not agree with
its basic thesis, is regarded by many as the most provocative
single statement about the mass media written in the past
two decades.   It confidently asserts that "the medium is the
message" and that the development of the electronic media
has created a totally new "wrap around" environment with
profound, though largely unrecognized, effects.   Although the
book is exceedingly broad in its content, there are several
references, general and specific, to political communication.
In a chapter entitled "Television: The Timid Giant," McLuhan
applies his "hot"-"cool" continuum for the classification of
media to television and makes reference to one of Richard
Nixon's appearances on the Jack Parr show and to the Kennedy-Nixon debates.

Mendelsohn, Harold, and Crespi, Irving.   Polls, Television,
        and the New Politics.   Scranton, Pa.:   Chandler Pub-
        lishing Co., 1970.
        This volume documents the role public opinion polls
play in political environments in the United States, ranging
from their effect on political leaders to their impact on the
formulation of foreign policy.   It also assesses the credi-

bility of voter-preference surveys, includes a chapter on the "partisan and manipulative" use of polls, and devotes attention to a study done in California which was designed to determine the influence of election day forecasts on those who had not yet voted. A final chapter is devoted to the indirect political effects of the mass media.

Mickelson, Sig. The Electric Mirror: Politics in an Age of Television. New York: Dodd, Mead and Co., 1972.
    Mickelson, former president of CBS-TV news, recounts the role of television in political campaigns from its early use in the 1952 Eisenhower presidential campaign through its use by Richard Nixon. His unique perspective allows him to interject many personal views on the performance of the television industry and on the use of television by those outside the industry. Although his discussions are analytical and descriptive and not based on any experimental data, Mickelson's insight into areas such as the effect of television on the outcome of elections, the mood of public opinion, the spread of violence, and the realities of image-building make interesting reading. Mickelson feels that television will continue to dominate political campaigning to the extent that political parties may soon establish their own permanent advertising firms. Mickelson has been quick to see the increased potential of cable television in politics and the potential of television technology in permitting instant feedback and polling of viewers.

Napolitan, Joseph. The Election Game and How to Win It. Garden City, N.Y.: Doubleday and Co., 1972.
    Replete with personal experiences and opinions by one of the nation's well-known professional campaign managers, this book provides interesting analyses of the way a professional consultant views electronic campaign technology from television commercials to political polling. Napolitan has great confidence in the ability of television (professionally, well-produced spots) to win elections and he recounts personal examples as support. His conclusions are based on personal observation and circumstantial evidence. One of the more interesting sections of the book is a detailed case analysis of the unsuccessful 1966 gubernatorial bid of Milton Shapp of Pennsylvania in which Napolitan describes the issue and media strategy of both the successful primary and the unsuccessful gubernatorial election efforts.

Nimmo, Dan. The Political Persuaders. Englewood Cliffs,
      N.J.: Prentice-Hall, 1970.
      This widely used book on political persuasion is con-
cerned with the influence of modern campaign techniques on
the electoral process. Sections are included on the importance and use of professional campaign management techniques, the role of campaign research with special emphasis
on polling, channels of campaign communication, and attitudinal effects and behavioral consequences of political campaigns. Appendices list campaign management personnel and
political pollsters. In a concluding chapter Nimmo posits a
"theory of perceptual effects" in which he argues that the
goal of campaign persuasion should not be to shift the views
of the committed but to shift the perceptions of those voters
with low involvement.

Perry, James M. The New Politics. New York: Clarkson
      N. Potter, Inc., 1968.
      Drawing on his six years of experience as a political
reporter for the National Observer, Perry discusses the take-
over of political campaigning by business and industrial technology. The "new politics," as he sees it, involves the increased use of professional campaign managers, pollsters,
computers, and television spot commercials. Most of the
discussion centers on case studies of the new technology as
used by particular candidates--for instance, George Romney's
1966 Michigan gubernatorial campaign(polling), Nelson Rockefeller's 1966 re-election campaign (television spots), and
Winthrop Rockefeller's 1966 Arkansas gubernatorial campaign
(computers and data processing).

Polsby, Nelson W., and Wildavsky, Aaron B. Presidential
      Elections: Strategies of American Electoral Politics.
      New York: Charles Scribner's Sons, 1968.
      Some regard this volume as the best single descrip-
tion and analysis of contemporary presidential elections. It
gives comprehensive attention to the strategic environment
in which presidential elections are held, the nominating process, the campaign, campaign reform, and the influence of
the ballot on the political system. By and large, the authors
take the position that campaigns probably do no more than
reinforce already existing tendencies. They delineate the
classic strategies of the underdog, acknowledge the need for
balance on issues which could erode the support of the faith-
ful while gaining the support of the uncommitted, and discuss
the difficulty of obtaining accurate feedback during a campaign.

Rogers, Everett M., and Shoemaker, F. Floyd. <u>Communi-</u>
<u>cation of Innovations: A Cross Cultural Approach.</u>
New York: The Free Press, 1971.
"The primary purpose of this book," say the authors,
"is to synthesize a series of generalizations from research
on the diffusion of innovations.... This book is essentially,
then, a distillation of the results of more than 1,500 diffusion publications." The authors develop a model of the diffusion process to which they relate the results of these
studies. This book is the most authoritative on the subject
and, although there are few direct references to political
communication, all new candidates and new political ideas
are innovations. The model developed by Rogers and Shoemaker can provide, with some modification, schema for
organizing some of the research on campaigning and should
stimulate much valuable research on diffusion in political
contexts.

Roll, Charles W., and Cantril, Albert H. <u>Polls: Their</u>
<u>Use and Misuse in Politics.</u> New York: Basic Books,
1972.
Written by two men with professional polling experience, this book is a "layman's guide" to political polls.
Polls can tell a political candidate whether or not to run,
identify strengths and weaknesses in his image, assess
trends, and target the weaknesses of the opposition. The
authors hold no illusions about the direct impact of polls on
the electorate, but they are concerned that survey procedures can be exploited by politicians. Particularly interesting
is the attention devoted to sampling techniques, interviewing,
potential bias in question construction, etc., providing a good
guide to interpretation of the meaning and reliability of political polls.

Rubin, Bernard. <u>Political Television.</u> Belmont, Calif.:
The Wadsworth Publishing Co., 1967.
This book documents the increasingly important role
of television in politics. Early chapters recount examples
of early television usage by politicians. Rubin's observations on the Kennedy-Nixon debates parallel those of many
others: Kennedy came out on top in the first debate and
was more at ease than his opponent. The supposed ability
of television to gloss over weaknesses and play up strengths
is also pointed out in a political (but non-election) context.
Concluding chapters discuss the role of television in the
1964 presidential campaign--primary election coverage, convention coverage, reporting candidate issue stands, and re-

porting election returns.

Scammon, Richard M., and Wattenberg, Ben J. The Real
    Majority. New York: Coward-McCann, Inc., 1970.
    This book develops three ideas in detail: voting de-
cisions are being made in America in response to social
situations such as high crime and racial unrest as well as
in response to economic issues; "the great majority of the
voters in America are unyoung, unpoor, and unblack; they
are middle-aged, middle-class, middle-minded"; those who
would win elections must steadfastly occupy the ideological
middle of the road. Those three main conclusions are based
upon election results, public opinion polls, and television
watching rather than extensive direct exposure to candidates
and the campaign trail. The presidential campaigns and
elections of 1968 are offered by the authors in support of the
three ideas mentioned above, and the mayoralty elections in
1969 are considered further confirmation. In general, this
book minimizes the role which the media play in political
decision-making, asserting that "demography is destiny."

Shaffer, William R. Computer Simulations of Voting Be-
    havior. New York: Oxford University Press, 1972.
    After a brief introduction which classifies voting be-
havior models into three theoretical levels of analysis (sociological, socio-psychological, and psychological), the author
discusses the use of computer simulation as a research
technique in the study of voting behavior. Utilizing data
gathered by the Survey Research Center on the 1964 presidential elections, Shaffer tests the predictive validity of two
models of voter decision-making: the Downsian rational
voter model and the SRC six-component model. Based upon
the results of these tests he builds a revised process model
of voting behavior. Of particular interest to students of political communication are the author's conclusions that "information costs" are not relevant to voting decisions and
that primary group interaction is a key determinant of electoral outcomes.

Thompson, Charles A. H. Television and Presidential
    Politics. Washington, D.C.: Brookings Institution,
    1956.
    This book examines the relationship of television to
the political process and analyzes the issues of public policy
which arise from the use of this medium. It focuses on the
growth of television as a political information source and on
the use of television at the national conventions and during

the political campaigns of 1952 and 1956. Suggestions for
the future use of television are also provided. Thompson
argues that Section 315 of the Federal Communications Act,
the Equal Time Provision, should be changed to "require
equal treatment by broadcasters of the major parties in
their campaigns for national office," leaving the other campaigns in the public service category.

Van Riper, Paul. Handbook of Practical Politics. New
    York: Harper and Row, 1967.
    One of the best known practical works on politics,
this book is designed to aid the ordinary citizen interested
in political participation. Day-to-day campaign activities are
outlined, including establishing a campaign headquarters, setting up county organizations, recruiting workers, raising
money, researching the issues and the opposition, polling,
and scheduling the candidate's time. The communication
aspects of a political campaign are covered in relation to
printed campaign literature, generating newspaper coverage,
radio and television usage, and various types of advertising.
Interpersonal aspects are also covered, especially in terms
of precinct canvassing and telephone campaigns.

White, Theodore H. The Making of the President 1964.
    New York: Atheneum Publishers, 1965.
    This is the second in what has come to be a quadren-
nial book by Theodore White on the presidential campaigns.
Beginning with the death of John F. Kennedy, it reportorially
traces and reflects upon the "multitudinous procession,"
which is presidential politics. Drawing upon first hand observations and two years of conversation with most of the
important luminaries, this book, like others by the same
author, is the most intimate account of the campaigns of
1964. The belated, ill-conceived Goldwater campaign is discussed, but not without passing respect paid to the "conserva-
tive with a conscience." One interesting feature of the chapter on the Johnson campaign is the many and varied persona
drawn by White out of the general style and speeches of the
candidate.

Wilhelmsen, Frederick D., and Bret, Jane. Telepolitics:
    The Politics of Neuronic Man. Plattsburgh, N.Y.:
    Tundra Books, 1972.
    "The reader of a book which claims to explore the
relations between politics and television has a right to know
where the authors stand. The authors stand nowhere. Today there is no place to stand, only to understand." So

state the authors as they begin a book which argues that television has created "neuronic" man who, in turn, murders
publicly, is intolerant, impatient, and has allowed a form
of government to develop which is more private than public,
and which is moving inexorably toward anarchy.   Drawing
heavily on the works of McLuhan, the authors have applied
the "medium is the message" doctrine to television and politics.   They support their "probes" with references to contemporary literary and philosophical sources.   "We see
Telepolitics," say the authors, "as an exercise in political
detection.   An early reader of this manuscript suggested it
be titled The Prince: Revisited, insisting that what we have
really written is a textbook of power, a how-to-do-it book
for the politician on the make."

Wyckoff, Gene.   The Image Candidates.   New York: Mac-
        millan Company, 1968.
        Proceeding from the basic premises that party identi-
fication is weakening, issues becoming less important, and
the number of the "politically unsophisticated" growing,
Wyckoff takes the position that the "image or personal character of the candidate" (particularly as portrayed by television) is now the critical factor in deciding elections.   Much
of the book reports the author's personal experiences as an
"image-maker."   Considerable attention is given to the author's interpretations and evaluations of the inherent capa-
bilities of television to project image and of the various
types of strategies and techniques which can be used.   The
author offers no quantitative evidence for his statements regarding the importance of television and image-making in winning elections.

5. GUIDE TO THE LITERATURE

One of the major weaknesses usually associated with a bibliography such as this one is the relatively short length of time during which it is of maximum value. The literature on political campaign communication is growing at such a rapid rate that there will be scores of new books and articles published between the time this bibliography is completed and the time it becomes widely available to researchers. Moreover, the mid-1970's appear to be years in which journalistic and scholarly activity in the area will continue to flourish, with consequent increases in the literature available. In an attempt to mitigate partially the effects of the inherent "timebound" nature of the entries provided here, we have prepared a brief guide to the literature. Its major purpose is to offer suggestions as to how the user may stay abreast of this burgeoning literature, using the bibliographic entries provided here as a point of departure.

Professional and Scholarly Journals[1]

On the assumption that the past is prologue, we have summarized, in Table I, the professional and scholarly journals in which we found relevant citations. The table does not include material from the French and German supplement, but does provide a general guide to the fields and journals which have contributed to the periodical literature.

As Table I indicates, the fields of journalism and broadcasting have contributed by far the largest body of relevant periodical literature. Forty-one per cent of the total number of articles cited came from these fields. Within journalism and broadcasting, the top five journals have contributed over 70 per cent of the total number of entries.

Public Opinion Quarterly, published by the American Association for Public Opinion Research,[2] is heavily interdisciplinary, tends to rely largely on articles reporting the

TABLE I

Frequency Distribution of Professional and Scholarly
Journals in which Articles on Political
Campaign Communication Were Published, 1950-1972

Fields and Journals	N	%	N	%
Journalism and Broadcasting			228	(42)[1]
Public Opinion Quarterly (POQ)[3]	79	(35)[2]		
Journalism Quarterly (JQ)	62	(27)		
Journal of Broadcasting (JB)	23	(10)		
Broadcasting (B)	13	(06)		
Columbia Journalism Review (CJR)	12	(05)		
Public Relations Journal (PRJ)	8	(04)		
Printers' Ink (PI)	7	(03)		
Journal of Communication (JC)	5	(02)		
Television Quarterly (TQ)	5	(02)		
Miscellaneous	14	(06)		
Political Science			105	(19)
American Political Science Review (APSR)	23	(22)		
Western Political Quarterly (WPQ)	20	(19)		
Congressional Quarterly Weekly Report (CQWR)	9	(08)		
Midwest Journal of Political Science (MJPS)	6	(06)		
Annals of the American Academy of Political and Social Science (AAAPSS)	5	(05)		
Miscellaneous	42	(40)		
Speech – Communication			99	(18)
Quarterly Journal of Speech (QJS)	28	(28)		
Today's Speech (TS)	13	(13)		
Central States Speech Journal (CSSJ)	11	(11)		
Southern Speech Journal (SSJ)	11	(11)		
Speech Monographs (SM)	8	(08)		

Fields and Journals	N	%	N	%
Speech - Communication (Cont'd.)				
Western Speech (WS)	9	(09)		
Moments in Contemporary Rhetoric and Communication (MCRC)	9	(09)		
Miscellaneous	10	(10)		
Psychology and Sociology			50	(09)
Journal of Social Psychology (JSP)	14	(28)		
Miscellaneous	36	(72)		
Miscellaneous Social Science			31	(06)
Miscellaneous Law			22	(04)
Miscellaneous Education			10	(02)
Total			545	(100)

[1]The numbers and percentages in this column refer to the total number of articles from the journals of that field or fields. For example, there were a total of 228 articles in the journals of Journalism and Broadcasting which is 42% of the total of the 545 found in all journals.

[2]The numbers and percentages in this column refer to articles which a single journal published in a field or fields. For example, 79 is 35% of 228, the total number of articles published in Journalism and Broadcasting.

[3]Whenever it has been necessary to abbreviate journal titles in the text of this Review, the abbreviations noted in this table have been used.

results of survey research and publishes more articles relevant to political campaign communication than any other journal. It is the most prestigious of the journals listed in the
journalism and broadcasting area. The last issue for each
year carries an index for that year.

The content of Journalism Quarterly is somewhat more
homogeneous than is that of Public Opinion Quarterly. About
half of the 65 articles noted in Table I are related to newspaper coverage of campaigns and generally rely on some
form of content analysis as their data gathering device. The
remaining half are concerned with the political effects of the
mass media, exposure patterns, bias in reporting, media
credibility, etc. This journal also provides a yearly index
in the last issue of each year, a quarterly annotated bibliography of articles in mass communication, and an annotated
list of books and pamphlets on journalistic subjects.

The Journal of Broadcasting has tended to concentrate
its relevant content on analyses of electronic media coverage
of campaigns, bias in reporting, convention coverage, and
some articles on the effects of political communication. It,
too, is indexed yearly.

Broadcasting is the news weekly of the broadcasting
industry and has tended to concentrate its relevant content
on the use of television in campaigns, with an occasional
article on the network television coverage of political events.
Columbia Journalism Review, [3] published by the Graduate
School of Journalism at Columbia University, has contained
several critical essays commenting on the political use of
both newspapers and the electronic media.

Although the journalism/broadcasting journals just
mentioned will continue to be the major contributors of
articles in the area, the Journal of Communication, published by the International Communication Association, may
show, over the next decade, a considerable increase in the
number of relevant articles published. The ICA recently
established a Political Communication division which may
generate more articles for its journal.

The field which has contributed the second largest
number of articles from 1950 to 1972 is political science.
It contributed 105 entries or 19 per cent of the total. We
make special mention of the American Political Science Review because of its generally high quality and because it ap-

pears to be a bellwether journal for relevant articles in political science. With articles on campaign strategy, campaign decision making, political opinion formation, the impact of political information on voting behavior, and the role
of political parties, among others, it provides an excellent
cross-section of the various types of articles which comprise
the contribution of political science. In the last few years,
it has reflected an increasing concern among political scientists regarding the role of communication variables in political decision making. One can predict, with a modest
degree of certainty, an increase in the number of relevant
articles in this journal, as well as from political science in
general.

Western Political Quarterly, published by the Western
Political Science Association, et al., carries a series of
articles shortly after each major election in the Western
states, some of which are usually relevant to political campaign communication.

Although Table I indicates that it has published only
five relevant articles, Midwest Journal of Political Science
bears watching as a journal which will probably appreciably
increase its contribution over the next few years.

Finally, in the political science section of Table I,
we have included Congressional Quarterly Weekly Report, not
as a scholarly journal, but as a publication which carries
articles on the day-to-day aspects of politics. Recent issues have contained articles on such matters as campaign
management, campaign spending reform, new broadcasting
regulations, and campaign techniques. CQWR includes more
detailed coverage than would a newspaper report on the same
subject, and publishes, each January, a complete author and
key-word index for the previous year's issues.

Relevant literature in speech-communication appears
most frequently in the Quarterly Journal of Speech, with ad-
ditional articles scattered across several other journals.
QJS and Speech Monographs are generally regarded as the
best in the field. Until recently the literature of speech-
communication has consisted largely of articles on the history
and criticism of campaign rhetoric. While this continues to
be true, increasingly there are articles which deal with more
inclusive topics such as the directions which political campaign research should take, the effects of the media, and
campaign strategy.

The regional journals mentioned in the speech-communication section of Table I, Western Speech, Southern Speech Journal, Central States Speech Journal, and Today's Speech, generally speaking, reflect the same trends as are evident in the Quarterly Journal of Speech. Speech Monographs is increasingly quantitative in its content, publishing relevant articles on such topics as candidate image and the effectiveness of campaign communication. Moments in Contemporary Rhetoric and Communication specializes in publishing student manuscripts. All nine entries in the bibliography came from the Fall 1972 issue. This journal is relatively new and is published at Temple University.

The psychology and sociology section of Table I indicates a limited number of contributions from these two fields, and this is an accurate impression, given the definitions and guidelines under which the entries were gathered. However, the user should keep in mind that these fields are seminal to some of the best thinking reflected in the literature of political science and communication fields. While there are relatively few articles dealing directly with campaigning, there are hundreds of articles dealing with concepts which indirectly shed much light on what happens in campaigns. Among these are selective exposure, selective perception, counter-attitudinal persuasion, and the diffusion of innovation. Thus, students of campaigning, particularly those with highly defined interests, will find it necessary to consult this body of literature, paying particular attention to the Journal of Social Psychology.

Finally, we offer a comment about the role that the indexes and abstracting services should play in one's attempts to keep up with the periodical literature of the field. A review of the introduction to this bibliography will indicate the key role which the indexes played in the gleaning of the entries presented here. Obviously, it behooves one to become familiar with indexes which generally contain items relevant to his interests.[4] Nevertheless, they have major limitations, the most significant of which are that they occasionally miss an important entry, and they are, by their very nature, always behind the field. They lag from a few weeks to a year behind the publications they monitor. The indexing and abstracting services are of value mainly because of their broad purview, which will produce articles which appear in a new or unusual journal of foreign publication. Direct monitoring of the best and most productive journals in one's major area of interest is essential if one is to stay abreast of the field.

Convention Papers, Dissertations, and Theses

Ideas in the intellectual environment of political campaign communication pass through the same general stages as do ideas in other areas of academic interest. They are conceived by scholars working alone or with a small group of students or colleagues. Out of the interactions which occur in these early stages may come a doctoral dissertation, a master's thesis, or a paper presented at a scholarly convention. Later, as they become more sharply focused, they may turn up in the periodical literature, and still later, in textbooks. Between each stage in this general process, months, and sometimes years, intervene. It is, therefore, necessary to acquire continuing access to relevant unpublished literature.

Every scholarly organization which has made a contribution to the literature on political campaign communication holds, at least once yearly, a convention at which scores of papers are presented. Any interested person, whether or not he attends the convention or is a member of the organization, may gain access to these papers. The following associations, [5] listed in order of the number of convention papers which are likely to be relevant to political campaign communication, are the most prominent: American Association for Public Opinion Research, Association for Education in Journalism, Speech-Communication Association, and American Political Science Association.

One can acquire the papers presented at these conventions while attending or by acquiring a copy of the program of each convention and writing the authors to request copies. Some groups are facilitating this process by making available a volume containing abstracts of all papers presented. The American Political Science Association publishes an advance copy of its annual fall convention program in the spring issue of PS, the quarterly newsletter of the profession. Information on the annual convention of the Speech Communication Association can be found in its bimonthly newsletter, Spectra.

Two other organizations, the American Association of Campaign Consultants and Campaign Associates, hold meetings which are interestingly different from those just mentioned. The AACC holds a symposium in Washington, D.C., after each major election at which pollsters, major candidates, and/or their representatives, along with campaign

consultants and media representatives exchange views. Until
recently no written record had been made of these symposia,
and they are limited to those participating and members of
the AACC. However, presentations from the 1972 meeting
were made available, at least in part, in the quarterly publication of the Association, Politéia.

The other group, Campaign Associates, is, according
to its monthly publication, Campaign Insight, the largest political campaign management firm in the country. This
group sponsors seminars in various cities around the country, designed largely for candidates and their staffs. Those
who attend receive study kits, sample news releases, budget
forms, and much advice on the day-to-day aspects of political
campaigning.

Another highly significant source of unpublished information on political campaign communication is, of course,
doctoral dissertations and theses. One hundred eleven references to dissertations and theses appear in Section 2 of
this bibliography. If one wishes to stay abreast of this literature, he must inevitably resort to American Doctoral Dissertations and to Dissertation Abstracts. American Doctoral
Dissertations is a complete listing of all dissertations ac-
cepted by American and Canadian universities, including,
therefore, many titles which are not in Dissertation Abstracts.
Some universities, the University of Chicago, for example,
do not send dissertations to University Microfilms, publishers of Dissertation Abstracts, and others allow some authors
to decide on their own. Thus, while Dissertation Abstracts
is not a complete index, it does provide a valuable abstract
for each entry which is usually written by the author of the
dissertation. For a fee, University Microfilms will do a
key-word search of its massive collection of dissertations
and mail the results.

Some fields have begun to publish specialized volumes
containing abstracts of theses and dissertations. Bibliographic Annual in Speech Communication is published by the
Speech Communication Association and contains abstracts of
dissertations, a section on graduate research in progress,
and specialized bibliographies. Journalism Abstracts, published by the American Association for Education in Journalism, provides much useful information on theses and dissertations in journalism and mass communication.

Finally, it should be mentioned that a relatively new organization, The Center for the Study of Television and Politics, has been established for the purpose of collecting, cataloging, and making available for scholarly purposes political campaign materials used on television. Affiliated with the New School for Social Research in New York City, the Center plans to convert film and video-taped campaign films into video-tape cassettes and make them available for study to anyone willing to sign a statement that the films will not be used in any future campaign.

Books

During the period covered by this bibliography, there were 196 books published which were relevant to the role of communication variables in political campaigns, and a substantial majority of these books were published in the 1960's and early 1970's. It seems safe to predict that at least 100 such books will be published in the next decade. Obtaining immediate access to these publications is not as easy as it should be because they are scattered across several disciplines, but we can make a few suggestions which may be helpful.

Several publications are available which list all new books being made available in this country. The political communication researcher will probably find that those which index by subject, such as Library of Congress Books: Subjects and Subject Guide to Books in Print, are the most useful. Forthcoming Books lists books which have been recently published, books which are soon to be published, and is indexed by subject. These publications are available in most university libraries, and one of them should be perused occasionally to find books that might otherwise be missed.

Periodical literature, both popular and scholarly, also provides much valuable data on new books. For example, The Washington Monthly carries ads announcing new political books and a regular feature entitled "Political Book Notes" which mentions as many as fifty public affairs books to be published each month. About half of the titles mentioned are accompanied by brief annotations. Books on politics are also advertised, listed, and sometimes reviewed in such diverse publications as Politéia, Campaign Insight, New York Review of Books, and the New York Times Review of Books.

Another excellent source of new book titles and book
reviews is, of course, the scholarly journals. Although the
time lag between publication and review is usually a year or
more, the best and most complete reviews of important new
books in any field are in the book reviews which appear in
the journals of that field. Most of the journals listed in
Table I regularly carry book reviews, and most of these reviews are indexed in Book Review Index. However, Book
Review Digest avoids most reviews appearing in scholarly
journals, but does cover rather comprehensively reviews
published in popular periodicals. The most comprehensive
book review index is International Bibliographie der Rezen-
sionen which indexes book reviews written in English, French,
and German by reviewed author, subject, and reviewing author.

A few of the journals, notably the American Political
Science Review, sell advertising space to book publishers.
These ads are a good source of information on revised editions and forthcoming books, and they can provide a good
indication of the publishers which seem to be active in one's
special area of interest. Book publishers also buy much of
the space made available in the convention programs of the
various scholarly organizations.

Popular Magazines and Newspapers

Political campaigns are events of such predictable
frequency and public importance that there is hardly a popular magazine in America that does not occasionally comment
on them. In the bibliography in Section 2, there are 449
entries from popular magazines. Those which produced ten
or more entries and which are still being published were:
Newsweek, New York Times Magazine, Time, Nation, U.S.
News and World Report, New Republic, Business Week, and
America. This literature tends to be much more impres-
sionistic than the literature in scholarly journals, but it is
obviously a better reflection of current public sentiment.
Because at least 25 divergent publications make an ongoing
contribution to this literature, we recommend an occasional
review of the Readers' Guide to Periodical Literature in
which most notable popular magazines are indexed.

While there are 64 entries in Section 2 from newspapers, no attempt was made to provide an exhaustive or
representative list of entries. Those who need, for what-

ever purpose, to remain informed on the political content of
the daily press should gain access to The Political Communication Bulletin, published monthly by the American Institute
for Political Communication. The Institute, which describes
itself as a "non-partisan, non-profit organization dedicated to
improving the flow of government and political affairs information to the American people through independent study,
analysis and reporting of the dissemination process," has
also published several books and monographs. The Political
Communication Bulletin takes a considerable proportion of
its material from the news and editorial columns of the
eastern press and from its own research. It also reports
on a variety of governmental activities related to political
communication, carries monthly reports on the national polls,
and reports polls conducted by legislators. In addition, anyone wishing to keep up with day-to-day developments in national campaigns should subscribe to at least one major daily
newspaper and review periodically the New York Times Index
which is a comprehensive guide to "the newspaper of record"
and is annotated.

Concluding this brief guide to the literature, we wish
to mention the Educational Resources Information Center
(ERIC) of the U.S. Office of Education, because it holds considerable potential as a source of up-to-date information on
the political communication process. An effort is now being
made by communications scholars from several areas of the
discipline to make available to ERIC books, conference papers, speeches, monographs, bibliographies, and unpublished
essays for storage and, in turn, for use by other educators
and scholars. ERIC's Document Reproduction Service will
make available for a fee copies of a document in its file on
microfiche or in hard copy. The number and significance of
the documents on political campaign communication available
through ERIC is limited, but it may grow considerably during
the next few years. If so, it could become of great aid to
those wishing to remain aware of significant, new thinking
on political campaign communication.

Notes

1. The 1539 entries in the bibliography in Section 2 can be
   categorized as follows: articles in professional and
   scholarly journals, 545; articles in popular magazines,
   449; books, 196; theses and dissertations, 111; articles in newspapers, 64; convention papers, 55; arti-

cles in books, 34; U.S. government publications, 22;
and miscellaneous, 63. In this Guide to the Literature, we discuss the items in the first six of these
categories.

2. See appendix, Professional and Scholarly Organizations,
   for an alphabetical listing of organizations which publish journals, hold conventions, or otherwise contribute to the literature.

3. There are several other journalism reviews which, although they are usually not indexed by any of the major indexes, contain critiques of political journalism
   written by the working press. Three such publications
   are: Chicago Journalism Review, St. Louis Journalism Review, and More: A Journalism Review. The
   publishers of these reviews are listed in the appendix.

4. The following is a list of 10 indexing and abstracting
   services which monitor the journals listed earlier in
   Table I, with an indication of the journals which each
   covers: Public Affairs Information Service Index -
   POQ, JQ, JB, CJR, WPQ, MJPS, CQWR; Social Sci-
   ences and Humanities Index - POQ, APSR, WPQ;
   Education Index - JC, QJS, SM; Psychological Ab-
   stracts - JC, JSP, CSSJ, SM; ABC Pol Sci - APSR,
   AAAPSS; International Political Science Abstracts -
   APSR; Historical Abstracts - SSJ; Current Contents:
   Behavioral, Social, and Management Sciences - APSR;
   Sociological Abstracts - JB; Business Periodicals In-
   dex - B. Today's Speech and Western Speech are ap-
   parently not monitored by any of the above.

5. Addresses for these groups can be found in the appendix.
   In addition to these national associations, there are a
   variety of regional associations, some of which hold
   conventions at which political communication is discussed. These, too, are listed in the appendix.

6. APPENDIX

Professional and Scholarly Organizations

American Association for Public Opinion Research, 817 Broadway, New York, New York, 10003. Publishers of Public Opinion Quarterly.

American Association of Political Consultants, Suite 618, 1028 Connecticut Avenue, N.W., Washington, D.C. 20036. Publishers of Politéia.

American Institute for Political Communication, 402 Prudential Building, Washington, D.C., 20005. Publishers of The Political Communication Bulletin.

The American Political Science Association, 1527 New Hampshire Ave., N.W., Washington, D.C., 20036. Publishers of The American Political Science Review, and PS.

Association for Education in Journalism, University of Minnesota, Minneapolis, Minnesota, 55455. Publishers of Journalism Quarterly.

Association of Working Press, 192 N. Clark St., Chicago, Illinois 60601. Publishers of Chicago Journalism Review.

Broadcasting Publications, Inc., 1735 DeSales St., N.W., Washington, D.C., 20036. Publishers of Broadcasting.

Campaign Associates, Inc., 408 Petroleum Building, Wichita, Kansas, 67202. Publishers of Campaign Insight: A Monthly Overview of Political Techniques.

Center for the Study of Television and Politics, Dr. Harry D. Gideonse, Chairman, Board of Directors, New

School for Social Research, New York, New York.
Collects campaign materials for scholarly use.

Central States Speech Association, Kenneth E. Anderson,
Business Manager, Department of Speech, University
of Illinois, Urbana, Illinois, 61801. Publishers of
The Central States Speech Journal.

Congressional Quarterly, Inc., 1735 K. Street, N.W., Washington, D.C., 20006. Publishers of Congressional
Quarterly Weekly Report.

Eastern Communication Association, Richard Bailey, Executive Secretary, Department of Speech, University of
Rhode Island, Kingston, Rhode Island, 02881. Publishers of Today's Speech.

Educational Resources Information Center (ERIC), U.S. Office of Education, 400 Maryland Avenue, N.W., Washington, D.C., 20202.

Focus/Midwest Publishing Co., P.O. Box 3086, St. Louis,
Missouri, 63130. Publishers of St. Louis Journalism
Review.

Graduate School of Journalism, 700 Journalism Building,
Columbia University, New York, New York, 10027.
Publishers of Columbia Journalism Review.

International Communication Association, B. Martin Hurley,
Business Manager, International Communication As-
sociation, P.O. Box 445, Flint, Michigan, 48501, or
Keith R. Sanders, Chairman, Political Communication
Division, International Communication Association,
Southern Illinois University, Carbondale, Illinois,
62901. Publishers of The Journal of Communication.

The Journal Press, Managing Editor, 2 Commercial Street,
Provincetown, Massachusetts, 02657. Publishers of
The Journal of Social Psychology.

Midwest Political Science Association, Professor Frank J.
Serauf, President, Department of Political Science,
University of Minnesota. Publishers of Midwest
Journal of Political Science.

The National Academy of Television Arts and Sciences, 54
West 40th Street, New York, New York. Publishers
of Television Quarterly.

Public Relations Society of America, 845 Third Avenue, New
York, New York, 10022. Publishers of Public Relations Journal.

Rosebud Associates, Inc., 750 Third Avenue, New York,
N.Y., 10017. Publishers of [More]: A Journalism
Review.

Southern Speech Communication Association, Jerry Tarver,
Executive Secretary, University of Richmond, Rich-
mond, Virginia, 23173. Publishers of Southern
Speech Communication Journal.

The Speech Communication Association, William Work,
Executive Secretary, Statler Hilton Hotel, New York,
New York, 10001. Publishers of The Quarterly
Journal of Speech, Speech Monographs, and Spectra.

University Microfilms, 313 North First Street, Ann Arbor,
Michigan, 48106. Publishers of Dissertation Abstracts.

The Washington Monthly, 1028 Connecticut Ave., N.W.,
Washington, D.C., 20036.

Western Political Science Association, Paul R. Murray,
Secretary-Treasurer, Department of Government,
Sacramento State College, Sacramento, California,
98519. Publishers of Western Political Quarterly.

The Western Speech Communication Association, Robert W.
Vogelsang, Executive Secretary, Portland State Uni-
versity, Portland, Oregon. Publishers of Western
Speech.

INDEX

Advance Men <u>See</u> Professional Campaign Consultants-
    Advance <u>Men</u>
Advertising <u>See</u> Political Advertising; Newspapers-Adver-
    tising
Advertising Agencies <u>See</u> Professional Campaign Con-
    sultants-Advertising Agencies
Agnew, Spiro 285, 457, 737, 793
Alabama 432, 1374
Alaska 1464
Attitude Change in Voting Behavior (<u>see also</u> Political Atti-
    tudes; Psychology in Voting Behavior) 103, 130, 206,
    207, 259, 752, 762, 853, 920, 1178, 1296, 1471, 1534

Bandwagon and Underdog Effects (<u>see also</u> Polling--Polls;
    Predictions) 070, 072, 265, 405, 493, 519, 1251,
    1314
Bias <u>See</u> Mass Media-Bias; Television in/and Politics-
    Bias; Newspapers-Bias
Bibliographies 020, 023, 147, 295, 364, 546, 698, 1089,
    1135, 1228, 1379, 1434
Black, Shirley Temple 428, 981
Broadcasting <u>See</u> Mass Media; Political Advertising;
    Political Broadcasting; Radio; Television in/and
    Politics
Brooke, Edward 115
Brown, Pat 116, 534, 775, 938, 1196
Buckley, William F. 551
Buttons <u>See</u> Campaign Paraphernalia-Buttons

Cable TV <u>See</u> Television in/and Politics-Cable TV
California 057, 091, 098, 116, 218, 256, 341, 383, 436,
    496, 576, 577, 638, 682, 775, 792, 812, 825, 847,
    1054, 1085, 1196, 1206, 1523
Campaign Management <u>See</u> Professional Campaign Con-
    sultants

Campaign Paraphernalia
  General 198, 823, 852, 941, 1459, 1535
  Billboards 806
  Buttons 043, 221, 227, 228, 414, 487, 1059, 1250, 1459
  Literature 267, 380, 626, 644, 792, 797, 1333, 1447, 1479
  Posters 1156
  Songs 980, 988, 1035, 1311
Campaigns See Political Campaigns; Presidential Campaigns
Candidates See Political Candidates; names of particular candidates
Cartoons, political 803, 889, 989, 1359
Charisma (see also Image) 276, 370, 736, 976, 1149
Coalitions, political 629
Colorado 075, 176, 669
Communication and Politics 026, 086, 129, 164, 173, 298, 367, 368, 422, 430, 438, 440, 469, 481, 535, 549, 593, 629, 632, 692, 782, 874, 925, 944, 955, 1033, 1110, 1142, 1227, 1360, 1367, 1456, 1507
Communication Theory in Politics 300, 333, 549, 910, 992
Comparative Politics 250
Computers (see also Technology)
  General 003, 005, 125, 277, 278, 303, 304, 312, 412, 446, 451, 774, 851, 861, 987, 995, 996, 1073, 1164, 1272
  Simulation 004, 005, 277, 327, 750, 933, 1009, 1114, 1278, 1463
Conflict, in politics 058
Conventions (see also Presidential Campaigns-Nomination)
  General 285, 316
  Newspaper Coverage 224, 396, 1273
  Television Coverage 015, 064, 158, 202, 345, 670, 856, 877, 896, 900, 942, 943, 959, 968, 970, 1021, 1055, 1158, 1265, 1273, 1282, 1452, 1493
Co-orientation in Political Communication 632
Credibility See Mass Media-Credibility

Daley, Richard 857, 952, 1521
Debates
  General 012, 101, 253, 268, 308, 510, 530, 551, 716, 719, 767, 785, 794, 832, 848, 876, 897, 923, 971, 1062, 1205, 1252, 1341, 1402, 1508
  Kennedy-Nixon Debates 092, 093, 119, 271, 365, 378, 389, 458, 508, 687, 705, 706, 707, 718, 719, 726, 765, 768, 895, 1088, 1171, 1203, 1205, 1225, 1244, 1259, 1308, 1312, 1350, 1351, 1372
Decision-Making in Campaigns 285, 631, 763, 778, 1197, 1245

Diffusion of Information See Information Diffusion
Direct Mail 040, 444, 1364, 1365
Dirty Politics 062, 135, 235, 325, 331, 342, 401, 402,
    478, 479, 552, 558, 583, 662, 666, 667, 696, 755,
    771, 804, 810, 901, 1053, 1061, 1154, 1235, 1275,
    1288, 1305, 1388
Dissonance Theory, in politics (see also Selective Exposure;
    Selective Perception) 265, 409, 410, 762, 1356, 1357
Douglas, Paul 328
Drama--Dramatization, in politics 1170, 1340

Eagleton, Thomas 172, 892, 1124, 1292
Economic Theory of Voter Choice (see also Voting Behavior)
    418, 1295, 1338
Editorials, Editorializing See Newspapers-Editorial En-
    dorsements; Television in/and Politics-Editorializing
Eggers, Paul 161, 1218, 1229, 1343
Ego-Involvement Approach, in voting (see also Psychology in
    Politics) 113, 993, 1296
Eisenhower, Dwight D. 011, 025, 101, 179, 200, 206, 249,
    261, 299, 335, 403, 503, 665, 756, 760, 931, 1049,
    1059, 1078, 1102, 1157, 1213, 1271, 1287
Election Eve Reporting See Predictions
Elites (see also Two-Step Flow of Communication) 014,
    264, 381, 427, 740, 849, 903, 952, 1186, 1526
Ellsworth, Robert 194
Entertainers, in politics 270, 461, 671, 1299
Entertainment, politics of 131
Equal Time (see also Mass Media-Regulation) 347, 571,
    802, 1386, 1419
Extremism, political (see also Ideology, political) 186, 578,
    579

Finance, campaign
    General 012, 013, 027, 028, 029, 030, 031, 032, 034,
        061, 077, 083, 088, 104, 110, 164, 191, 230, 276,
        309, 332, 356, 374, 426, 476, 477, 517, 569, 603,
        618, 622, 623, 624, 824, 830, 901, 922, 953, 1010,
        1053, 1054, 1123, 1129, 1179, 1185, 1234, 1277, 1280,
        1336, 1373, 1406, 1410, 1411, 1412, 1413, 1414, 1415,
        1416, 1417, 1423, 1425, 1426, 1429, 1446, 1448
    Regulation of Campaign Finance 031, 035, 083, 094, 137,
        204, 239, 240, 338, 484, 526, 605, 830, 839, 901, 953,
        1013, 1067, 1077, 1089, 1153, 1163, 1270, 1418, 1430,
        1432
    State Campaign Costs 006, 085
Florida 388, 463, 571, 1019 .

Fundraising (see also Finance, campaign) 036, 435, 517, 779, 820

Game Theory, in politics 628, 1300
Georgia 134
Goldwater, Barry 004, 057, 193, 195, 199, 339, 356, 459, 545, 597, 729, 778, 837, 844, 1000, 1208, 1274, 1473, 1490
Goodman, Robert 430
Gore, Albert 646
Grass Roots Politics (see also Personal Campaigning; Local and Precinct Level Campaigning) 011, 455, 729, 1047
Group Affiliation/Pressure 109, 130, 150, 249, 733, 935
Gruening, Ernest 1464

Hawaii 1342
Humor, in politics 281, 801, 915, 1130, 1329
Humphrey, Hubert H. 048, 067, 084, 113, 139, 188, 285, 391, 1032, 1406, 1439, 1491

Ideology, political 057, 120, 186, 456, 533, 578, 579, 682, 817, 1201, 1208, 1494
Illinois 857, 913, 965, 997, 1050, 1317
Image (see also Charisma) 052, 053, 054, 072, 137, 167, 175, 178, 189, 193, 194, 195, 201, 225, 296, 307, 334, 382, 399, 416, 436, 448, 467, 474, 475, 495, 503, 556, 559, 564, 567, 585, 589, 633, 640, 642, 657, 658, 665, 675, 697, 699, 746, 748, 749, 760, 768, 772, 789, 793, 805, 825, 826, 870, 873, 884, 885, 916, 919, 924, 989, 1004, 1005, 1006, 1011, 1015, 1020, 1024, 1028, 1049, 1063, 1140, 1144, 1166, 1178, 1196, 1202, 1207, 1216, 1217, 1218, 1229, 1238, 1244, 1257, 1259, 1260, 1279, 1287, 1318, 1330, 1358, 1372, 1391, 1466, 1529
Image Makers (see also Professional Campaign Consultants) 322, 430, 636, 901, 989, 1069, 1140
Incumbency 019, 450, 462, 1304
Indiana 212, 1517
Information Diffusion 361, 549, 1186, 1292
Information Sources (see also names of particular sources) 317, 318, 334, 454, 466, 495, 641, 642, 643, 727, 1492
Interpersonal Communication (see also Personal Campaigning; Local and Precinct Level Campaigning) 048, 071, 105, 130, 154, 155, 366, 389, 393, 455, 641, 642, 643, 702, 708, 764, 935, 963, 1186
Iowa 097, 1315

Issues 048, 052, 070, 178, 181, 189, 193, 195, 201, 206, 245,
    249, 256, 258, 263, 307, 394, 418, 427, 439, 463,
    495, 512, 589, 661, 675, 704, 735, 744, 768, 772,
    805, 853, 873, 880, 903, 931, 991, 1007, 1024, 1028,
    1107, 1114, 1159, 1207, 1257, 1279, 1295, 1342, 1355

Johnson, Lyndon 057, 193, 195, 315, 329, 356, 382, 459,
    545, 592, 729, 837, 1000, 1490

Kansas 194
Kefauver, Estes 1213
Kennedy, Edward 900, 1166
Kennedy, John F. (see also Debates-Kennedy-Nixon) 138,
    280, 372, 600, 819, 915, 1001, 1116, 1117, 1190,
    1224, 1489, 1498
Kennedy, Robert 525, 590, 736, 819, 1330, 1516
Kirk, Claude 388

Language, in politics 397, 433, 434, 549, 1219, 1221,
    1248, 1295, 1457
Lindsay, John 872, 1083, 1281, 1521
Local and Precinct Level Campaigning 144, 145, 354, 359,
    702, 764, 1522
Local Elections See State and Local Elections
Lodge, Henry Cabot 822, 1437, 1529
Louisiana 196, 483

McCarthy, Eugene 366, 590, 795, 1063
McGovern, George 145, 238, 541, 892, 900, 917, 1086,
    1141, 1394, 1495
McKay, Douglas 1398
McLuhanism 333, 485, 515, 546, 663, 842, 916, 926, 927,
    928, 929, 930, 1451, 1505
Magazines, coverage of political campaigns 1174, 1478,
    1503
Maryland 435, 721
Mass Media (see also Newspapers; Television in/and Poli-
    tics)
  General 012, 014, 026, 046, 047, 071, 076, 080, 102,
    105, 117, 128, 130, 135, 164, 171, 185, 238, 249,
    256, 273, 280, 287, 288, 291, 292, 297, 305, 306,
    334, 356, 393, 398, 400, 420, 422, 466, 482, 495,
    509, 511, 541, 567, 595, 598, 641, 642, 643, 652,
    655, 664, 680, 683, 704, 708, 715, 717, 732, 747,
    752, 761, 780, 784, 791, 796, 809, 815, 840, 842,
    843, 851, 860, 868, 874, 883, 884, 885, 893, 905,
    907, 908, 909, 920, 924, 947, 955, 958, 960, 965,
    1043, 1065, 1070, 1076, 1093, 1102, 1107, 1136,

Mass Media--General (cont'd)
1155, 1176, 1186, 1192, 1193, 1194, 1195, 1218, 1231,
1239, 1257, 1352, 1354, 1366, 1367, 1385, 1449, 1469,
1470, 1472, 1481, 1489, 1490, 1491, 1529, 1537
Agenda Setting Function 907, 908, 909
Bias 234, 533, 782, 962, 1183
Credibility 045, 050, 140, 266, 274, 464, 572, 652, 677,
678, 1192, 1477
Effects 048, 420, 460, 486, 652, 681, 751, 806, 842,
905, 944, 946, 1064, 1469, 1470
Regulation (see also Finance, campaign-Regulation; Political Broadcasting) 373, 475, 498, 506, 580, 912, 1143,
1164, 1386, 1419, 1420, 1421, 1422, 1424, 1427, 1428
Relative Use/Exposure 041, 071, 114, 144, 293, 352,
420, 456, 464, 572, 806, 906, 961, 1023, 1148, 1155,
1226, 1450, 1503
Massachusetts 613, 614, 818
Messages, political 206, 207, 486, 641, 642, 797, 831,
990, 1368, 1369, 1472, 1503
Methods and Techniques in Political Campaigns 008, 138,
163, 229, 241, 323, 329, 547, 603, 669, 688, 731,
778, 819, 828, 874, 1002, 1167, 1187, 1303, 1309,
1318, 1381, 1464, 1474, 1521
Michigan 141, 393, 1131
Minnesota 011, 021, 1523
Mississippi 006
Montana 714
Morse, Wayne 1398
Muskie, Edmund 697, 699, 798, 836, 902, 1034, 1509,
1518
Myth 490, 887

Neuberger, Richard L. 415
New Politics 047, 131, 165, 169, 214, 529, 594, 612, 736,
949, 951, 987, 1024, 1070, 1099, 1309, 1326, 1366,
1367, 1437, 1442, 1487, 1528, 1529
New York 010, 551, 1204, 1252, 1355
Newspapers (see also Mass Media)
Advertising 177, 178, 999, 1000, 1001, 1017
Bias 049, 141, 148, 149, 231, 232, 234, 286, 470, 533,
672, 753
Campaign Coverage 066, 067, 080, 091, 096, 097, 098,
100, 116, 124, 145, 161, 179, 192, 196, 197, 218,
224, 231, 232, 254, 255, 339, 344, 363, 442, 534,
587, 610, 637, 648, 712, 723, 754, 759, 799, 800,
813, 829, 855, 881, 882, 936, 1030, 1086, 1112,
1124, 1127, 1128, 1147, 1160, 1161, 1190, 1212,

Psychology in Voting Behavior (cont'd)
Values) 001, 222, 366, 409, 468, 471, 488, 504, 535,
545, 575, 582, 611, 613, 614, 627, 633, 725, 751,
752, 762, 817, 834, 835, 875, 890, 911, 920, 934,
939, 979, 982, 1137, 1155, 1173, 1201, 1202, 1208,
1362, 1363, 1471
Public Opinion 003, 024, 046, 129, 130, 160, 191, 287,
355, 423, 492, 500, 532, 639, 734, 781, 811, 815,
1041, 1233, 1514
Public Relations See Professional Campaign Consultants-
Public Relations
Public Speaking See Rhetoric and Public Speaking

Radio 283, 284, 367, 368, 421, 452, 460, 516, 542, 676, 1051,
1181, 1340, 1371, 1406, 1435, 1503, 1506, 1520
Reagan, Ronald 116, 181, 321, 436, 534, 825, 869, 938,
1144, 1175, 1191, 1196, 1370
Recruitment 180, 1022
Referendum 005
Regulation See Finance, campaign-Regulation; Mass Media-
Regulation
Research, in political campaigns 104, 277, 606
Rhetoric and Public Speaking 042, 053, 054, 060, 082, 087,
089, 101, 112, 133, 142, 172, 173, 179, 186, 188,
189, 190, 193, 194, 195, 208, 262, 281, 299, 315,
328, 342, 377, 390, 391, 392, 415, 417, 432, 454,
457, 481, 483, 490, 503, 520, 585, 597, 600, 601,
602, 604, 615, 616, 630, 646, 650, 697, 709, 737,
745, 746, 756, 777, 798, 836, 853, 857, 865, 866,
867, 868, 873, 919, 967, 983, 991, 1032, 1034, 1063,
1075, 1079, 1117, 1119, 1120, 1121, 1141, 1146, 1157,
1175, 1219, 1236, 1237, 1241, 1248, 1313, 1321, 1335,
1343, 1344, 1361, 1367, 1374, 1392, 1393, 1394, 1395,
1399, 1439, 1443, 1454, 1456, 1473, 1498, 1509, 1510,
1511, 1512, 1513, 1531, 1532, 1535
Rockefeller, Jay 976
Rockefeller, Nelson 210, 332, 346, 977, 1012, 1068, 1075
Romney, George 060, 393, 609

Selective Exposure 038, 068, 069, 102, 144, 410, 501, 502,
574, 578, 579, 676, 697, 699, 703, 704, 75°, 809,
920, 921, 924, 1024, 1169, 1255, 1256, 1258, 1263,
1348, 1366, 1368, 1369, 1526
Selective Perception 123, 222, 258, 326, 512, 535, 676,
743, 751, 809, 890, 918, 962, 993, 1024, 1154, 1201,
1205, 1259, 1263, 1279, 1298, 1310, 1348
Simulation See Computers-Simulation